Every Cyclist's Guide to Canadian Law

every cyclist's guide to
CANADIAN LAW

Craig Forcese & Nicole LaViolette

Every Cyclist's Guide to Canadian Law
© Irwin Law Inc., 2014

Published in 2014 by

Irwin Law Inc.
14 Duncan Street
Suite 206
Toronto, ON
M5H 3G8

www.irwinlaw.com

ISBN: 978-1-55221-384-1
e-book ISBN: 978-1-55221-385-8

Cataloguing in Publication data available from Library and Archives Canada

The publisher acknowledges the financial support of the Government of Canada through the Canada Book Fund for its publishing activities.

We acknowledge the assistance of the OMDC Book Fund, an initiative of Ontario Media Development Corporation.

Printed and bound in Canada.

1 2 3 4 5   18 17 16 15 14

Dedications

To all those who we have cycled with on roads and trails,
who have shared advice and experiences, and who have been part of
so many exhilarating rides, this book is for you.

Craig

To those citizens who have advocated, legislated, ridden,
and written to make roads safer for all their users.

Nicole

For Lisa, and for everyone who
has experienced infatuation with a bicycle.

Contents

Acknowledgements

Like all books, this one owes its existence to a peloton of people and organizations.

We are lucky to work in a supportive research environment. This book benefitted from the financial support of the Law Foundation of Ontario and the Faculty of Law, University of Ottawa, and we thank them for their generous support. Nicole was able to complete research and writing of the book during a sabbatical leave granted by the University of Ottawa, for which she is extremely grateful. We would also like to thank the law students who made valuable contributions to the book. Émilie Moniz is a tenacious and organized researcher who knew how to find and assemble the many legal sources needed to write the book. Cigdem Iltan spent many hours meticulously editing chapters and footnotes. Éliane Dupéré-Tremblay also provided invaluable editing assistance.

Let us also express our appreciation for the support that this project received from our publisher, Irwin Law. We would like to thank Jeff Miller for his enthusiasm for this project and Alisa Posesorski for overseeing the editing and proofreading work under a very tight timeline. Irwin Law is also very supportive of the decision to donate our royalties from the sale of the book to Share the Road Cycling Coalition in Ontario, whose work on bicycle safety we strongly support.

We are grateful to Jérémie Fournier, Catherine Gribbin, Sophie Matte, and Peter Showler, four of our colleagues from the legal profession who generously took time out of their busy schedules to help with the cover photograph. Putting their Lycra gear aside, they donned their legal robes and rode their bikes before a curious audience on a Gatineau bike path. We are very much indebted to Lisa Hébert for organizing a very professional photo shoot and orchestrating our legal models to capture the perfect visual representation of the themes of our book, law and bicycles.

As always, Craig extends thanks to his wife, Sandra, and daughter, Madeleine, for their patience during another summer of writing. Things he learned in writing this book he now imparts to Madeleine in the hope of inspiring another generation to venture forth safely and explore the world on two wheels.

Nicole wishes to express her appreciation to her partner, Lisa, and her family and friends for their encouragement and support, both for her cycling and her scholarly endeavours. Lisa has been a great two-wheeling companion, as have their dogs, who tolerated travelling to parks in a bicycle trailer. Nicole is grateful to her parents, who found a way to equip six children with bicycles; she still remembers the thrill of balancing on her bike for the first time at the moment her father let go. She is indebted to all of her bicycle comrades over the years, including friends from the Ottawa Bicycle Club, the Women's Time Trial Series, and the Olde Phartes. Finally, she is particularly grateful to Bob Hicks, who introduced her to the world of sport cycling, time trials, group riding, and, most of all, to the pure pleasure of the sport.

We would also like to acknowledge the work of Bob Mionske, a US attorney and expert on bicycle-related legal questions. His 2007 book, *Bicycling and the Law*, inspired us to write a book that would provide guidance to Canadian cyclists about their legal rights and duties.

Finally, we would like to underscore how much we enjoyed working together on a project that combined our legal knowledge with our passion for cycling. The time dedicated to the book did take us away from our bicycles at times, but somehow we still felt we were logging more kilometres by getting this project done. We feel it has equipped us to be better cyclists, and we hope it might do the same for you, the readers.

— Craig Forcese and Nicole LaViolette

Table of Legislation and Abbreviations

	Canadian Charter of Rights and Freedoms, Part I of the *Constitution Act, 1982*, being Schedule B to the *Canada Act 1982* (UK), 1982, c 11
	Citizenship Act, RSC 1985, c C-29
	Civil Code of Quebec, LRQ c C-1991
	Constitution Act, 1982, Schedule B to the *Canada Act 1982* (UK), 1982, c 11
NB CPWLA	*Consumer Product Warranty and Liability Act*, SNB 1978, c C-18.1
Ont CPA	*Consumer Protection Act, 2002*, SO 2002, c 30, Schedule A
Man CPA	*Consumer Protection Act*, CCSM c 200
Que CPA	*Consumer Protection Act*, CQLR c P-40.1
NS CPA	*Consumer Protection Act*, RSNS 1989, c 92
	Corporations Act, RSO 1990, c C.38
	Criminal Code, RSC 1985, c C-46
	Criminal Records Review Act, RSBC 1996, c 86
	Family Relations Act, RSBC 1996, c 128 [repealed]
Que HSC	*Highway Safety Code*, CQLR c C-24.2
NL HTA	*Highway Traffic Act*, RSNL 1990, c H-3
Ont HTA	*Highway Traffic Act*, RSO 1990, c H.8
PEI HTA	*Highway Traffic Act*, RSPEI 1988, c H-5
	Human Rights Code, RSBC 1996, c 210
	Human Rights Code, RSO 1990, c H.19
	Income Tax Act, RSC 1985, c 1 (5th Supp)
BC IVA	*Insurance (Vehicle) Act*, RSBC 1996, c 231
	Insurance Act, RSO 1990, c I.8
	Limitations Act, 2002, SO 2002, c 24, Schedule B
	Liquor Control and Licensing Act, RSBC 1996, c 267
	Liquor Licence Act, RSO 1990, c L.19
BC MVA	*Motor Vehicle Act*, RSBC 1996, c 318
NB MVA	*Motor Vehicle Act*, RSNB 1973, c M-17
NS MVA	*Motor Vehicle Act*, RSNS 1989, c 293
Can MVSA	*Motor Vehicle Safety Act*, SC 1993, c 16
NU MVA	*Motor Vehicles Act*, RSNWT (Nu) 1988, c M-16, as enacted for Nunavut, pursuant to the *Nunavut Act*, SC 1993, c 28 [*Nunavut Act*]
NWT MVA	*Motor Vehicles Act*, RSNWT 1988, c M-16
YT MVA	*Motor Vehicles Act*, RSY 2002, c 153
Ont MA	*Municipal Act, 2001*, SO 2001, c 25
Alta MGA	*Municipal Government Act*, RSA 2000, c M-26

Ont NPCA	*Not-for-Profit Corporations Act, 2010*, SO 2010, c 15 [not yet in force]
Alta OLA	*Occupiers' Liability Act*, RSA 2000, c O-4
BC OLA	*Occupiers Liability Act*, RSBC 1996, c 337
Ont OLA	*Occupiers Liability Act*, RSO 1990, c O.2
PEI OLA	*Occupiers' Liability Act*, RSPEI 1988, c O-2
NS OLA	*Occupiers' Liability Act*, SNS 1996, c 27
	Official Languages Act, RSC 1985, c 31 (4th Supp)
	Pawnbrokers Act, RSO 1990, c P.6
	Pawned Property (Recording) Act, SS 2003, c P-4.2
BC PIPA	*Personal Information Protection Act*, SBC 2003, c 63
PIPEDA	*Personal Information Protection and Electronic Documents Act*, SC 2000, c 5
Can PASA	*Physical Activity and Sport Act*, SC 2003, c 2
BC SGA	*Sale of Goods Act*, RSBC 1996, c 410
Ont SGA	*Sale of Goods Act*, RSO 1990, c S.1
	Societies Act, RSA 2000, c S-14
	Society Act, RSBC 1996, c 433
	The Automobile Accident Insurance Act, RSS 1978, c A-35
Sask CPA	*The Consumer Protection Act*, SS 1996, c C-30.1
Man HTA	*The Highway Traffic Act*, CCSM c H60
	The Manitoba Public Insurance Corporation Act, CCSM c P215
	The Municipalities Act, SS 2005, c M-36.1
	The Non-profit Corporations Act, 1995, SS 1995, c N-4.2
Man OLA	*The Occupiers' Liability Act*, CCSM c O8
Sask TSA	*The Traffic Safety Act*, SS 2004, c T-18.1
	Trade-marks Act, RSC 1985, c T-13
Alta TSA	*Traffic Safety Act*, RSA 2000, c T-6
	Trespass to Property Act, RSO 1990, c T.21

REGULATIONS

Bicycle Helmet Regulations, NS Reg 68/97

Bicycle Safety Helmet Exemption Regulation, BC Reg 261/96

Bicycle Safety Helmet Regulations, PEI Reg EC329/03

Bicycle Safety Helmet Specification Regulation, Alta Reg 59/2002

Bicycle Safety Helmet Standards Regulation, BC Reg 234/96

Helmet Regulations, NS Reg 99/2003

Immigration and Refugee Protection Regulations, SOR/2002-227

Licensing and Equipment Regulations, CNLR 1007/96

Motor Assisted Cycle Regulation, BC Reg 151/2002

Motor Vehicle Safety Regulations, CRC, c 1038

Motor Vehicles Regulations, YCO 1978/120

National Capital Commission Traffic and Property Regulations, CRC, c 1044

Operator Licensing and Vehicle Control Regulation, Alta Reg 320/2002

Pawned Property (Recording) Regulations, RRS c P-4.2 Reg 1

Pedicab Operation Regulations, NS Reg 183/2006

Provincial Parks (General) Regulation, Alta Reg 102/1985

Safety Helmets, RRO 1990, Reg 610

Societies Regulation, Alta Reg 122/2000

Use of Highway and Rules of the Road Regulation, Alta Reg 304/2002

Vehicle Equipment Regulation, Alta Reg 122/2009

Vehicles on Controlled-Access Highways, RRO 1990, Reg 630

Chapter 1

Introduction

Bicycles and cycling have been a feature of Canadian lives and roadways since the 19th century.[1] But there is no doubt that we are witnessing a new cycling boom in the 21st century. For example, commentators have repeatedly called cycling the "new golf," a comparison emphasizing the extent to which bicycle riding has become a preferred activity for movers and shakers who traditionally populate the greens.[2] For many people, however, cycling is much more than business networking in lycra. Bicycles are widely used today by Canadians for leisure, work, commuting, travel, exercise, and athletic competition. They are not only a source of recreation, but for an increasing number, a chief source of mobility.

Seemingly in direct proportion, news items regularly report on accidents involving cyclists, the value (or not) of mandatory helmet laws, doping scandals in professional cycling, and proposals for amendments to existing traffic laws to increase safety for cyclists. Municipalities are incrementally improving cycling infrastructure and bicycle routes, while legislatures debate legal reforms to acknowledge the needs and status of cyclists. Manufacturers are enjoying a boom in the sales and manufacture of bicycles and cycling equipment. The sport of cycling, with events like the Tour de France, has become not only popular entertainment, but also a common pastime for an increasing number of amateur cyclists. On top of actual bike racing, organized bicycle tours and rides, charity rides, and the latest European import, the "Grand Fondo" or "big ride," are now extremely popular. And cycling-related sporting disciplines, like triathlon, have witnessed a participation explosion over the last decade.

It is also true that more bicycles on the road have led to a multitude of conflicts between cyclists and other users. Between the two of us, we have logged tens of thousands of kilometres and hundreds of hours cycling on roads, paths, and trails, and we have witnessed lousy driving and lousy cycling. We've probably done our own fair share of both.

We've also heard and witnessed a lot of misinformed assertions, commentary, and opinion about what rules apply to whom — not just by drivers and cyclists, but also by law-makers and law enforcers.

Just as drivers decide whether to wear seatbelts or speak on hand-held devices, cyclists may decide to disregard the rules. That decision, however, does not make the rules any less legally binding, and every cyclist, and the parents of every kid on a bike, should know the law. If you choose to ignore it, then at the very least you should be aware that what you are doing constitutes a choice to disobey a rule. And if you don't like the rules, work to have them changed and improved.

In any case, we believe there is a growing interest in the laws that regulate cycling and we thought it was time to clear up a lot of misunderstandings and misinformation about the applicable legal standards. That is why we have written this book.

about this book

We offer this book as a one-stop shop for those who make, apply, regard, or disregard the laws that apply to cycling. It's a book for those who ride the roads, paths, and trails and those whose job may include regulating relations between — and adjudging the conduct of — those on bikes and those behind wheels. It is a guide for cyclists and legal practitioners with the emphasis on existing rules of law, although we discuss policy issues from time to time.[3]

In the chapters that follow, we provide a comprehensive overview of Canadian law applicable to bicycles across a wide range of issues — from riding a bike on the roads, to purchasing and using bicycles, to running a bike club, to racing in competitive cycling events. The main objective is to outline the rights and duties of cyclists. This, in turn, should contribute to two further goals: to educate cyclists, pedestrians, drivers, and the general public about the legal status of cyclists in Canada in order to encourage a better understanding of cycling and a safe use of the roads by everyone; and, to provide a tool for practitioners and judges who are increasingly encountering cases that involve bicycles and cyclists.

The book's style is hopefully 'user-friendly' for a non-legal audience, yet sufficiently rigorous for reference use by personal injury and municipal lawyers, club directors, coaches, sporting event planners, and others who may have a regular need for such a resource. We present legal issues in an accessible manner using a topical approach that is easily understood by readers with little or no legal background. Using straightforward and hopefully jargon-free explanations, we guide readers through the major legal areas specific to cycling. We have also inserted anecdotes and examples drawn from our own experiences as seasoned recreational and competitive cyclists.

In the balance of this chapter, we begin by covering some "legal basics." We need to do this because there is actually no such thing as "bicycle" or "cycling" law. No matter how hard you look, you won't find a federal or provincial statute entitled "An Act Respecting Bicycles and Cycling" that would guide you in every aspects of riding your bike. Simply put, there does not exist one branch of law that governs all things related to cycling. Instead, cycling is subject to rules emanating from a multitude of sources and this body of rules criss-crosses an assortment of different subject matters. Examples include tort law, contract law, property law, criminal law, insurance law, highway traffic law, human rights law, and non-profit corporation law. Throughout the book, we will examine, therefore, many different areas of the law, in both the private and public spheres. So we must begin with an effort to set the stage, describing basic legal terminology and key legal actors.

private and public law

"Private law" deals with the relations between persons, and in terms of cycling such rules touch upon a large number of subjects. It would include the rules governing the accident you had with a car, the agreement to purchase new wheels with your local bike store, the insurance agreement you signed to cover your bike in case of theft, or the selection of the provincial cycling team for the Canada Games.

"Public law" governs relations between governments and individuals. Governments lean towards regulating for the collective good. So they set rules about how everyone should safely use the roadways, what constitutes serious misconduct worthy of criminal or administrative sanctions, or what the tax contributions should be of athletes and cycling associations.

Cycling is a matter of both private and public law.

canadian constitutional system

Not only are the rules governing cyclists found in an array of branches of the law, they are also established by different levels of government.

Canada is a federation with two main levels of government. At the national level is the federal government. In addition, there are ten provincial jurisdictions. Each level, national and provincial, exercises its own authority and has its own distinct legislation. There are also three territorial governments who derive their legislative authority from a federal statute. In this way, the federal government has delegated to the territories similar powers to those possessed by the provinces.

Municipalities are local authorities that are established pursuant to provincial or territorial laws. As such, their legislative powers stem from laws adopted by the provinces and territories. Finally, it is also true that some indigenous territories now have powers to legislate on certain matters pursuant to self-government and land claims agreements signed with various First Nations.

The "division of powers" between the federal and provincial levels of government is outlined in the Canadian Constitution, specifically in the *Constitution Act, 1867*. Not surprisingly, bicycles and cycling are not mentioned in the Constitution — the bicycle as we know it today had not yet been invented in 1867. But the division of powers in the Constitution does determine which level of government regulates broad areas of the law that include matters relevant to bicycles and cycling. For instance, the federal Parliament has legislative authority over criminal law and taxation while the provincial legislatures have the exclusive power to make laws regarding "property and civil rights," in essence jurisdiction over all private law matters.

common law and civil law

Canada is also a legally pluralistic state where different legal traditions coexist, most notably civil law and common law. Thus, in the province of Quebec, private rights are governed by civil law principles, a legal tradition that originated in France. All other Canadian provinces and territories follow the common law legal tradition, a legacy which originated in England. Where relevant, we will try to highlight the differences between common law and civil law principles as they apply to the rules of riding a bicycle.

laws, regulations, caselaw

At the federal level and in common law provinces and territories, two sources of law apply to cyclists and bicycles: legislation and caselaw. Legislation consists of written texts (statutes or Acts) adopted either by Parliament or the legislatures. It also includes regulations made by the executive branch of government — government departments and agencies, among others. Regulations are a form of "delegated legislation" — that is, Parliament or the legislatures have used statutes to delegate to the executive responsibility for creating these regulations. The rules that govern cycling are often found in both statutes and regulations. Meanwhile, in all jurisdictions, courts are responsible for determining the precise meaning of this legislation when issues are litigated before them — they interpret legislation, applying it to particular disputes.

A second source of rules in all the provinces and territories except Quebec is what we call the common law, or caselaw. The common law is the set of legal rules established by court decisions; essentially, legal standards developed over time by the courts. Indeed, in common law jurisdictions, a significant part of the law is not statutory law or regulations. Caselaw consists primarily of previous court decisions by appellate courts (precedents) and the rationale or principle underlying the decisions (*ratio decidendi*) that must be followed by lower courts. In the absence of legislation, the common law is the default source of legal norms. Caselaw occupies a particularly important place in prescribing private law rules in common law jurisdictions (that is, everywhere except Quebec) and our book contains many references to key or illustrative court decisions.

canadian courts

The Canadian court system provides Canadians with a judiciary that has the power not only to confirm the rights and obligations of individuals, but also to enforce the rules set out in legislation and at common law. Courts exist in all of the provincial and territorial jurisdictions in Canada and their roles depend on their inherent constitutional or legislated mandate. (There are also separate "Federal Courts," but these do not feature in this book.)

Each province, the Northwest Territories, and Yukon have a provincial or territorial court whose mandate is limited to adjudicating matters within provincial or territorial legislation (or occasionally assigned to it by the federal Parliament). For instance, provincial courts hear traffic violation cases. In some provinces such as British Columbia, provincial courts include "small claims courts" dealing with disputes involving limited monetary amounts. Cases before the provincial or territorial courts are heard by a single judge.

Each province and territory also has a superior court with the jurisdiction and powers traditionally exercised by courts of common law in English law. The superior court has jurisdiction over both civil and criminal matters. In this book, many of the private law cases we cite are decisions of superior courts. In some provinces (such as Ontario), "small claims court" are branches of the superior court. The superior court also sits as a first-level court of appeal for decisions made by a provincial or territorial court, as appropriate. It is usually called the "Superior Court of Justice" (e.g., Ontario), "Supreme Court" (e.g., British Columbia) or the "Court of Queen's Bench" (e.g., New Brunswick and Manitoba).

All provinces and territories also have a Court of Appeal whose mandate is to hear cases that have been decided by lower courts. The Court of Appeal usually sits in three-judge bench — that is, three judges hear the appeal.

At the highest and final level of the Canadian legal system is the Supreme Court of Canada, located in Ottawa. The Supreme Court of Canada is the court of last resort in the country, and it hears appeals from the provincial and territorial courts of appeal. Although there are exceptions, typically seven or nine Supreme Court of Canada judges will hear these appeals. The Court's judgments are final.

structure of this book

All of these concepts and players appear in the pages that follow. In the next chapter, we begin with the most obvious topic: the laws that govern where and how you ride your bike. Here, our focus in on traffic rules at the provincial, territorial, and (occasionally) municipal level. If you don't know it already, you'll discover that riding your bicycle in Canada is almost as heavily regulated as driving your car.

In Chapter 3, we focus on what happens when these rules don't work as intended, and you are involved in a bicycle accident. Our focus is on bicycle collisions with motor vehicles, but we also examine other issues, such as bicycle accidents involving pedestrians and other cyclists and also the legal responsibilities of government to keep roads safe for cycling.

In Chapter 4, we discuss the bike that breaks, examining warranties and guarantees that govern consumer goods like bicycles and bicycle components. Then in Chapter 5, we walk through that most aggravating of occurrences: the stolen bicycle. Here, we examine scenarios in which your bicycle goes missing, and the legal issues that then arise.

In Chapter 6, we shift gears (so to speak) and examine the legal workings of an incorporated bicycle club, also highlighting the sort of legal issues that arise when a bike club (or anyone else) organizes cycling and cycling-related activities.

Finally, in Chapter 7, we look at the sport of bicycle racing, identifying the key actors and their roles in this complicated endeavour and then describing in detail the manner in which bicycle racing is organized and regulated.

Most readers won't sit down and read this book cover-to-cover. It is more likely that you'll have it at your elbow to use as a primer as issues in your cycling career arise. We hope that some chapters are never relevant because you never fall off your bike, it never breaks, and it is never stolen. But even then, these chapters suggest means of avoiding these mishaps. All told, we hope that this book will make your cycling safer, swifter, and more satisfying.

endnotes

1   For a recent discussion of 19th century cycling (and law), see Christopher Waters, "The Rebirth of Bicycling Law?" (2013) 91 Can Bar Rev 395.
2   Mark Hunter, "Is Cycling the New Golf?" *SLAW* (14 August 2014), online: www.slaw. ca/2014/08/14/is-cycling-the-new-golf/; Paul Luke, "Is Cycling the New Golf? From Fairway to Roadway and Back Again" *The Province* (31 March 2014); Oliver Moore, "Cycling is the New Golf: The Rise of an On-Trend Activity" *The Globe and Mail* (10 June 2012); "Cycling is the New Golf" *The Economist* (26 April 2013).
3   For an excellent guide to criticisms of these present rules, see Waters, above note 1.

chapter 2

Riding Your Bicycle

introduction

Many Canadians first learn to ride a bicycle when they are children. At that age, the ability to pedal away on a bicycle seems like an exhilarating and emancipating activity. Our parents and members of our communities often teach us basic rules about how to ride a bicycle on the road or on a trail, but for the most part, we consider cycling a freewheeling activity — one that provides fun and independence. As children, and later as adults, we are often oblivious to the fact that riding a bicycle is actually a highly regulated activity in Canada. In fact, cyclists and the equipment they use are subject to a large number of rules under federal, provincial, territorial, and municipal laws and regulations.

For the most part, the basic rights and duties of cyclists are found in highway traffic and safety laws and regulations at the provincial, territorial, and municipal levels of government. The full body of rules that regulates cycling also extends further to include many other types of statutes, regulations, and bylaws, and include court decisions as well. The first main chapter of this book outlines the most important legal rules that apply to riding a bicycle in Canada.

Some of you will disagree with a number of these rules. Mandatory helmet requirements galvanize serious debate. Bells on bikes are a source of mirth (and irritation during police bike-check blitzes) among many cyclists. Cyclists commonly disregard full stops at stop signs, a car-centric rule that many cyclists perceive as risky.

From time to time we discuss the merits of these rules below. But rules they are — if you do not like them, then knowing about them is the first step in changing them.

statutory definitions

A good number of law books, and almost all statutes, start with "definitions." A book on bicycling law is no different, and "what is a bicycle" is a surprisingly convoluted issue. This is especially the case on the margins — for instance, over the issue of whether power-operated two-wheel vehicles are entitled to "bicycle" status and should be allowed on, for instance, bicycle paths.

bicycle

There is no uniform legal definition of what constitutes a "bicycle" or a "cycle" in provincial and territorial laws. Some jurisdictions such as British Columbia,[1] Alberta,[2] Nunavut,[3] and the Northwest Territories[4] specify that a bicycle is a device with three characteristics: (1) it has any number of wheels; (2) it is propelled by human power; and (3) it can be ridden by a person. Manitoba law provides the same, but adds a qualification that a bicycle is propelled by human muscular power "through the use of pedals."[5] In all four Atlantic provinces[6] and in the Yukon,[7] a bicycle is a device propelled by human power upon which a person may ride, but laws in those jurisdictions generally restrict the legal definition to devices that have "two tandem wheels." Neither Ontario nor Quebec highway traffic laws describe what constitutes a bicycle despite referring to such vehicles throughout the legislation. In Saskatchewan, the relevant provincial law does not explicitly refer to bicycles, but the definition of a vehicle is broad enough to include them; the definition provides that a vehicle is "a device in, on or by which a person or thing is or may be transported or drawn on a highway."[8]

It is possible that provincial, territorial, or municipal regulations will adopt a slightly different definition of a bicycle depending on the purpose of the regulation. For instance, for the purposes of implementing a mandatory safety helmet requirement for youth, Alberta regulations define a bicycle as "a cycle propelled solely by human power on which a person may ride that has 2 wheels, and includes a bicycle with training wheels."[9]

unicycle, tricycle, and quadricycle

It is clear that some statutory definitions of a "bicycle" exclude unicycles, tricycles, and quadricycles. This is the case in New Brunswick, Prince Edward Island and Newfoundland and Labrador, where laws regulating highway traffic specify that a bicycle has "two tandem wheels."[10] In the Yukon, territorial legislation applies only to bicycles with two tandem wheels, or to a device that has three wheels, "but not more than three wheels."[11] In Nova Scotia, the definition of a bicycle includes devices with either two tandem wheels, or four wheels.[12] Ontario legislation specifically mentions that a "bicycle" includes a tricycle or a unicycle.[13] In other jurisdictions, a bicycle can have any number of wheels.[14]

power-assisted bicycle

Some provincial and territorial laws contain references to power-assisted bicycles, commonly called e-bikes, electric bicycles, electric assist bicycles, or electric scooters.[15] There exist many possible types of power-assisted bicycles as different technologies are available to equip these devices. However, according to federal regulations,[16] a power-assisted bicycle is defined by the presence of the following essential components:

(1) it has steering handlebars and pedals;
(2) it has a maximum of three wheels;
(3) it is capable of being propelled by muscular power;
(4) it has an electric motor with a 500W output or less for propulsion;
(5) the electric motor alone must not be capable of speeds in excess of 32 km/h on level ground; and

(6) it must bear a permanently-affixed label stating in both official languages that the vehicle conforms to the federal definition of a power-assisted bicycle.[17]

While the wording may differ, a number of provinces rely on the federal definition to describe a power-assisted bicycle.[18] Statutes in Alberta,[19] Manitoba,[20] and Ontario[21] explicitly refer to "power-assisted bicycles" or "power bicycles" in highway traffic legislation.[22] In Quebec, a "power-assisted bicycle" refers to a bicycle that has an electric motor.[23] In Nova Scotia, the definition of "bicycle" includes devices with electric motors.[24] In British Columbia, the term "motor-assisted bicycle" is used in relation to devices that meet the criteria of "power-assisted bicycles" under the federal regulations.[25]

In other Canadian jurisdictions, broad definitions of vehicle or motor-assisted bicycles may encompass power-assisted bicycles. For instance, this would appear to be the case in Prince Edward Island, where a "moped" or "motor assisted pedal bicycle" means a vehicle that: (1) has an electric motor or a motor having a piston displacement no greater than 50 cubic centimetres; (2) is not capable of obtaining speeds greater than 50 km/h; and (3) has no more than three wheels in contact with the ground.[26] In Saskatchewan, there are two categories of power-assisted bicycles. The first category is the "electric assist bicycle," which uses pedals and a motor at the same time. The second category is the "power cycle," which uses either pedals and a motor or a motor only, and is required to meet the federal standards for a power-assisted bicycle.[27]

motor-assisted bicycle

Motor-assisted bicycles are also known as mopeds, motorbikes, or limited-speed motorcycles. According to federal regulations,[28] a limited-speed motorcycle is defined by the presence of the following essential components:

(1) it has steering handlebars that are completely constrained from rotating in relation to the axle of only one wheel in contact with the ground;
(2) it has a maximum speed of 70 km/h or less;
(3) it has a minimum driver's seat height of 650 mm; and
(4) it does not have a structure partially or fully enclosing the driver and passenger, other than that part of the vehicle forward of the driver's torso and the seat backrest.[29]

While the laws regulating motor-assisted bicycles are not the subject of this book, we include the definition of these vehicles to clearly distinguish them from power-assisted bicycles. The distinction is important to make because the term "motor-assisted bicycle" may be used in legislation and regulations to refer to what is essentially a power-assisted bicycle, as is the case in British Columbia.[30] It may also be true that statutory references to "motor-assisted bicycles" are sufficiently broad and imprecise to encompass not only the limited-speed motorcycles described in the federal regulations, but also "power-assisted bicycles."[31]

In New Brunswick, a bicycle that could be pedaled, run from the electric, battery-powered motor, or a combination of battery and muscle power was considered a motor vehicle rather than a bicycle for the purposes of enforcing a driving suspension.[32]

other devices with wheels

In British Columbia, the definition of a bicycle specifically excludes "skate boards, roller skates or in-line roller skates."[33] Nova Scotia legislation exempts wheelchairs from the definition of a bicycle.[34] Pedicabs are also included in the definition of a vehicle for the purposes of highway traffic regulation in Nova Scotia. According to provincial regulations, a pedicab is a device with the following components: (1) it is designed to transport an operator and three or fewer passengers; (2) it has three wheels; and (3) it is propelled by human power, or human and mechanical power.[35]

legal requirements to ride a bicycle
minimum age

As a general rule, there is no minimum age to ride legally a conventional bicycle. However, some jurisdictions have set a minimum age requirement to operate a power-assisted bicycle. In Alberta, regulations state that the legal age for riding a power-assisted bicycle is twelve years.[36] Manitoba has set the minimum age at fourteen.[37] In Quebec, the minimum age to ride on an electric bicycle or tricycle is also fourteen years.[38] In Ontario[39] and British Columbia[40] the minimum age is set at sixteen years.

licensing

Every time a new controversy arises in media reporting about bicycles and cars — every summer in other words — some member of the car tribe insists that cyclists be licensed, to the chagrin of the pedaling clan. In fact, municipalities in at least some provinces can and have instituted licensing requirements for conventional bicycles. As a result, cyclists must consult local bylaws to verify whether they are legally required to obtain a licence. Regulations differ among municipalities. For instance, Toronto opted out of bicycle licensing programs all-together when it repealed its bylaw in 1957. In Regina, on the other hand, every bike is required by law to be licensed.[41]

Some provinces and territories require a licence to operate a power-assisted bicycle. In Saskatchewan, a device that meets the definition of a "power cycle" requires at least a learner's driving licence; the "electric assist bicycle," however, does not.[42] In Quebec, if under the age of eighteen, a power-assisted cyclist must hold a licence to drive a moped or motorized scooter, or a probationary licence to drive either a passenger vehicle or a motorcycle.[43] In Alberta, the regulations provide that "a person who is less than 18 years old shall not drive a power bicycle on a highway unless the person carries the consent of a parent or guardian . . . or holds a subsisting operator's licence."[44]

equipment requirements and prohibitions

safety helmets

Mandatory Helmet Laws

When Craig began racing bikes in the mid-1980s, hard shell helmets were rare (and hot, bulky, and oversized). Plus, none of the pros wore them, and so they were distinctly unfashionable. Now hard shell helmets are ubiquitous and cycling culture, like hockey culture, has generally warmed to the idea that blows to the head are not a good thing. This is a sensible view. A recent study of Ontario cycling fatalities from 2006–2010 found an "association between dying as a result of sustaining a head injury and not wearing a helmet. These results are consistent with a protective effect of helmets on cycling deaths."[45] This is a significant finding, and there is room for progress on this issue since 75 percent of Canadians between eleven and fifteen years old ride bikes, but only 25 percent wear helmets all the time. The proportion of children wearing helmets is better in provinces with mandatory helmet laws.[46] And indeed, other studies suggest mandatory bike helmet laws seem to lead to more helmet use generally.[47]

That said, there are still heated debates about whether helmets should be mandatory. Some of this debate falls into the "right to have wind in my hair" or "helmets muss my hairdo" camp. Others are more serious. For instance, bike share programs are now on the rise, but it is one thing to share a bike, and quite another to imagine that every tourist inclined to tootle about on a Bixi rental happens to have a helmet. It is even harder to imagine prospective riders receiving warmly the helmet dispensed from a vending machine, just returned by a sweaty earlier user.

Even more concerning are studies suggesting that helmet use increases risky behaviour. One recent experimental study affirmed a commonly expressed fear that cyclists riding with helmets perceive reduced risk, and ride faster.[48] Another study noted that helmet laws seem not to have injury reducing effects, and concluded (from Norwegian data) that helmet laws just discourage riding by less equipment-rich but generally slower and safer riding cyclists.[49] Australian[50] and New Zealand[51] studies showed little improved injury outcomes from mandatory helmet laws, and the Australian research measured a decline in cycling after the introduction of mandatory helmet rules. Indeed, the literature is rich with studies suggesting that bicycle helmet laws are at best useless and at worst counterproductive to net societal health.[52] Those studies are very persuasive, but then so are the studies that show the opposite: that bicycle helmets enhance net societal health.[53]

Potentially instructive are the findings of a 2013 study looking at hospitalization rates for cyclists before and after Alberta's mandatory helmet law for children: "Following the introduction of bicycle helmet legislation targeting those under the age of 18, the proportion of child bicyclist ED [emergency department] visits and child and adolescent bicyclist hospitalizations due to HIs [head injuries] declined to a greater extent than expected based on trends in pedestrian injuries. We also noted declines in the proportion of adult HI hospitalizations."[54] Helmets may not deserve full credit for these results — yet another study made similar findings based on Canadian hospital admissions data, but concluded that more important than mandatory helmet laws were "provincial and municipal safety campaigns, improvements to the cycling infrastructure, and the passive uptake of helmets."[55] Mandatory helmets laws are not, in other words, a silver bullet.

From all this, we think the Canadian evidence suggests helmets "work," in the sense that they save lives. But even we cannot agree on whether helmets should be mandatory (for at least adults). We both believe that educating cyclists is a critical step in encouraging them to don a cycling helmet. Nicole is unpersuaded, however, that mandatory helmet laws add much, as compared to the relative safety of cycling, and weighed against the knock-on effects on personal liberty and the possible reduction in cycling participation rates. Craig, for his part, places helmets in the same category as seat belts: a meaningful protection reducing tragic outcomes. He suspects dips in participation rates may be a temporary reaction where helmet culture is not yet well-established (and some of the comparative studies on this phenomena use figures that are a generation old). He is also less libertarian when it comes to public safety measures in a health system where we all foot the bill for unsafe choices.

But whatever one's personal philosophy on the question of helmet use, be warned: as discussed in Chapter 3, if you don't wear one and you crack your head, a court is likely to find you also were negligent in any lawsuit you bring against the driver who hit you.

Turning to the regulatory specifics, several provinces in Canada have made wearing a safety helmet while riding a bicycle mandatory. In British Columbia,[56] Nova Scotia,[57] Prince Edward Island,[58] and New Brunswick,[59] the compulsory helmet laws apply to cyclists of all ages. In Alberta[60], Ontario,[61] and Manitoba[62] only cyclists under eighteen years are legally required to wear a helmet. In Manitoba, the mandatory helmet law also applies to an individual under eighteen years of age when the youth or child is a passenger on a bicycle or in a child carrier attached to or towed by a bicycle.[63] The remaining provinces and territories do not have any laws regarding the mandatory wearing of a bicycle helmet. Some municipalities have, for their part, adopted bylaws that require cyclists to wear helmets. Cities with mandatory helmet bylaws include Vancouver,[64] Yorkton,[65] Sherbrooke,[66] Westmount,[67] Mount Pearl,[68] Corner Brook,[69] St. John's,[70] Inuvik,[71] and Whitehorse.[72]

Legislation mandating the wearing of bicycle safety helmets may be limited to on-road riding,[73] or it may be worded more broadly to cover both on-road and off-road riding.[74]

In British Columbia,[75] Alberta,[76] Saskatchewan,[77] Manitoba,[78] Ontario,[79] Québec,[80] and Nova Scotia,[81] anyone operating a power-assisted bicycle must wear an approved bicycle helmet at all times.

Exemptions from Mandatory Helmet Laws

British Columbia exempts some persons from wearing bicycle safety helmets. According to the provincial regulations, a cyclist is not required to wear a helmet if:

(1) it interferes with an essential religious practice;[82]

(2) if they are the operator or a passenger of a pedicab or quadricycle;

(3) ~~they are unable to wear a helmet for medical reasons; or~~

(4) if they are under the age of twelve years and are riding a non-chain driven three- or four-wheeled cycle designed for recreational use by children.[83]

There are also similar religious and medical exemptions in Nova Scotia, in addition to an exemption for a person who has a head measurement that exceeds 66 cm in circumference.[84] According to the Prince Edward Island regulations, the provincial Registrar can issue an exemption certificate to a person who has a head measurement that exceeds 64 cm in circumference, or to a person who should not be required, for any reason satisfactory to the Registrar, to wear a bicycle safety helmet.[85]

Helmet Standards

Some legislation sets out specific standards in relation to bicycle safety helmets. In New Brunswick and Nova Scotia,[86] where all cyclists must wear a helmet, the law specifies that the chin strap of the helmet is to be securely fastened under the person's chin.[87] Manitoba legislation specifies that persons operating a power-assisted cycle must wear a properly fitted and fastened helmet.[88] In British Columbia,[89] Ontario,[90] Nova Scotia,[91] PEI,[92] and Alberta,[93] regulations outline very specific standards, including a requirement that a bicycle safety helmet meet manufacturing safety standards such as those prescribed by the Canadian Standards Association or the Snell Memorial Foundation. Regulations also specify a number of additional legal requirements, including that a helmet have a smooth outer surface; an ability to absorb energy; and a chin strap. It must also be undamaged and properly fit the person wearing it.

Helmet Offences

Where the wearing of a bicycle safety helmet is mandatory, a person commits an offence if they operate or ride as a passenger on a bicycle or a power-assisted bicycle, and are not properly wearing a bicycle safety helmet.[94] It is also an offence for a parent or guardian to authorize or knowingly allow a youth to operate or ride as a passenger without properly wearing a bicycle safety helmet.[95] Persons convicted of such offences are liable to fines the amount of which will vary depending on the relevant provincial or municipal law.[96]

bells and horns

Look to your left and to your right at any organized cycling event and count the number of bells and horns mounted to bicycles. Commuter and lower-end bikes may have them, but generally not the glitzy sportif bikes. Many cyclists scoff at the idea. Craig, for one, finds the idea of a horn on a time trial bike (or frankly any bike) aesthetically unpleasing. Perhaps more mean-ingfully, neither of us can think of any purpose to be served by a device that may require us to adjust our grip in a manner that shifts our hand from brake to bell/horn (or in Ontario, "gong"), in a faintly pathetic effort to tin-kle at a city bus. And for those who might be in a position to hear anything above the music in their sound-proofed automobile, or the personal electron-ic devices used by many pedestrians, we both come equipped with a voice. This is especially true on bike paths, where pedestrians and other users may be warned of an approaching cyclist with a "passing on your left." The alternative is the indiscriminate and sometimes frenetic ringing of a bell signalling nothing other than the approach of someone whose hands may no longer be on his or her brakes. Moreover, we have both witnessed small children and adults respond to aggressively tinkled bells by jumping with fright into the path of the overtaking cyclist, causing near disasters.

In a search of the research database, we were unable to find any study advancing (or even assessing) the safety argument in favour of bells. And yet, five provinces require cyclists to mount a bell, horn or other audible warning device[97] on their bicycle: Alberta,[98] Ontario,[99] New Brunswick,[100] Prince Edward Island,[101] and Nova Scotia.[102] However, the three maritime provinces specifically prohibit the use of a "siren or whistle" on a bicycle.[103]

Some municipalities may also require bicycles to be equipped with an audible warning device. This is the case, for example, in Vancouver, where a municipal bylaw states that "[n]o person shall ride a bicycle upon a street unless the bicycle is equipped with a bell capable of being used as a warn-ing."[104] In Edmonton, cyclists are required to use a bell when passing other trail users on municipal park lands.[105]

Some provinces also specify the use to be made of an audible warning device: cyclists are required to give a warning when it is reasonably neces-sary to warn pedestrians and other drivers of their approach.[106]

brakes

Several provinces and territories require bicycles to be equipped with brakes.[107] Some laws specify that the brake system must enable the cyclist to block the rotation of the rear wheel sufficiently to skid on "dry, level and clean pavement,"[108] or be capable of "controlling the movement of and stopping the bicycle."[109] Under such regulations, a fixed-gear bicycle, or fixed-wheel bicycle, would fail to meet legal requirements as most fixed-gear bicycles only have a front brake, and some have no brakes at all.

lights and reflectors

The laws of every province and territory, except Saskatchewan and Nunavut, require bicycles to be equipped with reflectors and lights, principally if they are operated at night.[110] The laws can be specific about the type of lights and reflectors required, such as a white light at the front and red light or reflector at the rear.[111] In Ontario, it is currently expressly prohibited to equip a bicycle with a red flashing light,[112] a very common practice for many cyclists. But at the time of writing this book, changes to Ontario's law were possible.[113] The time period during which lights are to be used can also be specified. For instance, in British Columbia, lights and reflectors are to be used if a person is cycling "between 1/2 hour after sunset and 1/2 hour before sunrise."[114]

electronic equipment

Portable electronic equipment is increasingly carried and used by cyclists while riding. This includes mobile phones, portable media players, and equipment containing display screens that require input in order to function, such as GPS devices. The use of such devices while riding a bicycle is considered by some to be distracting and dangerous.[115] As a result, several Canadian jurisdictions have regulated or prohibited the use of electronic equipment while riding a bicycle.

One way the use of electronic equipment may be restricted is through highway safety laws that require individuals to drive with due care and attention. This obligation more often than not applies to cyclists.[116] If distracted while using an electronic device, a cyclist may commit the offence of careless riding, or riding without due care. For instance, Ontario's *Highway Traffic Act* defines careless driving as operating "a vehicle or street car on a highway without due care and attention or without reasonable considera-tion for other persons using the highway."[117]

In addition, as outlined in the next sections, legal restrictions on the use of electronic devices that explicitly apply to cyclists have been adopted in several provinces and territories.

Cellular Phones

Almost all provinces and territories have complemented the general duty to drive with care with specific prohibitions on the use of hand-held cell devices for talking, texting, or e-mailing. Only in Nunavut is it still legal to talk or text on cellphones while driving.[118] However, in most provinces and territories, the ban on cellphones only applies to drivers of motor vehicles. Only Alberta[119] and the Northwest Territories[120] have restrictions on using cellphones that extend to cyclists. In both of those jurisdictions, cyclists cannot use a handheld device unless they are using the cellular telephone in handsfree mode.[121]

Headphones and Ear Buds

In Manitoba, cyclists are prohibited from wearing, "on both ears, headphones which are used for the purpose of listening to a radio or a recording."[122] It is also illegal to wear headphones or earphones in Quebec.[123] The City of Van-couver also has a bylaw prohibiting the use of headphones while operating a bicycle.[124]

Global Positioning Systems (GPS)

In Alberta, the *Traffic Safety Act* prohibits individuals from using a global positioning system for navigation purposes while operating a vehicle on a highway. However, a cyclist can use a GPS if it "is programmed before the individual begins to drive or operate the vehicle," or if it "is used in a voice-activated manner."[125] If a GPS is portable, a cyclist can use the system while riding if it "is not held in the individual's hand, and is securely affixed to the vehicle in a manner that does not interfere with the safe operation of the vehicle."[126]

compliance with equipment and safety requirements

Cyclists are expected to conform to the equipment requirements specified in the law.[127] In Manitoba, a peace officer can stop and inspect a bicycle to determine if the bicycle is equipped as required by law.[128] In the Yukon, a peace officer may examine a bicycle to assess whether it is "fit and safe to be ridden."[129] A failure to comply with equipment and safety requirements could result in a cyclist being charged with "operating an unsafe vehicle."[130]

roadway rights and responsibilities

Most provincial and territorial laws provide that cyclists must comply with the same rules of the road that bind motor vehicle drivers.[131] This generally means that cyclists must follow the same rules as motor vehicles — for example, in relation to traffic lights, stop signs, yielding the right of way, and complying with road signs and signals. In *R v Moore*,[132] the Supreme Court of Canada held that under the British Columbia *Motor Vehicle Act*, a cyclist is under the same duties as the driver of a motor vehicle, which in turn meant that persons operating a bicycle were prohibited from proceeding against a red light at an intersection.

As a result, cyclists must be familiar with all of the rights and duties that apply to drivers of motor vehicles.

In addition, many highway traffic laws also list the explicit rights and duties of cyclists when riding on and off roads. The following sections outline the principal rules that apply specifically to cyclists.

stop lights and signs

If there is one, overarching complaint drivers seem to have of cyclists, it is that many disregard red lights and most seem to disregard stop signs. In one Australian study, 11 percent of cyclists disregarded red lights. The class of cyclists in this study most likely to appear as an accident statistic were the so-called "runners" — those who sailed through an already changed red light without pause.[133] We have no evidence on this point, but based on personal observations, we suspect that some portion of these runners are riding at night, clad in black, without lights or helmet, travelling against traffic and possibly inebriated.

The law is clear on this point: stop lights and signs apply equally to cyclists as to motor vehicles. Point final (or more fittingly, full stop). These requirements have the effect (in theory) of making all road users predictable in their response to traffic instructions. In his more vigilante moments, Craig has been known to chase down cyclists on group rides who blow through red lights, in order to educate them on this book's key finding. He is especially likely to do so in organized, but open road events in which everyone is wearing a number signifying common participation. In part, this is because he tires of all cyclists being blamed by drivers for the misdeeds of some cyclists. (As a motorist, he would not accept being painted a deviant because of the disreputable conduct of other drivers.) His traffic law advocacy produces few signs of improved behaviour, but does induce exhaustion as he tries to catch errant riders rolling through a sequence of stop lights at which Craig must stop each time. Nicole tends to roll her eyes, sigh, dutifully stop at the lights, and then pedal like hell to catch up with the misbehaving group.

That said, whatever the content of the law, there is vigorous room for debate as to its merits. As the accident data in Chapter 3 suggest, intersections can be particularly hazardous places for cyclists, and it is not clear to us that the hazard is always a product of disregard for the rules. A bicycle is most stable while in motion. A constantly stopping and starting bicycle is often a wobbly bicycle, one that is incapable of manoeuvring much at all at slow speeds. There is some risk that a cyclist otherwise able to match urban traffic speeds becomes to drivers an impediment to be passed, something that brings its own perils. It is also the case that stopping and starting expends significantly more energy. This in its own right is no excuse — people ride bicycles to improve fitness. But start and stop enough, and fatigue may affect reaction time.

Most people do not imagine there is much alternative to the current state of the rules. But in fact, this continent's alternative experiment is the so-called "Idaho stop." Since the 1980s, the Idaho code has read:

1) A person operating a bicycle or human-powered vehicle approaching a stop sign shall slow down and, if required for safety, stop before entering the intersection. After slowing to a reasonable speed or stopping, the person shall yield the right-of-way to any vehicle in the intersection or approaching on another highway so closely as to constitute an immediate hazard during the time the person is moving across or within the intersection or junction of highways, except that a person after slowing to a reasonable speed and yielding the right-of-way if required, may cautiously make a turn or proceed through the intersection without stopping.

2) A person operating a bicycle or human-powered vehicle approaching a steady red traffic control light shall stop before entering the intersection and shall yield to all other traffic. Once the person has yielded, he may proceed through the steady red light with caution. Provided however, that a person after slowing to a reasonable speed and yielding the right-

of-way if required, may cautiously make a right-hand turn. A left-hand turn onto a one-way highway may be made on a red light after stopping and yielding to other traffic. [134]

Put another way, Idaho law allows cyclists to treat stop signs as yield signs, and red lights as stop signs.

We imagine that a similar rule in Canada would drive some drivers to distraction, as it seems to privilege bicycles. It would have the effect, however, of regulating behaviour that is currently commonplace, but without any standard. Indeed, in our experience, informal driving conventions now seem almost to assume an Idaho style approach to stop signs. Both of us, in our obsessive compulsive effort to comply with stop sign rules, often disrupt traffic through a four-lane stop by actually stopping, while drivers try to wave us through. On the other hand, in the confused culture of bicycle and car interactions, we can't always be sure that the drivers in question will be of the "yield to cyclists" credo or the "you must stop or I'll yell at you and try to steer you off the road" orthodoxy. So confusion often reigns at intersections in Ottawa.

It is worth noting that there is some evidence the Idaho stop rules are safer, and associated with fewer (or less severe) collisions.[135] Whether similar patterns would recur in more densely populated and heavily trafficked regions is unknown. The matter is certainly worthy of further discussion and study.

signalling a turn

Cyclists have to indicate their intention to make a left turn, right turn, or a stop by using hand signals. Generally, the hand signal is made with the left arm and hand, and the manner in which this is done is described by the relevant provision of the law. In some jurisdictions, cyclists can use their right arm to signal a right turn.[136]

riding on the far right-hand side

Slow-moving traffic, including bicycles, can be required to travel in the right-hand lane of a highway, or as close as practicable to the right edge of the road, except when preparing to turn left or when passing another vehicle.[137] In Alberta, if a highway has a paved shoulder, a cyclist must ride on the right shoulder.[138] However, there is no requirement to ride on the part of highway that is not paved; this is explicitly provided for in Alberta and British Columbia laws.[139]

riding in single file

All provincial and territorial laws, except in Saskatchewan and Ontario, explicitly prohibit cyclists riding abreast another bicycle. Cyclists are required to ride single file except when overtaking another bicycle.[140] In Quebec, a single file cannot be composed of more than fifteen cyclists.[141] In New Brunswick, the prohibition on riding abreast does not apply to paths or parts of roadways set aside for the exclusive use of bicycles.[142]

Cyclists often disregard single file riding rules, especially when participating in organized or semi-organized group rides. Whether riding two-abreast (the standard for the Ontario bicycle club rides in which we participate) or as a pack (the standard for some of the crazier rides in which Craig has participated and the famous chain gang rides Nicole rode when living in Cambridge in the UK), group riding occupies more road space. Drivers tend to be offended by this. Cyclists may consider it safer — cars are forced to decelerate, and pass when safe, much as they would when encountering the slow-moving farm tractor or other powered vehicle. This, in the mind of some cyclists, is better than the car that insists on budging not a centimetre from its assigned course, and clips or comes close to clipping the solitary cyclist. In fact, we could find little empirical literature one way or another on group riding and safety. The single greatest preoccupation in an Australian study on the subject was groups running red lights[143] — something we have witnessed. We would add that stop signs are particularly difficult for group riding — the start and stop breaks up groups and causes mass confusion for both riders and drivers at stop signs. In practice, the (illegal) practice of many groups in our experience is for group leaders to announce an intersection as clear (or not) allowing the riders to sail through (or not). In other words, group riders often adopt an Idaho approach.

riding on sidewalks

Provincial and territorial laws generally prohibit cyclists from riding on sidewalks,[144] unless authorized by a specific bylaw or otherwise directed by traffic signs or traffic control devices.[145] Traffic laws in Ontario, Saskatchewan, and the Yukon do not specifically prohibit riding on sidewalks. Restrictions on cycling on sidewalks can also be regulated by municipal bylaws.[146] For instance, the City of Toronto only allows cyclists with a tire size of 61 cm or 24 inches or less to ride on the sidewalk, essentially permitting only young children to cycle on the sidewalk.[147] Other municipalities prohibit all cyclists from riding on sidewalks.[148] Some regulations may specifically allow a peace officer or a newspaper carrier to ride a bicycle on a sidewalk.[149]

riding on designated bicycle pathways

Parts of a roadway may be designed for the use of cyclists or designated as bicycle pathways. Areas dedicated to cycling traffic may include the paved shoulders of a roadway; a marked lane on a roadway reserved for the exclusive use of cyclists; segregated bicycle lanes or paths which are physically separated from motor vehicles; and designated roadways, shared by both cyclists and motorists.[150]

In all of the Atlantic provinces, whenever a useable bicycle lane or path has been established adjacent to a roadway, cyclists are required to ride within the bicycle lane,[151] unless, as provided for in Nova Scotia, it is impracticable to do so.[152] Riding in cycling lanes or paths is also required in the Northwest Territories[153] and Nunavut[154]. In Alberta, if a highway has paved shoulders, cyclists are required to ride on the right shoulder.[155] Numerous municipalities have designated bicycle lanes or pathways, but for the most part, it is not mandatory for cyclists to use them.[156]

If cyclists must ride in designated bicycle pathways, conversely, motor vehicles are prohibited from driving or stopping in a bicycle lane.[157] If for some lawful reason a motor vehicle must move into a bicycle lane, for example to avoid a hazard or to pass a left turning vehicle, the law may require them to yield the right of way to any cyclist.[158]

Some municipalities such as Toronto have recently allowed e-scooters — electrically assisted scooters with token and useless pedals — to use bike lanes. These decisions have ignited controversy. As one Toronto city report noted "The likelihood of being injured when struck by a 120 kg vehicle [the maximum e-bike weight] travelling at 32 km/h [the maximum speed] is probably far greater than if struck by a lighter bicycle travelling at a slower speed."[159] This preoccupation has led some regulators to ban the machines on bicycle pathways.

The National Capital Commission runs Ottawa's chief recreational pathways. On those pathways, e-scooters are banned: "[v]ery often, the electric bike with a non-conventional appearance is much heavier than a conventional-type electric bicycle, and therefore poses greater risks to safety in the event of a collision."[160] Craig has been known to cite NCC regulations at full voice to e-bike riders who have silently raced down on him at 32 km/h and 120 kg as he runs along the recreational trails. He is unsure whether this is an effective strategy.

riding between two lanes of vehicles

Traffic laws in Quebec specifically prohibit cyclists from riding "between two lines of vehicles moving on contiguous lanes."[161]

speeding

In some jurisdictions, speeding limits on roadways and related offences apply to motor vehicles only, and not bicycles. For instance, under the Ontario *Highway Traffic Act*, the prohibition on speeding states that "[n]o person shall drive a motor vehicle" at a rate of speed greater than prescribed by law or regulation.[162] In other provinces and territories — for example, Alberta, Saskatchewan, and the Yukon — speeding prohibitions apply to a person driving a "vehicle," which is defined broadly enough to include a bicycle.[163]

There may be speeding limits on designated bicycle pathways and trails. For instance, a Calgary bylaw states that persons cannot ride a bicycle at a speed greater than 20 kilometres per hour in a municipal park.[164] The bylaw further states that rate of speeds should not be unreasonable, for instance with regard to the "nature, condition and use" of the pathway or trail, or the volume and type of traffic on the pathway.[165]

prohibited highways

Cyclists may be prohibited by law from using specific highways and roadways.[166] For example, Ontario prohibits riding a bicycle on controlled-access highways.[167] At the time of writing, there were proposals that would allow cyclists to use the paved shoulders on some separated provincial highways, to promote safer opportunities to cycle.[168] Generally, traffic signs will identify the roads upon which cyclists must not ride. Municipalities may also ban cyclists from highways under their jurisdiction.[169] However, the Alberta Court of Queen's Bench quashed one such municipal ban in 1997, holding that the Rocky View municipal bylaw that prohibited bicycles from operating on a specific road discriminated against cyclists, and there was no statutory authorization in provincial law permitting such discrimination.[170]

cycling road signs and markings

Cyclists have to obey road signs and traffic signals.[7] In fact, specific signs and signals have been developed for cyclists and cycling pathways. Green is now the colour adopted in North America as the standard colour for cycling signs and facilities. The following are a few examples of cycling road signs:

Designated Bike Route
Indicates streets that form a part of a bicycle route.

Diamond Lanes
Indicates that lanes are reserved for use by specific vehicles such as buses, taxis, and bicycles.

Bicycle Parking
Indicates where bicycle racks or supervised bicycle parking may be found.

Cyclist Dismount
Indicates the need to get off a bicycle for safety reasons.

Advanced Stop Lines (also known as Bicycle Boxes)
Indicates area where cyclists may get into position for turning or going straight when the signal turns green, ahead of other motor vehicle traffic.

One Way Except for Bicycles
Indicates that cyclists can ride against the flow of traffic on a one-way street.

Bicycle with Arrow
Indicates that the direction of a bicycle route is changing.

Sharrows
Reminds drivers to share the road when driving or cycling.

Shared Pathway
Indicates an off-street pathway shared by pedestrians and cyclists. Cyclists must yield to pedestrians.

Cycling Prohibited
Indicates that riding a bicycle is prohibited on the roadway.

riding off-road

Rules regarding off-road riding can be found in both regulations and voluntary codes of conduct.

The National Capital Commission has adopted a regulation that forbids cycling on property under the jurisdiction of the federal agency — for instance, Gatineau Park, Quebec — other than on a driveway or a bicycle path set aside for this purpose.[172] A similar restriction exists in provincial regulations in Alberta: cyclists can only ride on roads and trails within provincial parks.[173] In Calgary, a bylaw regulating the use of municipal parks and pathways also requires that cyclists ride only on a pathway, trail, or park roadway.[174]

In terms of voluntary rules, the International Mountain Bicycling Association has developed guidelines to promote safety and responsible conduct for riding bicycles off-road.[175] Mountain bike facilities such as the Silver Star Bike Park in British Columbia, and Blue Mountain's Bike Park in Ontario also have codes of conduct that cyclists are expected to follow.[176] The same is true of some national parks: for instance, Banff National Park has some guidelines about riding bicycles in the park.

motor vehicles passing bicycles

Provincial laws are typically fairly ambiguous on motorists passing cyclists. In Manitoba, traffic laws require drivers to pass to the left at a safe distance when overtaking a bicycle, and to avoid returning to the right until they have safely cleared the bicycle.[177] Drivers overtaking a bicycle in Ontario are required to "turn out to the left so far as may be necessary to avoid a collision," while the cyclist is expected to turn out to the right to allow the faster vehicle to pass.[178] Quebec also requires drivers to pass bicycles safely.[179]

Nova Scotia applies a different approach, in emulation of a number of US states. In 2011, Nova Scotia enacted rules requiring motor vehicles to pass cyclists at a safe distance by leaving "at least one metre open space between the vehicle and the cyclist."[180] The law also provides that motor vehicles may cross the centre line in order to pass a cyclist, when safe to do so.[181] At the time of writing, there was the possibility that Ontario would introduce a similar "one metre" law.[182]

Cycling safety advocates seem to favour these laws. That said, there is some question as to whether these laws mean much, if enforcement is uneven. A study of Maryland's experience with a "three foot rule" assessing video footage of car passing practices concluded cyclists in Baltimore "were routinely passed at a distance of three feet or less while cycling during morning and evening commutes, which indicates that the three-foot law is not being followed and cyclist safety may be compromised."[183] Risk factors for close passes included narrowing lane width and absence of bicycle lanes. (It is worth noting other studies suggesting that drivers actually pass closer when there is a cycle lane, seeing no reason to deviate around cyclists where there are marked lanes.)[184]

passing on the right

Cyclists passing stalled traffic on the right hand side is an almost universal practice. And yet highway safety laws sometimes bar passing on the right. For instance, in British Columbia, passing on the right is generally prohibited except, for instance, where there is "one or more than one unobstructed lane on the side of the roadway on which the driver is permitted to drive."[185]

On the other hand, Nova Scotia law specifically allows cyclists to pass on the right of a vehicle, if it is safe to do so.[186] For example, a cyclist would be permitted to pass on the right, between a line of cars stopped at a red light and the curb.

We return to cyclists passing on the right in Chapter 3 — it is a relatively common issue when courts are asked to partition responsibility between driver and cyclists in lawsuits.

passing a streetcar or a bus

In Ontario, a cyclist must stop two metres behind the rear-most open door when a streetcar is stopped, and wait for passengers to board or depart and reach the curb.[187] It is also prohibited to pass a streetcar on the left.[188] All vehicles in Ontario, including bicycles, must also yield the right of way to the driver of a bus who has indicated his or her intention to enter into a traffic lane from a bus bay.[189]

car door collisions

Collisions with car doors are a serious danger to cyclists.[190] Motorists have a duty to avoid opening car doors into passing cyclists, an action labelled as "dooring." Indeed, regulations exist that prohibit motorists from opening car doors without ascertaining first that this manoeuvre is safe.[191] In Ontario, for example, a driver could be charged under sections of the *Highway Traffic Act* that requires motorists to take "due precautions" when opening a car door so as not to endanger any other person or vehicle.[192] Usually, the offence simply requires that a driver was careless when opening their door, and not that they intended to break the law or intentionally injure a cyclist. The penalty is by and large a light fine.[193] However, at time of writing, the Ontario Legislature was debating a change in the law that would increase the fine range for convictions of dooring of cyclists from $60–$500 to $300–$1,000.[194]

riding while impaired

Operating a motor vehicle while impaired — for example, under the influence of drugs or alcohol — is a criminal offence in Canada, but riding a bicycle while impaired is not.[195]

While a cyclist cannot be charged under federal criminal laws, provincial laws do impose some restrictions on cycling and drinking. First, some provinces specifically forbid drinking alcohol while riding a bicycle. In Manitoba, a person who is drunk is prohibited from riding a bicycle on a highway or bicycle facility.[196] In Quebec, the law states that "[n]o person may drink alcoholic beverages while riding a bicycle."[197] Second, most provincial laws require individuals to drive with due care and attention and this obligation applies to cyclists.[198] As a result, a cyclist who rides while impaired may commit an offence of careless riding, or riding without due care. For instance, Ontario's *Highway Traffic Act* defines careless driving as operating "a vehicle or street car on a highway without due care and attention or without reasonable consideration for other persons using the highway."[199] Finally, a drunken cyclist could be charged under provincial liquor laws for being intoxicated in a public place,[200] or for consuming alcohol outside of a licensed establishment — for instance, in the case of a cyclist who is drinking while riding.[201]

hitching a ride on another vehicle ("bumper hitching" or "skitching")

It is illegal in most provinces and territories for a cyclist to be towed on a bicycle by holding onto or attaching themselves to a moving vehicle.[202] In Quebec, the law further states that a cyclist is prohibited from holding onto a power-assisted bicycle.[203]

positioning on the bicycle

Several provincial and territorial laws specify the position a cyclist must maintain while riding a bicycle. A person must keep at least one[204] or both hands[205] on the handlebars, except when making a signal; a person must keep both feet on the pedals,[206] and must sit on and astride the seat.[207]

passengers

According to traffic laws in most provinces and territories, a bicycle must not be used to carry more persons than the number for which the cycle was designed or constructed by its manufacturer.[208] Nova Scotia law is very specific in prohibiting cyclists from carrying passengers upon "the handlebar, frame or tank of any such vehicle or side-saddle on any such vehicle."[209] Manitoba law qualifies this prohibition by permitting a child passenger, if the child is under the age of six years and is on a seat designed for carrying infants on bicycles.[210]

carrying objects that interfere with the operation of a bicycle

In some jurisdictions, cyclists are prohibited from carrying objects that may interfere with the proper operation and control of the bicycle.[211]

riding naked

In Canada, criminal laws prohibit indecent acts and public nudity if it offends "against public decency or order."[212] There are no statutory definitions of what constitutes an indecent act, or what offends public decency, so courts have been left to decide what state of undress is "indecent," and thereby unlawful. For instance, courts have found that nude swimming is not offensive,[213] and toplessness is not an indecent act.[214]

Several Canadian cities have been the site of World Naked Bike Rides.[215] These events bring together participants in a clothing-optional bike ride intended to promote bicycling and to protest the "indecent exposure of people and the planet" to the pollution of motor vehicles. Full and partial nudity is encouraged. In 2011, Ottawa police informed cyclists participating in the World Naked Bike Ride that they risked arrest if they rode completely naked and encouraged riders to wear some level of clothing.[216] In Vancouver, a man was arrested when he insisted that he and his three-year-old son ride naked in the 2008 World Naked Bike Ride.[217]

When a radio station held a contest in which a woman agreed to ride a bicycle nude down a main street in Winnipeg for a chance to win a cash prize, the Canadian Broadcast Standards Council found the station in breach of the Canadian Association of Broadcasters Code of Ethics. The Council held "that a nude woman (or, the Council assumes, a nude man) cycling down the principal avenue of one of the nation's largest cities could reasonably be expected to constitute a distraction for drivers," and as a result, the activity caused a "public disturbance or inconvenience" in violation of the broadcasting Code of Ethics.[218]

parking

Parking regulations may prohibit motor vehicles from parking in ways that impede cyclists. For example, in Nova Scotia, motor vehicles may not park in a bike lane.[219]

There are occasional legal restrictions on where a cyclist may park a bicycle,[220] although these may not be closely enforced. For example, a regulation that prohibits cyclists from locking their bicycles to parking meters is rarely enforced in Vancouver.[221] Some bicycle racks may be reserved for bicycle couriers and have a specific time limit on how long a bicycle may be parked.[222] We discuss bicycle parking further in Chapter 5.

Some municipalities have adopted rules, guidelines, or standards that apply to the development of, and the equipment to be used in, parking facilities for bicycles.[223]

stopping and providing identification

In some provinces, territories, and municipalities, cyclists may be stopped by police for breaking traffic laws, or when they are involved in an accident.[224] One Ontario court concluded the "highway" governed by that province's highway safety law does not extend to stopping cyclists using a sidewalk for infractions, like the absence of lights.[225] But before lightless cyclists leap on sidewalks at the appearance of a police cruiser, they should appreciate that municipal law and dangerous driving provisions may reach that conduct.

Once (properly) stopped, a cyclist who fails to cooperate with police by, e.g., correctly identifying oneself, may be charged.[226] In Ontario at least, this does not mean cyclists must carry identification — a (truthful) oral response suffices.[227] In some provinces — Nova Scotia, for instance — police may arrest without warrant a person (including a cyclist) that they find committing a highway safety act offence,[228] while in jurisdictions such as Ontario, an arrest power only arises if the person fails to identify themselves properly.[229]

A failure to cooperate can also be a crime and not just a traffic offence. In *R v Moore*,[230] a cyclist went through an intersection against a red light in the City of Victoria. A police constable stopped him to give him a traffic ticket.

riding your bicycle » **33**

The cyclist refused, however, to provide his name and address. As a result, the constable charged him with unlawfully and wilfully obstructing a peace officer in the execution of his duty, contrary to the *Criminal Code*. The Supreme Court of Canada held that a cyclist who refuses to accede to a constable's request for his identification is in fact obstructing a police officer in the performance of his or her duties.

remaining at the scene of an accident

As discussed more fully in Chapter 3, some laws specify that cyclists must remain at scene of an accident and render all possible assistance.[231]

conclusion

We have all seen him: the inebriated, un-helmeted, nighttime cycling wraith in the black hoodie, astride the camouflaged and unlit bicycle weaving down the sidewalk, and unexpectedly darting across a red-lighted intersection, against traffic. This person is clearly a leading contestant for the Darwin Awards. He is also violating a long list of traffic safety laws. He can be ticketed, fined, sometimes arrested, and (as we discuss more in the next chapter) probably criminally charged. He may not care very much.

For the rest of us, however, there are the rules. We don't agree with all of them — some are useless and others may actually be counterproductive. But most are designed to make cyclists both visible and predictable. In the contest between bicycle and car, this sort of defensive riding is probably the best offence. In the next chapter, we discuss what happens when this strategy doesn't work.

endnotes

1   *Motor Vehicle Act*, RSBC 1996, c 318, s 119(1) [*BC MVA*].
2   *Use of Highway and Rules of the Road Regulation*, Alta Reg 304/2002, s 1(1)(c).
3   *Motor Vehicles Act*, RSNWT (Nu) 1988, c M-16, as enacted for Nunavut, pursuant to the *Nunavut Act*, SC 1993, c 28 [*Nunavut Act*] [*NU MVA*].
4   *NWT MVA*, s 1.
5   *The Highway Traffic Act*, CCSM c H60, s 1(1) [*Man HTA*].
6   *Motor Vehicle Act*, RSNB 1973, c M-17, s 1 [*NB MVA*]; *Motor Vehicle Act*, RSNS 1989, c 293, s 2(c)(i) [*NS MVA*] (Nova Scotia law also specifies the size of the wheels required to meet the definition of a bicycle); *Highway Traffic Act*, RSPEI 1988, c H-5, s 1(a.1) [*PEI HTA*]; *Highway Traffic Act*, RSNL 1990, c H-3, s 2(e) [*NL HTA*].

7   *Motor Vehicles Act*, RSY 2002, c 153, s 1(1)(a) [*YT MVA*].

8   *Traffic Safety Act*, RSA 2000, c T-6, s 2(1)(ccc) [*Alta TSA*]. The City of Saskatoon
    bylaws do have a definition of a bicycle: "Bicycle" means any muscular-propelled,
    chain-driven wheeled device in, on, or by which a person is or may be transported
    or drawn; City of Saskatoon, Bylaw No 6884, *The Bicycle Bylaw* (19 December 2011),
    s 2(b).

9   *Vehicle Equipment Regulation*, Alta Reg 122/2009, s 1(1)(c).

10 *NB MVA*, s 1; *PEI HTA*, s 1(a.1); *NL HTA*, s 2(e).

11 *YT MVA*, s 1(1)(b).

12 *NS MVA*, s 2(c)(i).

13 *Highway Traffic Act*, RSO 1990, c H.8, s 1(1) [*Ont HTA*].

14 *BC MVA*, s 119(1); *Alta TSA*, s 1(1)(i); Alta *Use of Highway and Rules of the Road
    Regulation*, s 1(1)(c); *NU MVA*, s 1; *NWT MVA*, s 1.

15 See *Motor Vehicle Safety Regulations*, CRC, c 1038, s 2(1).

16 The definition is contained in the *Motor Vehicle Safety Regulations*, s 2(1). These
    federal regulations are promulgated by Transport Canada pursuant to the *Motor
    Vehicle Safety Act*, SC 1993, c 16 [*Can MVSA*], and they set out manufacturing and
    importation standards for motor vehicles.

17 See *Motor Vehicle Safety Regulations*, s 2(1):

    "*power-assisted bicycle*" means a vehicle that:
    (*a*) has steering handlebars and is equipped with pedals,
    (*b*) is designed to travel on not more than three wheels in contact with the
           ground,
    (*c*) is capable of being propelled by muscular power,
    (*d*) has one or more electric motors that have, singly or in combination, the
           following characteristics:
           (i)   it has a total continuous power output rating, measured at the shaft of
                  each motor, of 500 W or less,
           (ii)   if it is engaged by the use of muscular power, power assistance im-
                  mediately ceases when the muscular power ceases,
           (iii) if it is engaged by the use of an accelerator controller, power assist-
                  ance immediately ceases when the brakes are applied, and
           (iv)   it is incapable of providing further assistance when the bicycle attains
                  a speed of 32 km/h on level ground,
    (*e*) bears a label that is permanently affixed by the manufacturer and appears
           in a conspicuous location stating, in both official languages, that the
           vehicle is a power-assisted bicycle as defined in this subsection, and
    (*f*) has one of the following safety features,
           (i)   an enabling mechanism to turn the electric motor on and off that is
                  separate from the accelerator controller and fitted in such a manner
                  that it is operable by the driver, or
           (ii)   a mechanism that prevents the motor from being engaged before the
                  bicycle attains a speed of 3 km/h; (bicyclette assistée).

18 See *Man HTA*, s 1(1); Alta *Use of Highway and Rules of the Road Regulation*, s 1(1)(o).

19 *Alta TSA*, s 1(1)(i).

20   *Man HTA*, s 1(1).

21   *Ont HTA*, s 1(1).

22   This is the case in Manitoba: *Man HTA*, s 1(1); in Nova Scotia: *NS MVA*, s 2(c)(ii); in Alberta: *Use of Highway and Rules of the Road Regulation*, s 1(1)(o); and in Ontario: *Ont HTA*, s 1(1).

23   *Highway Safety Code*, CQLR c C-24.2, art 4 [*Que HSC*].

24   *NS MVA*, s 2(c)(ii).

25   *Motor Assisted Cycle Regulation*, BC Reg 151/2002.

26   *PEI HTA*, s 1(k.2).

27   Saskatchewan Government Insurance, "Saskatchewan Motorcycle Driver's Handbook: A Guide to Safety" (Regina: Saskatchewan Government Insurance, 2014) at 71, online: www.sgi.sk.ca/motorcyclehandbook.

28   The definition is contained in the *Motor Vehicle Safety Regulations*, s 2(1). These federal regulations are promulgated by Transport Canada pursuant to the *Can MVSA* and set out manufacturing and importation standards for motor vehicles.

29   See *Motor Vehicle Safety Regulations*, s 2(1):

> "limited-*speed motorcycle*" means a motorcycle that
>   (*a*)   has steering handlebars that are completely constrained from rotating in relation to the axle of only one wheel in contact with the ground,
>   (*b*)   has a maximum speed of 70 km/h or less,
>   (*c*)   has a minimum driver's seat height, when the vehicle is unladen, of 650 mm, and
>   (*d*)   does not have a structure partially or fully enclosing the driver and passenger, other than that part of the vehicle forward of the driver's torso and the seat backrest; (*motocyclette à vitesse limitée*).

30   BC *Motor Assisted Cycle Regulation*. For a discussion of the definition of "motor assisted bicycle" in the British Columbia law, see *R v Ryan*, 2012 BCPC 67.

31   See *PEI HTA*, s 1(k.2); *NL HTA*, s 2(mm); *YT MVA*, s 1(1).

32   Bruce Bartlett, "No Criminal Intent, Man Not Guilty: Judge Court Suspended Driver Genuinely Believed Battery Operated Bicycle Did Not Meet Definition Of Motor Vehicle, Jurist Rules" *Telegraph-Journal* (14 January 2011) C2.

33   *BC MVA*, s 119(1).

34   *NS MVA*, s 2(c)(i).

35   *Pedicab Operation Regulations*, NS Reg 183/2006, s 2(b).

36   *Operator Licensing and Vehicle Control Regulation*, Alta Reg 320/2002, s 9(1).

37   *MAN HTA*, s 145(2).

38   *Que HSC*, art 492.2. Article 492.2 stipulates that a person needs to be eighteen to have the right to ride a power-assisted bicycle, unless that person has a licence to drive a moped. It is possible to have a licence to drive a moped at fourteen: *Que HSC*, art 67.

39   *Ont HTA*, s 38(1).

40   *BC MVA*, s 182.1.

41   City of Regina, Bylaw No 9900, *The Regina Traffic Bylaw* (1997), s 80.

42   *Saskatchewan Motorcycle Driver's Handbook*, above note 27 at 71.

43   *Que HSC*, art 67.

44 Alta *Operator Licensing and Vehicle Control Regulation*, s 9(2).
45 Navindra Persaud & Dorothy Zwolakowski, "Nonuse of Bicycle Helmets and Risk of Fatal Head Injury: A Proportional Mortality, Case-Control Study" (2012) 184(17) CMAJ E921 at E922. For other similar findings, see, e.g., Peter Cripton et al, "Bicycle Helmets Are Highly Effective at Preventing Head Injury during Head Impact: Head-form Accelerations and Injury Criteria for Helmeted and Unhelmeted Impacts" (2014) 70 Accident Analysis & Prevention 1.
46 Colleen Davison et al, "Bicycle Helmet Use and Bicycling-Related Injury among Young Canadians: An Equity Analysis" (2013) 12 International Journal for Equity in Health 48.
47 Mohammad Karkhaneh et al, "Bicycle Helmet Use Four Years after the Introduction of Helmet Legislation in Alberta, Canada" (2011) 43(3) Accident Analysis & Prevention 788.
48 Ross Owen Phillips, Aslak Fyhri, & Fridulv Sagberg, "Risk Compensation and Bicycle Helmets" (2011) 31(8) Risk Analysis 1187.
49 Aslak Fyhri, Torkel Bjornskay, & Agathe Backer-Grondahl, "Bicycle Helmets: A Case of Risk Compensation?" (2012) 15(5) Psychology and Behaviour 612.
50 Dorothy L Robinson, "Helmet Laws and Health" (1998) 4 Injury Prevention 170.
51 DL Robinson, "Changes in Head Injury with the New Zealand Bicycle Helmet Law" (2001) 33 Accident Analysis and Prevention 687.
52 See, e.g., Piet de Jong, "The Health Impact of Mandatory Bicycle Helmet Laws" (2012) 32(5) Risk Analysis 782.
53 See, e.g., William Meehan et al, "Bicycle Helmet Laws Are Associated with a Lower Fatality Rate from Bicycle-Motor Vehicle Collisions" (2013) 163(3) The Journal of Pediatrics 726; DS McNally & S Whitehead, "A Computational Simulation Study of the Influence of Helmet Wearing on Head Injury Risk in Adult Cyclists" (2013) 60 Accident Analysis & Prevention 15.
54 Mohammad Karkhaneh et al, "Trends in Head Injuries Associated with Mandatory Bicycle Helmet Legislation Targeting Children and Adolescents" (2013) 59 Accident Analysis & Prevention 206 at 211.
55 Jessica Dennis et al, "Helmet Legislation and Admissions to Hospital for Cycling Related Head Injuries in Canadian Provinces and Territories: Interrupted Time Series Analysis" (2013) BMJ 346:f2674 at 4.
56 *BC MVA*, s 184. The law in BC is being challenged as unconstitutional: "Vancouver Man Challenges Bike Helmet Law" *CBC [British Columbia]* (12 August 2011), online: CBC www.cbc.ca/news/canada/british-columbia/story/2011/08/12/bc-vancouver-helmet-law.html. A previous legal challenge to the mandatory helmet law was unsuccessful: *R v Warman*, 2001 BCSC 1771.
57 *NS MVA*, s 170A.
58 *PEI HTA*, s 194(2)(a.1).
59 *NB MVA*, s 177(3).
60 Alta *Vehicle Equipment Regulation*, s 111(1).
61 In Ontario, the *Ont HTA* states in s 104(2.1) that "[n]o person shall ride on or operate a bicycle on a highway unless the person is wearing a bicycle helmet that complies with the regulations and the chin strap of the helmet is securely fastened

under the chin." However, the regulations restrict the application of this provision to persons under the age of eighteen by providing that: "A person who is 18 years old or older is not required to comply with subsection 104(2.1) of the Act. O. Reg. 411/95, s 1" (*Safety Helmets*, RRO 1990, Reg 610, s 5).

62 *Man HTA*, s 145.0.1.

63 *Ibid.*

64 City of Vancouver, Bylaw No 2849, *Street and Traffic Bylaw*, ss 60D-60E. The regulations specify that a bicycle safety helmet must be worn on any path or way designated in Schedule C of the bylaw.

65 City of Yorkton, Bylaw No 10/2000, *Traffic Bylaw*, s 67(5).

66 City of Sherbrooke, Bylaw No 1, *Règlement général de la Ville de Sherbrooke*, s 5.1.67.1.

67 City of Westmount, By-law No 1162, *By-Law to Render the Wearing of a Protective Helmet Mandatory for Cyclists and In-line Skaters* (4 July 1994), s 3(2).

68 City of Mount Pearl, *Bicycle, Scooter, Skateboard and Similar Objects Regulations* (6 August 2001), s 3.

69 City of Corner Brook, *City of Corner Brook Bicycle Helmet Regulations* (21 April 2008), s 2(a).

70 City of St John's, By-law No 1332, *Bicycle Helmet By-law* (25 April 1994), s 2.

71 City of Inuvik, By-law No 2515/TR/11, *Highway Traffic By-law* (9 November 2011), s 40(2).

72 City of Whitehorse, Bylaw No 2013-35, *Bicycle Bylaw* (28 October 2013), s 4(2)(h).

73 *BC MVA*, s 184 ("[a] person commits an offence if that person operates or rides as a passenger on a cycle on a highway and is not properly wearing a bicycle safety helmet . . .").

74 *NS MVA*, s 170A(2) ("[n]o person shall ride on or operate a bicycle unless the person is wearing a bicycle helmet . . ."); Alta *Vehicle Equipment Regulation*, s 111(1) ("[n]o person who is less than 18 years old shall operate or ride as a passenger on a bicycle unless that person is properly wearing a safety helmet").

75 *BC MVA*, s 184.

76 Alta *Vehicle Equipment Regulation*, s 108.

77 *Saskatchewan Motorcycle Driver's Handbook*, above note 27 at 66.

78 *Man HTA*, s 145(4).

79 *Ont HTA*, s 103.1(2).

80 *Que HSC*, s 492.2.

81 *NS MVA*, s 170A(1).

82 See also *Dhillon v British Columbia (Ministry of Transportation and Highways, Motor Vehicle Branch)* (1999), 35 CHRR D/293 (BCHRT).

83 *Bicycle Safety Helmet Exemption Regulation*, BC Reg 261/96, s 3.

84 *Helmet Regulations*, NS Reg 99/2003, s 5.

85 *Bicycle Safety Helmet Regulations*, PEI Reg EC329/03, s 2(3)(a).

86 *NB MVA*, s 177(3); *NS MVA*, s 170A.

87 *NB MVA*, s 177(3); *NS MVA*, s 170A(2).

88 *Man HTA*, s 145(4).

89 BC *Bicycle Helmet Exemption Regulation*.

90 Ont *Safety Helmets*.

91   *Bicycle Helmet Regulations*, NS Reg 68/97.

92   PEI *Bicycle Safety Helmet Regulations*.

93   ~~*Bicycle Safety Helmet Specification Regulation*, Alta Reg 59/2002; Alta *Vehicle Equipment Regulation*, s 112.~~

94   See, e.g., Alta *Vehicle Equipment Regulation*, s 115; *NB MVA*, s 177(4.1).

95   See, e.g., Alta *Vehicle Equipment Regulation*, Alberta, s 111(2); *NB MVA*, ss 177(4) & 177(4.1).

96   See, e.g., *Que HSC*, art 504; *NB MVA*, s 177(4.2).

97   Ontario law mentions "alarm bell, gong or horn," *Ont HTA*, s 75(5).

98   Alta *Vehicle Equipment Regulation*, s 60.

99   *Ont HTA*, s 75(5).

100   *NB MVA*, s 181(2).

101   *PEI HTA*, s 107(2).

102   *NS MVA*, s 183(5).

103   *NB MVA*, s 181(2); *PEI HTA*, s 107(2); *NS MVA*, s 183(5).

104   City of Vancouver, *Street and Traffic Bylaw*, above note 64, s 60B.

105   City of Edmonton, Bylaw No 2202, *Parkland Bylaw* (consolidated 25 November 2003), s 12(1.1).

106   Alta *Use of Highway and Rules of the Road Regulation*, s 83(2); *Ont HTA*, s 75(5). In PEI, the law requires a "vehicle" to use an audible warning when passing another vehicle and the definition of "vehicle" is worded to include bicycles: *PEI HTA*, s 154(1)(a).

107   *BC MVA*, s 183(8); Alta *Vehicle Equipment Regulation*, s 113(2); *Ont HTA*, s 64(3); *Que HSC*, art 247; *NB MVA*, s 181(3); *Licensing and Equipment Regulations*, CNLR 1007/96, s 25(11); *YT MVA*, s 217(2).

108   *BC MVA*, s 183(8); *Ont. HTA*, s 64(3); *Que HSC*, art 247; *YT MVA*, s 217(2).

109   NL *Licensing and Equipment Regulations*, s 25(11); *NB MVA*, s 181(3).

110   *BC MVA*, s 183(6); Alta *Use of Highway and Rules of the Road Regulation*, ss 55(1)(b), 55(1)(f)(i), and 55(2); *Man HTA*, s 149(1); *Ont HTA*, s 62(17); *Que HSC*, arts 232–33 and 424; *NB MVA*, s 181(1); *NS MVA*, s 174(6); *PEI HTA*, s 107(1); NL *Licensing and Equipment Regulations*, s 22; *YT MVA*, ss 178(1)(b) and 217(1); *NWT MVA*, s 143.1.

111   Alta *Vehicle Equipment Regulation*, s 113(1); *Ont HTA*, s 62(17); *Man HTA*, s 149(1); *Que HSC*, arts 232–33; *NS MVA*, s 174(6); *PEI HTA*, s 107; NL *Licensing and Equipment Regulation*, s 22.

112   *Ont HTA*, s 62(14).

113   Bill 31, *Transportation Statute Law Amendment Act (Making Ontario Roads Safer)*, 2014, 1st Sess, 41st Leg, 2014, cl 22(2) [Bill 31].

114   *BC MVA*, s 183(6). Similar nighttime requirements are found in other jurisdictions: Alta *Vehicle Equipment Regulation*, s 113; *Man HTA*, s 35(11); *Ont HTA*, s 62(17); *Que HSC*, art 233; *NB MVA*, s 181(1); *NS MVA*, s 174(1); *PEI HTA*, ss 96–96.1.

115   "Mobile Phone Use and Listening to Music While Cycling Increases Crash Rate" (2010) 44 Research Activities 3, online: www.swov.nl/rapport/Ss_RA/RA44.pdf.

116   See *BC MVA*, s 183(14); *Alta TSA*, s 115(1); *Man HTA*, s 75; *NWT MVA*, s 154(1).

117   *Ont HTA*, s 130. The definition of "vehicle" includes a bicycle.

118 "Nunavut Drivers Sole Exemption from Cellphone Laws" *CBC News [North]* (1 December 2011), online: www.cbc.ca/news/canada/north/story/2011/12/01/north-distracted-driving-laws.html.

119 *Alta TSA*, s 115.1.

120 *NWT MVA*, s 155.1.

121 *Alta TSA*, s 115.1(2); *NWT MVA*, s 155.1(3).

122 *Man HTA*, s 215.

123 *Que HSC*, art 440.

124 City of Vancouver, *Street and Traffic Bylaw*, above note 64, s 60A.

125 *Alta TSA*, s 115.3(2).

126 *Ibid*, s 115.3(3).

127 *Que HSC*, arts 212 and 249.

128 *Man HTA*, s 150.

129 *YT MVA*, s 217(3).

130 *Ont HTA*, s 84; *PEI HTA*, above note 6, s 91.

131 *BC MVA*, s 183(1); Alta *Use of Highway and Rules of the Road Regulation*, s 75; *Man HTA*, s 145(1); *Ont HTA*, s 1(1) (defines a bicycle as a vehicle); *NB MVA*, s 176; *PEI HTA*, s 194(1); *NL HTA*, s 129(1); *YT MVA*, s 211(1). See also *R v Moore* (1978), [1979] 1 SCR 195 [*Moore*].

132 *Ibid*.

133 M Johnson et al, *Cyclists and Red Lights: A Study of Behaviour of Commuter Cyclists in Melbourne*, online: www.casr.adelaide.edu.au/rsr/RSR2008/JohnsonM.pdf.

134 Idaho Code, s 49.720.

135 Jason Meggs, *Bicycle Safety and Choice: Compounded Public Cobenefits of the Idaho Law Relaxing Stop Requirements for Cycling* (2010), online: meggsreport.files.wordpress.com/2011/09/idaho-law-jasonmeggs-2010version.pdf; Brandon Whyte, *The Idaho Stop Law and the Severity of Bicycle Crashes: A Comparative Study* (2013), online: www.brandonwhyte.com/assets/mastersprojectbrandonwhyteprintquality.pdf.

136 *BC MVA*, s 183(17) (can use right arm for right turn); Alta *Use of Highway and Rules of the Road Regulation*, s 11; *Traffic Safety Act*, SS 2004, c T-18.1, s 234(2) [*Sask TSA*]; *Man HTA*, ss 125–26 (can use right arm for right turn); *Ont HTA*, s 142 (can use right arm for right turn); *Que HSC*, art 490; *NB MVA*, ss 162(4) and 164; *NS MVA*, s 119; *PEI HTA*, ss 178–80; *NL HTA*, ss 114 and 133; *YT MVA*, s 156; *Motor Vehicles Regulations*, YCO 1978/120, s 62(1).

137 *BC MVA*, s 183(2)c); Alta *Use of Highway and Rules of the Road Regulation*, ss 3(1) and 77(2); *Man HTA*, ss 109(2) and 145(5); *Ont HTA*, s 147; *Que HSC*, art 487; *NB MVA*, s 179(1); *NS MVA*, s 171(4); *PEI HTA*, s 194(2)(b); *NL HTA*, s 129(2)(b); *YT MVA*, s 213(2); *NWT MVA*, s 246(1)(b); *Motor Vehicles Act*, NU MVA, s 246(1)(b). Municipalities may also have similar bylaws. See, for example, City of Ottawa, By-law No 2003-530, *By-law Regulating Traffic and Parking on City Highways*, s 96(1).

138 Alta *Use of Highway and Rules of the Road Regulation*, s 77(4).

139 *BC MVA*, s 183(3); Alta *Use of Highway and Rules of the Road Regulation*, s 77(4)(b).

140 *BC MVA*, s 183(2)(d); Alta *Use of Highway and Rules of the Road Regulation*, s 78(a); *Man HTA*, ss 145(6)–(7); *Que HSC*, art 486; *NB MVA*, s 179(2); *NS MVA*, s 171(6);

PEI HTA, s 194(2)(c); NL HTA, s 129(2)(c); YT MVA, s 215; NWT MVA, s 246(1)(c); NU MVA, s 246(1)(c).

141 ~~Que HSC, art 486.~~

142 NB MVA, s 179(2).

143 Marilyn Johnson, Jennie Oxley, & Max Cameron, Cyclist Bunch Riding: A Review of the Literature (Clayton, VIC: Monash University Accident Research Centre, 2009), online: www.mcgroup.monash.edu.au/miri/research/reports/muarc285.pdf.

144 BC MVA, s 183(2)(a); Alta Use of Highway and Rules of the Road Regulation, s 13; Man HTA, s 145(8) (no person shall operate on a sidewalk a bicycle with a rear wheel the diameter of which exceeds 410 mm); Que HSC, art 492.1; NV MVA, s 191.1; NS MVA, s 171(2); PEI HTA, s 194(2)(a); NL HTA, s 129(2)(a); NWT MVA, s 246(1)(a); NU MVA, s 246(1)(a).

145 BC MVA, s 183(2)(a); Alta Use of Highway and Rules of the Road Regulation, s 13; Man HTA, s 145(9); Que HSC, art 492.1; YT MVA, s 126(1)(b) (municipalities may make bylaws regulating use of sidewalks).

146 See, e.g., City of Ottawa, By-law Regulating Traffic and Parking on City Highways, above note 137, s 84.

147 City of Toronto, Bylaw No 313-27, Toronto Municipal Code, c 313, Streets and Side-walks, s 313.27C.

148 See City of Edmonton, Bylaw No 5590, Traffic Bylaw (consolidated on 3 July 2013); City of Vancouver, Street and Traffic Bylaw, above note 64.

149 City of Calgary, Bylaw 26M96, Being a Bylaw of the City of Calgary to Control and Regulate Traffic on Streets Within the City, ss 3(2) and 41(2).

150 In an Ontario case, the City of Toronto was found partly liable for injuries sustained by a cyclist when the city failed to repair a multi-use street that still had signs indicating that it was a bicycle route although the designation was cancelled several years earlier: Evans v Toronto (City), [2004] OJ No 5844 (Sm Cl Ct).

151 NB MVA, s 179(3); NS MVA, s 171(3); PEI HTA, s 194(2)(i); NL HTA, s 129(1)(i).

152 NS MVA, s 171(3).

153 NWT MVA, s 246(2).

154 NU MVA, s 246(2).

155 Alta Use of Highway and Rules of the Road Regulation, s 77(4)(a).

156 For example, in Ottawa, cyclists are not required to use a recently built segregated bike lane: City of Ottawa, "Suggested Bike Lane Pilot Project: Project Overview," online: www.ottawa.ca/en/city_hall/planningprojectsreports/public_consult/bikelane/faq/index.html. See also Toronto Municipal Code, c 886, Footpaths, Pedestrian Ways, Bicycle Paths, Bicycle Lanes and Cycle Tracks (a person may ride a bicycle on a bicycle path or in a bicycle lane).

157 See, e.g., NS MVA, s 131A. See also Toronto Municipal Code, s 886-6(10).

158 See, e.g., NS MVA, s 131A.

159 See Toronto, Staff Report, Electric Bikes: Proposed Polices and By-Laws (2013), online: www.toronto.ca/legdocs/mmis/2014/pw/bgrd/backgroundfile-65205.pdf.

160 National Capital Commission, Rules for Electric Bikes ("E-Bikes"), online: www.ncc-ccn.gc.ca/places-to-visit/parks-paths/rules-electric-bikes-e-bikes.

161 Que HSC, art 478.

162 *Ont HTA*, s 128; See also *BC MVA*, s 146(1).

163 *Sask TSA*, s 199; *Alta TSA*, s 115(2)(p); *PEI HTA*, s 176; *NL MVA*, s 110; *YT MVA*, ss 137–38; *NWT MVA*, ss 169 and 171; *NU MVA*, ss 169 and 171.

164 City of Calgary, Bylaw 20M2003, *Being a Bylaw of the City of Calgary to Regulate the Use of Parks and Pathways and to Regulate Activities in and on Parks and Pathways*, s 32 [*City of Calgary, Park and Pathways Bylaw*].

165 *Ibid*, s 33.

166 *BC MVA*, s 183(2)(h); *Man HTA*, s 150(5); *Vehicles on Controlled-Access Highways*, RRO 1990, Reg 630, s 1(1); *Que HSC*, art 295(4); *PEI HTA*, s 194(2)(h); *NL HTA*, s 129(1)(h).

167 Ont *Vehicles on Controlled-Access Highways*, s 1(1).

168 Bill 31, above note 113, cl 47, which reached second reading before the 2014 Ontario election.

169 See, e.g., *BC MVA*, s 124.2(1); *YT MVA*, s 126(2)(b).

170 *Elbow Valley Cycle Club v Rockyview (Municipal District No 44)* (1997), 201 AR 128 (QB).

171 See, e.g., *Que HSC*, art 488.

172 *National Capital Commission Traffic and Property Regulations*, CRC, c 1044, s 16.

173 *Provincial Parks (General) Regulation*, Alta Reg 102/1985, s 27(2).

174 *City of Calgary, Park and Pathways Bylaw*, above note 164, s 30.

175 International Mountain Bicycling Association, *Rules of the Trail*, online: www.imba.com/about/rules-trail.

176 The *Silver Start Bike Responsibility Code*, online: http://summer.skisilverstar.com/s/bike-responsibility-code; *Mountain Bike Responsibility Code*, online: www.bluemountain.ca/mtnbike.htm#re.

177 *Man HTA*, s 114(1).

178 *Ont HTA*, s 148(6). Ontario is also considering amending the *Highway Traffic Act* to include a one-metre passing rule for vehicles when passing cyclists: Ontario, Ministry of Transportation, *Draft Cycling Strategy For Consultation on the Environmental Registry* (Toronto: Ministry of Transportation, 2012) at 17, online: www.raqsa.mto.gov.on.ca/techpubs/eps.nsf/8cec129ccb70929b852572950068f16b/db68ce058968597d85257ac3005f6877/$FILE/Draft%20Cycling%20Strategy%20-%20FINAL%20CLEAN%20VERSION.pdf.

179 *Que HSC*, art 341.

180 *NS MVA*, s 171B(1).

181 *Ibid*, s 171B(2).

182 Bill 31, above note 113, cl 50, which reached second reading before the 2014 Ontario election.

183 David C Love et al, "Is the Three-foot Bicycle Passing Law Working in Baltimore, Maryland?" (2012) 48 Accident Analysis and Prevention 451 at 455.

184 John Parkin & Ciaran Meyers, "The Effect of Cycle Lanes on the Proximity between Motor Traffic and Cycle Traffic" (2010) 42(1) Accident Analysis and Prevention 159.

185 *BC MVA*, s 158.

186 *NS MVA*, s 114(2).

187 *Ibid*, s 166(1).

188 *Ibid*, s 166(2).

189　*Ibid*, s 142.1.

190　The City of Toronto's Transportation Services Division conducted a study of colli-
~~sions between cyclists and motor vehicles in 1998 and 1999, and found that 11.9~~
percent of crashes were the result of a motorist opening a door into a passing
cyclist: City of Toronto, *City of Toronto Bicycle/Motor-Vehicle Collision Study* (2003),
online: www1.toronto.ca/city_of_toronto/transportation_services/cycling/files/
pdf/car-bike_collision_report.pdf. Since 2012, Ontario no longer keeps track of the
number of "doorings" since a 2012 change in the definition of a collision, which no
longer includes stationary vehicles: Alexandra Kazia, "Cycling Website to Record
Toronto 'Dooring' Accidents" *CBC News [Toronto]* (8 August 2013), online: CBC.ca
www.cbc.ca/news/canada/toronto/story/2013/08/08/toronto-door-prize-data-
gathering.html.

191　*Que HSC*, art 430; *Ont HTA*, s 165 (requires motorists to take "due precautions");
YT MVA, s 202(1); Alta *Use of Highway and Rules of the Road Regulation*, s 86.

192　*Ont HTA*, s 165 (the section requires motorists to take "due precautions" before
opening the door of a motor vehicle on a highway "to ensure that his or her act will
not interfere with the movement of or endanger any other person or vehicle"). In
Ontario, the violation comes with two demerit points and a fine: *Demerit Point System*, online: www.mto.gov.on.ca/english/dandv/driver/demerit.shtml.

193　In Ontario, the fine is $85: *Ont HTA*, Schedule 43. In Quebec, a motorist was fined
$30 for dooring and seriously injuring a cyclist: Gabriel Béland, "Cycliste heurté
par une portière: des pénalités plus sévères demandées" *La Presse* (12 May 2011),
online: Cyberpresse www.lapresse.ca/actualites/quebec-canada/justice-et-faits-
divers/201105/12/01-4398534-cycliste-heurte-par-une-portiere-des-penalites-plus-
severes-demandees.php.

194　Bill 31, above note 113.

195　*Criminal Code*, RSC 1985, c C-46, s 253. Section 253 states specifically that the law
only applies to motor vehicles. However, if a power-assisted bike is considered
a motor vehicle, then criminal charges including impaired driving could be laid
against an impaired cyclist.

196　*Man HTA*, s 227(1).

197　*Que HSC*, art 489.

198　See *BC MVA*, s 183(14); *Alta TSA*, s 115(1); *NWT MVA*, s 154(1).

199　*Ont HTA*, s 130. The definition of "vehicle" includes a bicycle.

200　See, e.g., *Liquor Licence Act*, RSO 1990, c L.19, s 31(4); *Liquor Control and Licensing
Act*, RSBC 1996, c 267, s 41(1).

201　See, e.g., Ont *Liquor Licence Act*, s 31(2); BC *Liquor Control and Licensing Act*, s 40(1).

202　*BC MVA*, s 183(2)(h); *Man HTA*, ss 145.1(1) and 145.1(3)(d); *Ont HTA*, ss 160 and
178(4); *Que HSC*, art 434; *NB MVA*, ss 178(1) & 178(2); *NS MVA*, s 169; *PEI HTA*, s
195; *NL HTA*, s 130; *YT MVA*, s 214; *NWT MVA*, s 248; *NU MVA*, s 248.

203　*Que HSC*, art 434.0.1.

204　*BC MVA*, s 183(2)(e); *Que HSC*, art 477; *NB MVA*, s 180; *NS MVA*, s 171(1); *PEI HTA*,
s 194(2)(d); *NL HTA*, s 129(1)(d); *NWT MVA*, s 246(1)(d); *NU MVA*, s 246(1)(d).

205　Alta *Use of Highway and Rules of the Road Regulation*, s 77(1)(a); *YT MVA*, s 213(1)(a);

206 Alta *Use of Highway and Rules of the Road Regulation*, s 77(1)(b); *NS MVA*, s 171(1); *PEI HTA*, s 194(2)(j); *YT MVA*, s 213(1)(b);

207 *BC MVA*, s 183(2)(f); Alta *Use of Highway and Rules of the Road Regulation*, s 77(1)(c); *Man HTA*, s 146; *Que HSC*, art 477; *NB MVA*, s 177(1); *PEI HTA*, s 194(2)(e); *NL HTA*, s 129(2)(e); *YT MVA*, s 213(1)(c); *NWT MVA*, s 246(1)(e); *NU MVA*, s 246(1)(e).

208 *BC MVA*, s 183(2)(g); Alta *Use of Highway and Rules of the Road Regulation*, s 77(1)(d); *Man HTA*, s 147(1); *Ont HTA*, s 178(2); *Que HSC*, art 485; *NB MVA*, s 177(2); *NS MVA*, s 169(1); *PEI HTA*, s 194(2)(f); *NL HTA*, s 129(2)(f); *YT MVA*, s 213(1)(d); *NWT MVA*, s 246(1)(f); *NU MVA*, s 246(1)(f).

209 *NS MVA*, s 169(1).

210 *Man HTA*, s 147(2).

211 *Man HTA*, s 147(3); *NB MVA*, s 180; *PEI HTA*, s 194(2)(g); *NL HTA*, s 129(1)(g).

212 *Criminal Code*, s 174.

213 *R v Benolkin* (1977), 36 CCC (2d) 206, 1 WCB 313 (Sask QB).

214 *R v Jacob* (1996), 31 OR (3d) 350, 142 DLR (4th) 411 (CA).

215 In 2004, Conrad Schmidt, a social activist, filmmaker, and writer living in Vancouver, created what has become known as the World Naked Bike Rides. The rides have since been held annually: "World Naked Bike Ride Hits Halifax" *CBC News [Nova Scotia]* (12 June 2011), online: CBC www.cbc.ca/news/canada/nova-scotia/story/2011/06/12/ns-world-naked-bike-ride.html; Larissa Cahute, "Cyclists Bare Almost All for Naked Bike Ride" *Ottawa Sun* (11 June 2011), online: Ottawa Sun www.ottawasun.com/2011/06/11/cyclists-bare-almost-all-for-naked-bike-ride; Antonia Zerbisias, "World Naked Bike Ride: Toronto Cyclists Bare Down" *The Star* (12 June 2012), online: The Star www.thestar.com/news/gta/article/1212606--world-naked-bike-ride-toronto-cyclists-bare-down.

216 Cahute, above note 215; "Nude Cyclists Protest Arrest at Vancouver Naked Bike Ride" *CBC News* (23 August 2008), online: CBC www.cbc.ca/news/canada/british-columbia/story/2008/08/23/naked-cyclists.html.

217 *Ibid.*

218 The Council also found the broadcast breached provisions of the Code that prohibit demeaning and degrading attitudes towards women: *CJKR-FM re a radio contest (Nude Bicycle Riding)* (18 November 1999), 98/99-0476, online: www.cbsc.ca/english/decisions/1999/991118a.php.

219 *NS MVA*, s 143(2).

220 See, e.g., *City of Toronto Municipal Code*, c 743, s 743-9P, discussed more fully in Chapter 5.

221 Matthew Burrows, "City of Vancouver Not Strict about Bikes Locked to Parking Meters" *Straight.com* (11 July 2012), online: www.straight.com/article-729436/vancouver/city-vancouver-not-strict-about-bikes-locked-parking-meters.

222 "Bike Rack Time Limit Outrages Vancouver Cyclist" *CBC News [British Columbia]* (2 August 2013), online: CBC www.cbc.ca/news/canada/british-columbia/story/2013/08/02/bc-vancouver-bike-rack.html.

223 See, e.g., City of Vancouver, Streets and Transportation, *Bicycle Parking*, online: www.vancouver.ca/engsvcs/transport/cycling/parking/index.htm; City of Calgary, Bylaw No 1P2007, *Land Use Bylaw*, ss 116 and 125.

224 See, e.g., *Man HTA* s 65(2); *Ont HTA*, s 218; *Que HSC*, art 170; *NB MVA*, s 127; *NS MVA*, s 97(3); *PEI HTA*, s 232(2); *NL HTA*, s 169(6)(c); City of Vancouver, *Street and Traffic By-Law, above note 64, s 60F.*

225 *R v Green*, [2004] OJ No 5757 (Ct J).

226 See, e.g., *R v Ramos*, 2010 ONCJ 303 (applying Ontario law).

227 *R v Graham*, [2000] OJ No 465 (SCJ); *R v Cassidy*, [2007] OJ No 4269 (SCJ).

228 *NS MVA*, s 261.

229 *Ont HSA*, s 218.

230 Above note 131.

231 See, e.g., *BC MVA*, s 183(9); *Ont HTA*, ss 199(1) and 200(1); *Que HSC*, arts 168–69; *NS MVA*, s 97(1); *PEI HTA*, s 232(1); *NL HTA*, ss 169(6)(a)–169(6)(b).

Chapter 3

Falling Off Your Bicycle

introduction

Every year brings a new rash of headlines about fatal collisions involving bicycles and cars. Cycling, as a sport or a mode of transportation, can be risky. Those risks are compounded when cyclists, pedestrians, or motorists disregard the highway safety laws discussed in Chapter 2. But even in the best circumstances, accidents can happen. Not all accidents are, however, equal. Some may be unavoidable. Others reflect carelessness or even malice. Careless and malicious "accidents" attract the attention of the law in two main ways.

First, carelessness or malice can be viewed by our justice system as criminal conduct, and attract charges that could lead to prison, fines, or other penalties.

Second, individuals can bring lawsuits before our courts to seek compensation for injuries or damage caused by careless or malicious conduct.

Either way, we are all legally required to ride our bicycles, or drive our motor vehicles, with utmost care, and if we fail to do so, we may face legal consequences. This chapter outlines what legal rules apply when you have an accident while riding your bicycle. It begins by first trying to outline the risks involved in riding a bicycle. It then examines interactions between cyclists and motorists that cross the line into criminal conduct, before focusing on civil liability for various forms of bicycle accidents.

this chapter's takeaways

» Cycling is generally a safe activity, but it does have risks. Riding a bicycle is certainly not a death wish, but there are very real hazards and dangers that come with cycling. Cyclists and other road users need to appreciate those risks, and cooperate in reducing them. Fewer accidents mean fewer complicated and costly interactions with the justice system.

» If you are involved in a collision or crash, there are steps you need to take at the scene of the accident. Understand them, and understand the legal obligations on you as a cyclist, as well as those on everyone else involved.

» Various forms of lousy driving are criminal offences, and motorists can go to jail or face fines.

» Various forms of lousy driving violate provincial and territorial highway safety laws and municipal bylaws, and motorists can go to jail or face fines.

» Various forms of lousy cycling violate provincial and territorial highway safety laws and municipal bylaws, and cyclists can go to jail or face fines.

» Leaving the scene of an accident is a criminal offence, as well as a violation of provincial highway safety laws, and motorists can go to jail. These hit and run rules also extend to cyclists who leave the scene of an accident.

» In many provinces and territories, obtaining compensation for injuries caused by an accident may require a lawsuit. Road users owe each other duties of care, and can be liable to one another if they violate them. How much blame goes to a cyclist or driver in a collision between a motor vehicle and a cyclist is influenced by their actual behaviour, including whether they are following the "rules of the road." In some provinces, it is assumed that the driver is at fault, and he or she bears the onus of proving he or she did not act negligently.

» Motor vehicle or home insurance policies may insure a cyclist injured in a collision with a motor vehicle — check your policy. But don't assume that those policies also cover damage to the bicycle itself — check again.

» Cyclists can be held liable for crashing into pedestrians and other cyclists.

» Governments, including municipalities, can be liable to cyclists for poor road repair, and to a lesser extent, dangerous recreational trails.

» Occupiers of rural land or land with private recreational trails can be liable to cyclists, but often only for conduct that constitutes reckless disregard for safety.

understanding the risks

We start this chapter with a discussion of the risks involved in cycling for one principal reason. Understanding the risks of the activity, and reducing them to avoid accidents, is in our view, the best way to avoid falling off your bike. This, in turn, will keep you far away from our justice system. As we hope you will gather from this chapter, keeping you and your bike in one piece is a better option than being involved in a criminal or a civil proceeding before the courts.

Cycling is generally a safe activity, especially for those who obey highway traffic laws. But riding a bicycle does come with risks, although there is much disagreement about the extent to which it is a dangerous mode of getting around. Indeed, it can be hazardous to even discuss the dangers of cycling. Many of us have had heated exchanges on the topic during bike club rides, especially if we dared lay some blame on cyclists themselves.

Meanwhile, pointing out to drivers the dangers of some of their practices can also ignite an altercation. We have both experienced individual or group rides that were almost brought to an end when aggressive drivers responded to commentary (politely, if loudly shared) on their untoward driving practices. In one case, a driver passed the group with which Craig was cycling and then repeatedly slammed on his brakes in front of the riders. Nicole was almost sideswiped by a truck on a quiet rural road, and after raising her arm in a questioning gesture, the driver stopped further ahead and told her that cyclists had no right to be on the road because "they don't pay taxes." Similar confrontations have happened to many other riders — including Canadian Olympians.[1]

While the issue attracts debates, we think it is important to highlight the hazards facing those of us who like to ride our bicycles. Collisions with motorists, pedestrians and other cyclists, or crashes caused by the dreaded off-leash dog or startled horse, are among the most serious risks confronting cyclists. Moreover, every cycling club has members who have been struck by objects directed from a passing vehicle. Some people have even shot at cyclists[2] (and indeed others have used their bikes in ride-by-shooting incidents).[3] For most cyclists the dangers are less dramatic but nonetheless just as hazardous: potholes[4], bridge crossings[5], expansion joints[6], sewer grates[7], streetcar tracks[8], and rail crossings[9], to name but a few.

Some of our examples above are extreme, and they are not intended to suggest that the risks of cycling outweigh the well-known social, health and environmental benefits of riding a bicycle. But the bottom line is this:

cyclists and bikes are particularly susceptible to accidents caused by road hazards and careless and dangerous conduct. There is no disputing that a cyclist straddling a few kilos of aluminum or carbon is much more vulnerable than anyone encased in a Volvo, even when riding at modest speeds. To sum it up in a single, breathless sentence: a bicycle is a few tubes propelled forward on thin tires, mounted by an exposed (often helmeted but otherwise unarmoured) human, moving at high speeds on roadways (the conditions and quality of which vary) that are also frequented by large metal boxes moving at even higher speeds and steered by sometimes distracted, careless, inebriated or impatient drivers, many of which have not read Chapter 2 and seem disinclined to view a bicycle as lawfully present on a roadway.

And even this statement fails to capture the range of risk. Craig recently tumbled on a car-free trail from a basically stationary mountain bike with a jammed derailleur, knocking his (fortunately helmeted) head on a nearby rock, scuffing elbow and shin and generally freaking out his family. No harm was done, but even this type of benign tumble poses more risk of injury to a cyclist than the automobile equivalent of Nicole bumping her responsibly seat-belted self into a curb, while encased in her sensible, highly-safety rated Subaru.

A quick Internet search produces many facts and figures on cycling safety, some quite discouraging. For instance, the chief cause of sports and recreational injury hospitalizations in Ontario in 2002–03 was bicycling.[10] Sixty cyclists were killed on average per year in Canada between 2004–06[11] and an average of fifty-four fatalities per year during 2007–2011.[12] But measuring what figures like these really mean in terms of *risk* is complex, and past efforts are not always satisfactory, to our minds. We have tried to compile and analyze a variety of studies to draw some conclusions. Not surprisingly, a substantial amount of research has been conducted on cycling safety and accidents.[13] If you like number crunching, see the accompanying text box for an overview of the existing statistics and research.

That said, we resist the idea that cycling reflects some kind of death wish. As responsible adults rationalizing a sometimes risky activity that is more leisure than necessity, we find attractive studies that conclude that the health benefits of cycling for life expectancy exceed the life lost by dying early in an accident.[14]

We also believe that the statistics cited in the text box are not (or at least not entirely) representative of unalterable laws of nature: while the laws of physics make human bodies fragile and metal and concrete hard, one hitting the other also has a lot to do with human design and behaviour. Some solutions are systemic — better cycling infrastructure — and some personal, like when, where and how one cycles. For instance, we strongly believe most everyone can acquire solid bike handling and riding skills by enrolling in the many learn to ride programs offered by municipalities and cycling clubs. And the very act of making the choice to ride may have knock-on effects: there is some reason to believe that the more people cycle, the safer cycling becomes.[15]

But the bottom line is that whatever precautions individuals or society take, people do fall off bicycles. In the balance of this chapter, we discuss when a fall is a legal matter, something that every cyclist (and driver) should know.

falling off bicycles, in numbers

some sobering numbers

To repeat a few figures from the beginning of this chapter: the chief cause of sports and recreational injury hospitalizations in Ontario in 2002–03 was bicycling.[16] Sixty cyclists were killed on average per year in Canada between 2004–06[17] and an average of fifty-four fatalities per year during 2007–2011.[18] Fifty-four fatalities per year between 2008–2011 represented about 2.3 percent of all fatalities among road users.[19] Drawing on this kind of statistic, one study notes that while cyclists constituted 2.5 percent of all traffic fatalities in 2006, cycling that year represented a mere 1.3 percent of commuter traffic.[20] In the most recent data available at the time of this writing, the equivalent figures were 2.6 percent of traffic fatalities[21] and 1.3 percent cycling commuter traffic in 2011.[22]

We discuss below why a focus on commuting may mislead, but many studies concentrate on this form of cycling in measuring risk. For instance, a 1999 study of bicycle commuters in Toronto reported 300 collisions (or 0.25 per cyclist) over the preceding three years and 203 falls (0.17 per cyclists) during the preceding twelve months. This translated into a collision rate of 8.2 and a fall rate of 12.9 every 1,000,000 km (a combined rate of 21.1).[23] The combined accident rate of 21.1 per 1 million km reported in the Toronto study works out to an accident every 4,739 km. The average commuter in that study covered 1,312 km per year.[24] This suggests that the average commuter experienced an accident once every 3.6 years, a figure somewhat higher than, but broadly consistent with other, more recent studies from other North American cities.[25]

These numbers on the risks of cycling commuting are distressing. They may be enough to make the average person pause before grabbing their bicycle pump. But context is important. We are not statisticians by any measure, but there are obvious objections to gauging risk with an eye to bicycle commuting. For one thing, automobiles cover distance more quickly than bicycles, and accident rate per unit *distance* may not be that useful a measure for cyclists trying to assess risk — over a given distance, drivers will generally spend less time in the hurly burly of kinetic motion. The *duration* of exposure to risk may, in other words, be a more indicative measure — cyclists may just be out there in traffic longer during their daily commute than drivers.

Even more critically, pointing to these studies as a proxy for *overall* cycling risk seems to discount that fact that cycling for many riders is (either, or in addition) a recreational activity, and not transport to and from work. Indeed, recreational cyclists may cumulatively log more time on the road than commuting riders. A 1999 Toronto survey found that 48 percent of the population over fifteen engaged in utilitarian or recreational cycling. Of these, 338,000 people were "utilitarian" cyclists riding to work, school, shopping, running errands, or "going visiting." In comparison, 862,000 people road for fitness, of which 548,000 rode *solely* for recreation.[26] In other words, recreational cycling dwarfed the proportion of workers who commute by bicycles (the latter amounting to only 159,000 persons in the Toronto survey).

There is no reason to believe that these proportions are a Toronto-specific finding or that they have changed with time. Nor is there any reason to believe that commuters individually or cumulatively log more miles or time on two wheels than recreational cyclists, some of whom may ride very far indeed.

Moreover, commuters may brave more difficult road and traffic conditions than do recreational cyclists. The latter seem more likely to gravitate to bike pathways (of modest use to commuters because many don't go where commuters must travel) or country roads specifically selected with an eye to minimizing risk. It is also true that Toronto is a more dangerous city for cycling than other Canadian cities.[27] Put another way, commuting (especially in Toronto) may be more dangerous than recreational cycling.

Finally, Census figures from 2006 suggest that young men fifteen to twenty-four were the most frequent bicycle commuters (at 3.3 percent as opposed to the overall rate of 1.3 percent). Notably, this is an age group that may be more prone to making risky choices, whatever their chosen form of transportation. For instance, while drivers in the sixteen–twenty-four group constituted 12.4 percent of all licensed drivers, 22.1 percent of all driver and 30.5 percent of all passenger deaths in 2011 were among those aged fifteen–twenty-four.[28]

These observations strike us as consistent with Transport Canada's list of cycling accident risk factors, all of which seem to us more likely to arise more often in cyclist commuting than in recreational cycling. It is worth being attentive to this list:

» *Afternoon rush hour*: In 2001, almost 24 percent of cyclists seriously injured and 17 percent of those killed were struck during afternoon rush hour, between 4 and 6 pm. In 2004–06, a total of 49 percent of fatal accidents occurred between 3 and 9 pm.

» *Intersections with traffic control signals*: In 2001, accidents at intersections with traffic control signals accounted for 30 percent of cyclist deaths and 38 percent of cyclist serious injuries. Intersections more generally were the site of 39 percent of deaths and 64 percent of serious injuries.

» *Cities and fast rural roads*: In 2001, urban areas accounted for 56 percent of cycling deaths and 85 percent of serious cycling injuries. Rural road with speed limits of 80 km/h or higher accounted for 44 percent of cycling deaths.

» *Night*: In 2001, nighttime riding accounted for 30 percent of cycling fatalities. The figure for fatal accidents in 2004–06 was 34 percent.

» *Age*: Fatality rates were 39 percent higher and serious injury rates 99 percent higher among cyclists twenty-four years of age or younger than for the population as a whole. In 2004–06, 18 percent of cyclists' fatalities were under the age of sixteen. However, this number constituted a significant improvement over traffic deaths in this age group between 1996–2001.

» *Big trucks*: In 2004–06, 19 percent of cycling fatalities stemmed from collisions with heavy trucks.[29]

This entire discussion is no *apologia* for careless and occasionally masochistic cyclists weaving their way down roads populated, at least in part, by lousy drivers. Nor is it a "don't worry, be happy" response to the indisputable risks of cycling. It does mean, however, that the above-noted 2.6 percent of traffic fatalities associated with cycling stems from a much, much bigger pool than the (national rate) of 1.3 percent of commuters who travel by bicycle. Comparing the two is like contrasting *all* automobile accidents with the proportion of people driving Honda Civics (including many converted into boom-boxes for young men) during urban rush hours, and concluding that Civics are very dangerous indeed.

It may be useful, therefore, to contextualize risk by contrasting *rates* of injury between cycling and other life events. In 2008–09 in Ontario, cycling incidents amounted to 3 percent (or 136) of hospitalizations and 2 percent (or nine) of all in-hospital deaths.[30] Each of these deaths and injuries is one too many, but there were more hospitalizations (9 percent) and deaths (8 percent) caused by assault and injury purposely inflicted by another person.[31] Meanwhile, "unintentional" falls were the cause of 38 percent of hospitalizations and 44 percent of all in-hospital deaths.[32]

Of particular note, 287 pedestrians were hospitalized after being struck by motor vehicles, and fifty-four were killed.[33] Overall in Canada in 2011, pedestrians constituted 15.7 percent of all traffic fatalities (as opposed to the above-noted 2.6 percent figure for cyclists). This does not necessarily mean you are more likely to be mowed down as a pedestrian than as a cyclist — there are more pedestrians than cyclists, and so the base of persons who may suffer injury is greater. But this figure does further underscore the implausibility of the apples and oranges comparison of automobile to *commuter* pedestrian accident statistics. That methodological approach makes walking look positively lethal: in 2011, 5.7 percent of workers commuted to work on foot.[34] If that figure is compared to 2011 pedestrian traffic fatalities, the ratio of commuters to deaths is 2.75, much higher than the equivalent figure of 2 for cyclists.

and a pinch of common sense

But even with this valiant effort to contextualize accidents, we would be foolish not to acknowledge the risks. The bottom line is that even in bicycle-friendly Holland, casualties per billion kilometres were 4.7 times greater for those travelling by bicycles than by cars (although again, a more relevant statistic might be "duration of exposure" not "distance travelled," given the different rate at which a car and a bicycle get from A to B).[35]

the mechanics of an accident scene

First things first: what should happen in the aftermath of an accident? Obviously, where there are serious injuries, the priority of drivers, cyclists, and bystanders is to call 911 for emergency medical assistance. Beyond that, the following are commonly suggested as the best responses to an accident involving a cyclist, to be done by either those involved in the accident or by helpful bystanders:[36]

- » Call the police and wait for them to arrive;
- » Ask witnesses for their names and contact information;
- » Where a motor vehicle is involved in the accident, collect the driver's name, contact information, insurance information, vehicle description, and licence plate number;
- » If injured, even if you feel that your injuries are not all that severe, visit a hospital emergency room or your doctor as soon as possible and ask for official documentation of the injury and your physical condition after the accident; and,
- » If the bicycle or other gear is damaged, obtain an estimate of the cost of repairing the damage or replacing the equipment from a bike shop.

It is also sensible to conduct activities at the accident site in a manner that does not imperil other road users. Obviously, it is not advisable to move injured persons whose wounds may be aggravated in this manner. On the other hand, as the Ontario government advises, "[i]f it is safe to do so, move your vehicle to the side of the road, out of traffic. If your vehicle cannot be driven, turn on your hazard lights or use cones, warning triangles, or flares, as appropriate."[37] It is also useful to record the scene with a digital camera — something with which more and more cyclists now ride.

Some of these accident response items deserve further discussion, as they are not only sound advice, but actually rest on specific legal duties.

In most jurisdictions, motorists involved in an accident *must* report an accident to the police if someone is injured or there is property damage that exceeds a specified amount. Moreover, the motorist must remain (or immediately return) to the accident scene, render all possible assistance and supply in writing his or her name, contact information, licence number, and vehicle registration and permit information and often insurance data. Failing to abide by these rules is generally considered an offence.

Some provinces assign similar responsibilities to cyclists indirectly, by giving cyclists the same rights and duties as drivers. Others include detailed rules for cyclists. In British Columbia, for instance, where an accident involving a bicycle causes direct or indirect injury to a person or property, the cyclist must remain (or immediately return) to the scene of the accident, render all possible assistance, and provide his or her identifying and contact information to anyone injured or suffering property damage.[38] Unlike in many other provinces, there is no statutory obligation to call the police. However, where they are present, police must complete a written accident report and file it with the Insurance Corporation of British Columbia

(ICBC) for any accident involving the "presence or operation of a cycle on a highway or sidewalk" that directly or indirectly causes death or injury to a person or sufficient property damage.[39]

Notably, a cyclist failing to cooperate with police by, for example, refusing to divulge name and address can be charged with violating their duties under some highway traffic laws.[40]

The general requirements of various provincial and territorial laws concerning accident scenes are set out in Table 3-1.

TABLE 3-1: PROVINCIAL AND TERRITORIAL LAWS GOVERNING CONDUCT AT THE SCENE OF AN ACCIDENT[41]

Rule	NL	NS	NB	PEI	QC	ON	MB	SK	AB	BC	YK	NWT
Driver must stop vehicle at scene of the accident	✓	✓	✓	✓	✓	✓	✓		✓	✓	✓	✓
Driver must provide identifying information	✓	✓	✓	✓	✓	✓	✓	✓	✓	✓	✓	✓
Driver must provide proof of insurance or financial responsibility card	✓				✓	✓	✓	✓	✓	✓	✓	✓
Driver must give person injured reasonable assistance (often specified to include transport to medical help)	✓	✓	✓	✓	✓	✓			✓	✓	✓	✓
When a person has been injured, a motor vehicle driver involved in the accident must call a police officer					✓							
Where accident results in death or injury or damage to property usually above a specified amount (e.g., $1000), the driver must make a report to a police officer	✓	✓	✓	✓		✓	✓	✓	✓		✓	✓
Cyclist must remain or return to the scene of the accident	✓	*	*	*		*	*			✓		
Cyclist must give reasonable assistance	✓	*	*	*		*				✓		

Rule	NL	NS	NB	PEI	QC	ON	MB	SK	AB	BC	YK	NWT
Cyclist must give identifying information	✓	*	*	*	*	*				✓		
When accident injures a cyclist, cyclist must report accident to police officer (if capable of doing so)								✓				
Where accident results in death or injury or damage to property above a specified amount, the cyclists must make a report to a police officer	✓	*	*	*	*	*						
Offence to violate some or all of these rules	✓	✓	✓	✓	✓	✓	✓	✓	✓	✓	✓	✓

* Cyclists are implicitly governed by the same rules as drivers of motor vehicle, because the definitions of vehicle and driver are broad enough to capture bicycles and cyclists or because of express language that applies the duties of motor vehicle drivers to cyclists.[42]

crime and punishment

Once an accident involving a motor vehicle happens, the law says a lot about whether the conduct of individuals is blameworthy or not. Canada's *Criminal Code* is a federal statute that applies across the country. It contains a host of offences that might be implicated by careless or malicious operation of a motor vehicle. Some are generic offences that really do not depend on the presence of a motor vehicle. For instance, intentionally running someone over with a car triggers the homicide provisions in the same way as would killing someone with any other form of weapon. Such intentional use of a motor vehicle to visit harm or injury on a cyclist is discussed below in the section on "road rage." Other likely offences are criminal negligence causing injury[43] or death.[44]

Perhaps most relevant are instances where motorists fail to meet duties that are imposed on motorists *per se*. The *Criminal Code* has a long list of offences that apply only when a "motor vehicle" is involved, with motor vehicle defined as any vehicle other than railway equipment propelled by means other than muscular power.[45]

Criminal Code offences most relevant to possible collisions between motorists and cyclists are summarized in Table 3.2.

TABLE 3.2: MOST RELEVANT *CRIMINAL CODE* OFFENCES

Offence	Summary of Offence
Dangerous operation (better known as "dangerous driving")	Operating a motor vehicle "in a manner that is dangerous to the public, having regard to all the circumstances, including the nature, condition and use of the place at which the motor vehicle is being operated and the amount of traffic that at the time is or might reasonably be expected to be at that place."[46]
Street racing	Street racing is "operating a motor vehicle in a race with at least one other motor vehicle on a street, road, highway or other public place."[47] A person who "by criminal negligence" causes death to another person while street racing is liable to life in prison.[48] Where that street racer causes bodily harm, the penalty is imprisonment for up to fourteen years.[49]
Impaired driving	Operating a motor vehicle or having care or control of that motor vehicle, whether it is in motion or not, while "the person's ability to operate the vehicle . . . is impaired by alcohol or a drug; or . . . having consumed alcohol in such a quantity that the concentration in the person's blood exceeds eighty milligrams of alcohol in one hundred millilitres of blood."[50]
Failure to stop at the scene of an accident	With the intent to escape civil or criminal liability, and having care, charge or control of a vehicle that is involved in an accident with a person or vehicle, fails to a) stop, b) give his or her name and address or c), where any person appears to require assistance or has been injured, offer assistance.[51]

dangerous driving

It is worth focusing on the first of these offences — the dangerous operation of a motor vehicle. The relevant *Criminal Code* provision makes it an offence to operate a motor vehicle "in a manner that is dangerous to the public, having regard to all the circumstances, including the nature, condition and use of the place at which the motor vehicle is being operated and the amount of traffic that at the time is or might reasonably be expected to be at that place."[52]

More than this, to be convicted of this offence, the driver's behaviour must constitute "a marked departure from the standard of care that a reasonable person would observe in the same situation."[53] Obviously, the range of behaviour violating this standard is variable and the caselaw contains a host of examples of what constitutes a deadly use of motor vehicles.

The danger and risk posed by the driver's behaviour in reported cases tends to be obvious. For instance, dangerous driving may exist where a motorist operates a vehicle without clearing away condensation that obscures vision through the front windshield.[54] It is also dangerous driving to steer deliberately a vehicle slowly towards a curb, knowing that a cyclist is on the curbside of the vehicle.[55] More than that, the motorist acts criminally in driving at a speed that is excessive in the circumstances.[56] This may be true even if it is never proven how the accident actually occurred; all that is necessary is that the prosecutor shows that the motorist was driving too fast to deal with any emergency.[57] More extreme examples include a motorist overtaking another vehicle at twice the posted speed limit, losing control, and striking a cyclist.[58]

The penalty for dangerous driving varies according to the injury caused. Driving dangerously without causing any injury is punishable by up to five years in jail. Dangerous driving causing bodily injury may be punished with imprisonment of up to ten years. Dangerous driving causing death bears a penalty of up to fourteen years.

In respect to the offence involving dangerous driving causing death, a conviction does not require that the motorist had intent to cause death or injury or even that the actual fatality or injury was unanticipated or unlikely. Nor does it matter if there were other contributing causes to that accident — all that matters is that the motorist's operation of the vehicle was more than a *de minimis* contributing cause of the death.[59]

A classic example of dangerous driving is the case of *R v Vandorp*.[60] In this case, the Ontario court made the following finding of fact:

> Mr. Vandorp and his mother, for one reason or another, did become upset with [cyclist] Mr. Broughten for something he did while still out on the public roadway and before the turn into the parking lot. Perhaps it's because they didn't think Mr. Broughten was following the rules of the road; perhaps it was because, as Mr. Vandorp says, he passed them along the curb too closely, and in an unsafe manner. Perhaps it was because he was sitting out in the middle of the road not moving. It's hard to know for sure, based on the evidence I heard.
>
> Mr. Vandorp then proceeded to follow Mr. Broughten into the parking lot, not necessarily to hit him. Notwithstanding [one witness's] impression that he was trying to hit the cyclist intentionally, I don't believe he did

intentionally, and with a specific purpose, try and hit Mr. Broughten, but rather was attempting to intimidate him by making it known he was upset by following him too closely. The act of following closely, which in turn enabled his mother to continue her verbal tirade was, I find, the purpose. This immature, outrageous, and dangerous behaviour in the result not only caused a dangerous situation but caused actual harm. It could have been worse.

The fact Mr. Vandorp at no point applied pressure to his brakes; the fact he at no point attempted to manoeuvre his vehicle out of the line being travelled by the bike; and the fact he either was travelling too quickly throughout the parking lot or at some point accelerated, all assist me in coming to this conclusion.[61]

As a result of the driver's conduct, the cyclist was "ejected from the bike and did suffer some injuries."[62] And as a result of his conduct, the driver was convicted: "It was criminal driving and behaviour that should attract the stigma associated with a criminal conviction and punishment."[63]

A more tragic conviction for dangerous driving causing injury to cyclists occurred in Ottawa, the city where we both live. This case is notable both for the number of victims and because the driver's conduct bore few of the hallmarks of outrageous conduct, of the sort detailed above. In *R v Luangpakham*,[64] a weary driver returning from a night of socializing (but apparently not drinking) dozed off at the wheel, and struck five cyclists riding single file in a bike lane of a roadway with two driving lanes on each side. He then departed the scene (a separate offence described below), leaving "five seriously injured cyclists, their bicycles twisted and bent and their bodies broken and bleeding."[65] The driver had no criminal record. There was no evidence of recklessness, excessive speed, and the accused was remorseful. He was sentenced to nine months in prison, and a further fifteen months for leaving the scene of the accident.

careless driving

Provincial and territorial laws also usually contain regulatory offences that sanction poor driving. These sanctions are not as severe as those found in the *Criminal Code* and do not result in a criminal record, but are still significant legal prohibitions. Examples of specific offences include "dooring" and driving while using electronic devices. In Ontario, for example, a driver can be charged under sections of the *Highway Traffic Act* that requires motorists to take "due precautions" when opening a car door so as not to endanger any other person or vehicle.[66] Meanwhile, all provinces and territories (other than Nunavut) have specific prohibitions on the use of hand-held cell devices for talking, texting, or e-mailing.

The broadest provincial offence is, however, "careless driving." For instance, under the Ontario *Highway Traffic Act*, operating a vehicle on a highway without "due care and attention or without reasonable consideration for other persons on a highway" is an offence associated with a fine of between $400 and $2,000 and/or imprisonment for up to six months. Conviction may also result in the suspension of a licence for up to two years.[67] "Highway" under Ontario law is basically any non-private roadway.

This careless driving standard requires drivers to exercise a "reasonable amount of skill" in the handling of their vehicles or, put another way, behave like an "ordinary prudent person." The test is, therefore, whether the motorist "in the light of existing circumstances of which he was aware or of which a driver exercising ordinary care should have been aware, failed to use the care and attention or to give to other persons using the highway the consideration that a driver of ordinary care would have used or given in the circumstances."[68] As this statement suggests, what constitutes due care varies according to, e.g., road conditions. The court must also consider that the conduct is of "such a nature that it can be considered a breach of duty to the public and deserving of punishment."[69]

Other jurisdictions have similar offences in their highway and vehicle laws.[70] The test in each varies slightly but creates a similar standard as exists in Ontario. In British Columbia, for example, the threshold is whether the manner of driving, in all the circumstances, "departs from the accustomed sober behaviour of a reasonable" person.[71]

Leaving the scene of an accident

Most people have heard of the obligation that those involved in an accident remain at the scene. As noted, this is a requirement of most provincial motor vehicle laws. More than this, failure to remain at the scene is also a serious criminal offence under the federal *Criminal Code*. Specifically, a person may be convicted if, while having care, charge or control of a vehicle that is involved in an accident with another person or vehicle, fails to stop and give his or her name and address and, when someone has been injured, offer assistance, if the failure to stop is one with the intent to avoid liability.[72] In everyday language, we call this failure to stop a "hit and run."

The criminal offence has several key elements. First, and obviously, there has to be an "accident." But the accident does not have to be accidental — it can include both intentional and unintentional occurrences.[73] Moreover, while an accident obviously includes an outright collision, there need not be actual contact between a vehicle and a bike for there to be an accident. For instance, where a motorist knows he or she has forced a cyclist off the road, and nevertheless fails to stop and leaves the scene, that motorist may be guilty of a hit and run.[74] There need not be an injury or damage for the elements of the offence to arise.[75]

Third, the failure to stop must be done with the intent of avoiding liability, whether criminal or civil. On this issue, there is a presumption that a motorist acts to escape liability where they fail to perform one of their obligations; that is: stop; offer assistance where there is an injury; or give name and address.[76]

In *Luangpakham*,[77] discussed above, the court underscored the importance of stopping at the scene of the accident in sentencing the offender:

> . . . it is important that there be this strong statement from the Court denouncing and deterring if not Mr. Luangpakham himself, certainly the public generally, not only of dangerous driving but particularly of leaving the scene of the accident. All drivers must know of their duty to stop and render assistance if they are involved in an accident where any person has been injured or appears to need assistance. There are other duties too that are set out for all drivers in an accident, including leaving your name and address, but the sentence imposed here will reflect that fact, that that very important duty was not met here.[78]

As noted above, the offender was sentenced to fifteen months for the hit and run.

extreme acts: "road rage"

Dangerous or careless driving creates obvious perils for cyclists. Less common but even more perilous are instances where a driver intends to cause injury to a cyclist. While not a legal term or art, we call these sorts of acts "road rage." Earlier in this chapter, we described some examples of conflicts between cyclists and motorists that truly rise to the level of road rage.

Dangerous driving can capture such road rage incidents. But a motorist who intentionally strikes a cyclist with their vehicle is potentially culpable for a range of other criminal offences, including murder. In one case, for example, an offender stole a vehicle and then, moments later, intentionally struck a cyclist, at least in part on the dare of his friends in the vehicle. He later pled guilty to manslaughter.[79]

Even in circumstances where the results of the motorist's actions are less dire, he or she may be convicted for such things as assault with a weapon — the weapon being their vehicle. In one British Columbia case, a cyclist stopped at an intersection for a red light. The motorist approached from behind and told her to get out of the way and threatened to hit the cyclist. When the cyclist failed to move, the motorist pressed the bumper of his vehicle against the rear wheel of the bicycle, causing the cyclist to skip forward but not otherwise causing any damage or injury. The cyclist then moved aside, and the motorist left. The motorist was convicted of assault with a weapon, as well as leaving the scene of an accident.[80]

cyclists and criminal culpability

The discussion above has focused on driver culpability for lousy driving and road rage incidents. There is, of course, another side to the coin: egregious behaviour by cyclists. Both of us have witnessed poor and even dangerous behaviour by cyclists. Craig for one has even considered investing in a cycling jersey for group rides, emblazoned with "I'm not responsible for stupid's foul language and inattention to traffic rules."

It is true, of course, that when a cyclist mishandles his vehicle, she or he generally only puts himself or herself at risk of injury. But there are exceptions. Pedestrians, for example, are vulnerable to errant or speeding cyclists, and serious injuries have resulted from such collisions.[81] A careless or malicious cyclist can also harm other cyclists. More than this, it is not unknown for a motorist to be pursued and assaulted by a cyclist vigilante. In one Alberta case, a cyclist felt an elderly driver exiting a driveway had cut him off, causing him to fall. In response, he then attacked the driver through the car window. He was convicted of criminal assault.[82] In a famous 2009 incident involving a cyclist and a car driven by a former Ontario attorney-general, an altercation between cyclist and driver ignited a tragic sequence of events in which the cyclist was ultimately killed, the driver criminally charged, and the charges ultimately dropped after the prosecutor concluded that the cyclist has exhibited "an escalating cycle of aggressiveness toward motorists."[83]

All of this is to say that there is no limit to the trouble a cyclist can find him or herself in by running amok. But it is worth asking here about the extent to which errant cycling attracts the same sort of dangerous or careless driving or driving-related penalties as does an imprudent motorist. Many cyclists may be under the impression that while drivers have obligations under these laws, cyclists have only rights.

On that point, they would be wrong. The short answer is that the *Criminal Code* concept of dangerous driving (although not the broader concept of criminal negligence) is confined to "motor vehicles" and thus excludes conventional bicycles. But careless driving under, e.g., the Ontario *Highway Traffic Act*, has a greater reach. The Ontario provision applies, simply, to "vehicles," a concept that includes a bicycle. In other words, operating a bicycle on a highway (again, essentially any non-private roadway) without "due care and attention or without reasonable consideration for other persons on a highway" is an offence associated with a fine of between $400 and $2,000 and imprisonment for up to six months. And cyclists have been charged under this provision: in a relatively recent case, a cyclist was charged for striking a pedestrian at an intersection in Toronto.[84] Likewise, in Quebec a cyclist was convicted of violating that province's *Highway Safety Code*, after "riding a bicycle . . . and cross[ing an] intersection diagonally while the light was red and motorists were honking at him."[85]

Several other provincial laws follow this pattern, and impose careless driving prohibitions on cyclists because the definition of a "vehicle" is (at least in principle) broad enough to encompass bicycles[86] or because of provisions that make cyclist obligations equivalent to those of drivers in most instances.[87] (Some other provinces include cyclist-specific due care language, but without making violations of that duty an offence.[88])

It is also notable that the *Criminal Code* offence of failing to stop at the scene of an accident applies to those who have care, charge or control of a "vehicle," not simply a "motor vehicle." The striking omission of "motor" means the provision extends to other vehicles. As discussed in Chapter 2, a bicycle is commonly considered a vehicle under provincial highway traffic laws. In fact, in 2013, a Toronto cyclist was charged with leaving the scene of an accident after striking a pedestrian and causing a brain injury that resulted, ultimately, in death. If convicted, he faces a sentence of life in prison.[89]

Municipal bylaws may also include sanctions. For instance, riding a bicycle on a sidewalk may be an offence under municipal law, penalized by fines, or even the prospect of incarceration.[90]

suing and being sued

Criminal culpability is only one part of the equation. Bicycle mishaps and accidents are also often the source of civil claims. This is possible because under our laws, everyone has a duty not to injure others. If a person harms another person or damages their property, they are liable to pay compensation for the harm suffered by the injured party. This branch of private law is called tort law in common law provinces, and civil responsibility in Quebec. It determines in what circumstances, and with what consequences, one person may be liable for injuring or harming another person.

"Plaintiffs" — those wronged — may bring lawsuits against "defendants" — those who do the wrong — so long as filed prior to the expiry of "limitations periods." The latter are time limits on such lawsuits. They vary between jurisdictions, and sometimes are affected by the identity of the defendant. For instance, in Ontario, the general limitation period is two years after a reasonable person would know of the injury (almost always, the day on the incident causing the injury).[91] But where the defendant is a municipality, tort lawsuits are impermissible (subject to exceptions) unless the municipality has been served with written notice of the claim within ten days of the injury.[92]

Remedies for tort wrongs are the payment of damages. These come in different guises — compensatory damages are the most common and aim to restore the injured person to the position she or he would have been in had the wrongful conduct never occurred. Aggravated damages are more infrequent and compensate for humiliation, embarrassment or distress precipitated by the defendant's conduct. Courts award punitive damages where the defendant's actions are so outrageous as to prompt a severe punishment. Aggravated and punitive damages are more common where the defendant intentionally (rather than carelessly) causes an injury.[93]

In common law jurisdictions, tort law is developed for the most part by the courts, rather than by law-makers. In Quebec, the civil responsibilities of individuals are found in the *Quebec Civil Code*. The general principle, however, is the same for all Canadians: the law imposes a general duty on everyone (both human beings and corporations) to take reasonable care to avoid causing injury or harm to others.

In this section, we will review the legal rules that govern civil lawsuits in three main areas: collisions between motorists and cyclists; accidents involving cyclists and pedestrians, or between cyclists; and, finally, cycling accidents resulting from the negligent conduct of governments.

accidents between cyclists and motorists

Civil lawsuits may be an important means of obtaining full compensation for collisions with motor vehicles that cause the death or injury of a cyclist. This is true in all provinces and territories except for Manitoba and Quebec. In those two jurisdictions, a comprehensive no-fault public automobile insurance system precludes lawsuits as a means to supplement public insurance payouts, to be discussed more fully in the section on insurance.

There are various legal bases for civil lawsuits, but the most likely is a claim for negligence. We will describe the elements of a claim for negligence as it applies in common law provinces and territories, the principles having derived for the most part from court decisions.

Negligence and the Duty of Care

Boiled down to its essence, a claim for negligence is a tortious "cause of action" that arises where a person owes another a "duty of care" and the person's behaviour then transgresses an acceptable "standard of care," causing injury to another person or their property. In negligence law, one person owes another a duty of care where "one could reasonably contemplate that carelessness on his or her part might cause damage to the other."[94] Drivers steering vehicles on roads frequented by cyclists have this duty, as indeed cyclists have to other road users. And, as we will discuss later, municipal and provincial governments also have a duty of care to cyclists who use the roads they build and maintain.

The Standard of Care

When it comes to interactions between motorists and cyclists, the standard of care expected of a driver "is not one of perfection, but whether the driver acted in a manner in which an ordinarily prudent person would act."[95] Cyclists, likewise, have an obligation not to contribute to their own peril. A cyclist who is injured while failing to take reasonable care of his or her own safety contributes — and indeed may be the sole source — of that injury. What "reasonable care" means will vary according to the circumstances. Road, weather and lighting conditions are all relevant considerations. Moreover, as discussed further below, a failure to comply with the rules of the road may trigger a duty to take extra care.

Special issues in the application of the standard of care may arise with young children. Children on bicycles generally lack the seasoned judgment of adults, knowledge of the rules of the road and bike handling skills. Drivers must be particularly wary of the erratic riding and sudden appearances of children on bicycles, and the law may impose a standard of extra vigilance where motor vehicles are driven near children. As one New Brunswick court observed:

> When an accident occurs between a child on a bicycle and a motor vehicle operator, the first issue to be determined is whether it was reasonably foreseeable that the child (or, depending on the facts of the case, any child) may act so as to constitute an imminent danger, and therefore place a duty on the motorist to take steps to be able to take preventative or evasive action if necessary. Where a child's behaviour is reasonably foreseeable, the onus is high on motorists to show that all reasonable measures were taken to avoid the accident. Such measures which may be required of drivers are: to adjust vehicle speed according to the circumstances; to take evasive action, including braking; to keep a proper lookout and to warn others of one's presence (namely, by timely sounding of the driver's horn). The analysis of liability and onus on drivers is similar with respect to children cycling as for those running into the street, with the additional element that children on bicycles, in addition to being impulsive, may also be unskilled riders.[96]

In cases involving cyclists and motorists, there are a number of more specific patterns involving the application of the rules on negligence.

Apportioned Liability

First, in many bicycle and motor vehicle collisions, there is often an element of fault by both parties — both cyclist and motorist were careless.

In one fairly typical case stemming from an accident in British Columbia,[97] the plaintiff cyclist was riding along a sidewalk routinely used by both cyclists and pedestrians. The day was clear with excellent visibility. The defendant driver stopped prior to executing a right turn from a shopping mall lot. Failing to see the approaching cyclist, he proceeded with the turn, and the cyclist collided with the side of his vehicle.

In apportioning liability in this case, the court noted that both cyclist and motorist had duties to take reasonable care. The driver need not meet a standard of perfection, but must act in fashion consistent with an ordinarily prudent person. Where, as in this case, the driver failed to see a cyclist approaching on a clear day and proceeded to make a turn causing a collision, he did not act in a normally prudent manner.

At the same time, the cyclist acted wrongly in riding on the sidewalk — something that violated the highway safety laws. He assumed that the driver had seen him, and did not attempt to make eye contact with the driver. The cyclist's failure to take reasonable care for his own safety was a contributing cause of the accident. The court divided blame for the accident, concluding that the driver was the substantial (but not sole) cause of the accident. Liability was, therefore, apportioned 75 percent to the driver and 25 percent to the cyclist.

As this case suggests, much in negligence cases turns on the specific circumstances of the accident. Otherwise similar accidents may produce different legal outcomes depending on seemingly minor distinctions. For instance, courts have held drivers liable for striking a cyclist appearing suddenly in front of the driver at a crosswalk. A reasonable driver approaching a marked crosswalk should have been alert to the possibility of pedestrians or cyclists. On the other hand, a similar abrupt appearance elsewhere on the road, away from crosswalks, may not give rise to the same caution, and thus potential liability.[98]

Likewise, while it may be careless for a cyclist to ride at night without a headlight, the failure to do so does not eliminate the liability of a driver that strikes that cyclist at a well-lit intersection in which the driver should have seen the rider.[99] Courts have also held that a cyclist who suffers a concussion but fails to wear a helmet is partially to blame for that outcome.[100]

Rules of the Road as a Benchmark

Second, while provinces vary in the emphasis placed on them, a failure to abide by the rules set out in provincial and territorial highway traffic or motor vehicle acts provides a measuring stick against which to gauge the reasonableness of motorist and cyclist behaviour. At least some courts have imposed the onus to disprove their own negligence on cyclists where they have violated the rules of the road.[101] Others have specified that an individual violating traffic rules is subject to an increased duty of care.[102]

Still, it should be noted that abiding by the rules of the road does not definitively determine the question of responsibility. That is because, in deciding negligence cases, "a court must determine whether, and to what extent, each of the players in an accident met their common law duties of care to other users of the road. In making that determination, a court will be informed by the rules of the road, but those rules do not eliminate the need to consider the reasonableness of the actions of the parties."[103]

Some courts have assigned blame to cyclists where they violate the careless driving prohibitions in highway safety laws.[104] Other courts have pointed to more specific rules violated by cyclists.[105] For instance, highway safety rules may specify circumstances in which one vehicle must yield to another. A vehicle entering traffic from a laneway, for example, is expected to yield to oncoming traffic. A failure to yield may have a bearing in apportioning responsibility for an accident.[106]

Another recurring issue is the responsibility of cyclists involved in an accident while passing stopped cars on the right. This may be a dangerous manoeuvre, especially when approaching an intersection in which facing traffic may be turning left. Likewise, the cyclist moving along the right side of stopped traffic may not be visible to a motorist intending to turn right. The circumstances in which one vehicle may pass another on the right are limited under highway safety laws. Nevertheless, it is commonplace for cyclists to make their way to the front of a column of gridlocked traffic by passing on the right. In fact, the increasing use of advanced stop lines, also called bike boxes (see "Cycling Road Signs and Markings" in Chapter 2), encourages cyclists to move to the front at a stop light to take advantage of a head start when the traffic signal changes from red to green. Along with many cyclists, Craig has certainly imagined he travels up an invisible bike lane to the right of stalled traffic, exercising his right not to linger in their exhaust. On the other hand, such behaviour is sometimes viewed as a contributing (if not definitive) element of the accident, and again liability is apportioned between driver and cyclists accordingly.

As impractical as it may seem, everything may depend on the province in which you pass on the right. There are several cases in British Columbia and Alberta where courts assigned blame to cyclists passing on the right in violation of the rules of the road.[107] However, courts are not consistent on this question. New Brunswick and Nova Scotia courts have concluded "it would be illogical to say a cyclist must pass on the left in traffic when he is required to drive on the extreme right."[108] This is an especially cogent conclusion where provincial highway safety laws allow cyclists to pass on the right.[109]

As a final point on this issue, rules of the road may not apply in cycling specific events, but it all depends. In deciding whether the rules of the road apply to a cycling specific event, Ontario courts have considered whether the road is completely closed (in which case the rules do not apply) or whether they are also open to emergency or other vehicles (in which case they do apply).[110]

Onus of Proof

A third issue involves who has the burden of proof in a negligence case. Cyclists who violate highway traffic laws and regulations, for instance by passing on the right, or riding on sidewalks or across crosswalks, may be partially to blame for the accident — but that does not automatically exonerate the drivers who strike them. Everything still hinges on the level of care exhibited by the driver.[111] Further, someone has to provide evidence to a court to determine if a motorist in fact met the level of care.

Some provinces impose special obligations on drivers in relation to other road users. In Manitoba, "[w]here loss or damage is sustained by any person by reason of a motor vehicle upon a highway the onus of proof that the loss or damage did not arise entirely or solely through the negligence or improper conduct of the owner or driver is upon the owner or driver."[112] Cyclists in collisions are entitled to this reverse onus.[113] Similar rules exist in Prince Edward Island, Alberta, and Ontario.[114] These provisions mean that the driver has to prove that their negligence was not the cause of the accident, changing the onus of proof as compared to conventional negligence claims.[115]

Insurance

Finally, the world of tort law is informed also by provincial and territorial insurance rules. Unlike motor vehicles, bicycles do not need to be insured. This means that it is not illicit to operate a bicycle without insurance coverage. Nevertheless, a cyclist may still have a claim for insurance coverage if injured in an accident with a motor vehicle. It is, therefore, useful to have a basic understanding of the complex world of motor vehicle accident insurance.

First, Canada divides into two broad classes: provinces with government-run, public automobile insurers who are the sole (or in Quebec, at least partial) provider of auto insurance;[116] and, provinces where insurers are private companies. British Columbia, Saskatchewan, Manitoba, and Quebec are in the first category, while the other provinces and territories are in the second.

Public automobile insurers provide a package of benefits for injury or death, coverage against third-party liability and (except in Quebec) property damage.[117] These benefits are paid, no matter who is at fault in the accident, and in Manitoba and Quebec, injured parties have no further right to sue a negligent driver for more compensation.

Second, automobile insurance of some sort is mandatory in all provinces and territories, although the minimum level of coverage each driver must buy varies from place to place. In jurisdictions other than Manitoba and Quebec, those injured by a driver may sue that driver to recover damages that exceed this minimum coverage.

The bottom line is that drivers are supposed to be insured everywhere in Canada, and face penalties if they are not. That said, accidents with uninsured drivers can happen. Some provinces have government-run funds that serve as "payers of last resort" in situations where the injured cyclist is unable to claim against a negligent driver or his or her insurance company. These funds are particularly important where a driver is un- or underinsured or the accident is a hit and run.

If a cyclist is injured in a motor vehicle accident, the insurance process will vary in each province and territory, according to that jurisdiction's rules. For instance, in British Columbia, the process for collecting from an uninsured driver or in a hit and run case involves the ICBC and includes a number of specific procedural steps that an injured person must follow in seeking compensation.[118]

In Ontario, cyclists injured by a motor vehicle must first claim against their own auto insurance company, should they have one. Otherwise, they claim against the insurer of the motor vehicle involved in the accident. In other instances — where, for example, the driver is uninsured or the accident was a hit and run — the cyclist may submit a claim to the provincial Motor Vehicle Accident Claims Fund (MVACF).[119]

Not surprisingly, Ontario law seeks to limit the number of circumstances in which the latter fund will be called upon. The MVACF is intended as a payer of last resort. To minimize the need to call upon the fund, the province requires motor vehicle insurance policies to include specific terms. Most notably, Ontario motor vehicle insurance policies must provide for payment of the amounts that the insured individual is legally entitled to recover from the driver of an uninsured or unidentified vehicle for bodily injuries caused by being struck by a vehicle.[120] Put another way, if you're a driver, your policies must include coverage for injuries caused by being struck by uninsured motorists or in hit and run situations, even when you are riding your bicycle rather than driving your car. Being "struck" obviously means being hit by the motor vehicle.[121] But the courts have interpreted the expressions generously to include both circumstances involving collisions (regardless of who hits whom)[122] and near misses in which a cyclist in injured in the course of taking evasive action.[123]

It should be noted that the preceding discussion is really about personal injury: a cyclist is hurt in a collision with a motor vehicle. But claims for personal injury are one thing, and compensation for damage to your very expensive $10,000 carbon-frame, electric-shifted, racing bike quite another. While an injured cyclist claims first against his or her own motor vehicle insurer (should they have one) for personal injuries in a province like Ontario, that insurance policy need not (and may not) extend to property damage to the bicycle itself. Cyclists should do what Craig did after writing this section: check with your insurer to see if your policy includes damage to your precious two wheel vehicles.

If the cyclist's property damage is not covered by motor vehicle insurance, he or she may claim against the driver's insurance. There may also be a claim under the cyclist's home insurance, depending on its terms.

Indeed, the latter may be the only source of insurance in accidents that do not involve motorists — running your mountain bike off a trail, for instance, or crashing into a lamppost. But even if coverage reaches this far, the dollar limits on the insurance, after deductibles, may be quite low, leaving the sportif rider with the cracked $3,000 disk wheel out of pocket. Bicycle specific insurance policies or riders on existing policies do exist and may be worth careful consideration. For cyclists competing in sanctioned competitive cycling events, club insurance policies may offer additional coverage.

accidents between cyclists and pedestrians or other cyclists

Pedestrians and cyclists do collide, as do cyclists with each other, creating additional circumstance in which negligence principles may govern civil liability. The most likely scenario involves collisions between pedestrians and cyclists travelling on sidewalks or shared trails.[124] The fact that cyclists are not supposed to be on sidewalks makes courts more likely to assign fault to the cyclist.[125]

In collisions with other cyclists (for instance, during a cycling event) one consideration in assigning liability is the nature of the sporting activity. As one Ontario court has observed "[t]he nature of the risks inherent in a given activity is relevant to what the proper standard of care is in a specific situation. Put differently, the question of what constitutes reasonable care is affected by what risks a person participating in a sporting event could reasonably have expected to face."[126] In that case, two cyclists on a charity ride collided and crashed. The court opined on the standard of care in such a case, in reasons that are worth reproducing in detail:

. . . when the Plaintiff decided to participate in this ride, he assumed the usual risks associated with the sport. He agreed with the risks including the actions of reasonable cyclists who he could expect to follow the known rules governing group rides. He did not, however, agree to accept the risks associated with conduct that did not accord with the usual rules. . . . It is sufficient if the Plaintiff proves that the conduct of the Defendant fell short of what a reasonable cyclist participating in a group ride for charity would do or refrain from doing. . . . By its nature cycling is not a contact sport or one that involves physical encounters with opponents such as football or rugby. . . . That said, it is a sport which is done at a fast rate of speed, wearing little protective gear and there are various risks that are inherent in participating in an organized bicycle race. A rider might, for example, hit a pothole with a resulting loss of control and being thrown off the bike, sustaining injury. Or a cyclist might blow a tire and fall off the bike or perhaps skid on wet pavement, losing control of the bike and suffering injury. These eventualities might be viewed as risks inherent in participation in the sport of cycling. However, negligent conduct cannot be viewed as a risk that a participant agrees to accept by engaging in a sport.[127]

The court then noted "one of the cardinal rules of participating in a group ride is that a cyclist must not make any sudden movements, must maintain a steady pace and signal any movements."[128] Here, the defendant's conduct "consisted of making a sudden movement while riding in a group, failing to maintain a straight line, failing to signal his intention to move and moving directly into the path of the Plaintiff when he could have moved out to the right."[129] This, the court concluded, violated a standard of care expected of riders in a pace line, and was therefore negligent conduct.

As already noted, these sorts of accidents would generally not be covered by motor vehicle insurance, and so riders may wish to consider more specialized coverage that would reach their participation in recreational and sporting events. We discuss insurance for sporting events also in Chapters 6 and 7.

accidents caused by negligent governments

Road Safety

When he raced bikes in Ontario as a junior, Craig's entire cycling team once wiped out after a race on a municipal bridge surfaced with a (wet) metal grate, whose presence was not signalled by any warning sign. No one was seriously hurt, but he did wonder idly who would be at fault if there had been injuries. More recently, he has cursed each time he has swerved around the handful of sewer grates in his municipality whose gaps continue to be oriented towards the direction of travel — and which are more than ample enough to swallow up his narrow, 700c road tires.

Cyclists sometimes crash because roads are in lousy condition, raising questions about whether the government is on the hook for damages. Government liability for negligence is a complicated and arcane area.[130] For our purposes, it suffices to say that governments may be held liable for their negligence in maintaining roadways and cycling infrastructure. Municipalities and provincial and territorial governments with road-related responsibilities have a duty to maintain roads to ensure reasonably safe conditions. The duty exists at common law,[131] and in Quebec, in the provincial Civil Code.[132]

A BC court held that "[t]he duty is to keep the roads in a reasonable state of repair such that those using them may, exercising ordinary care, travel upon them with safety. The standard of care is to be assessed in light of all the surrounding circumstances, including the nature of the road, where it is situated, the amount of traffic, the requirements of the public who use the road, budgetary constraints, and the availability of qualified personnel."[133] A Manitoba court, for its part, described the government's duty as protecting road users from unreasonable harm by taking reasonable steps to fix problems of which the government ought to be aware.[134]

Accordingly, courts have emphasized that governments must make reasonable efforts to prevent injury to road users stemming from hazardous conditions, be they transitory (e.g., ice and debris) or permanent (e.g., road design).[135] For instance, governments may be liable for negligent roadway inspections where they do not consider curb hazards peculiar to cyclists, especially in circumstances where a cyclist might have reason to negotiate a curb in crossing a roadway.[136]

Of course, the government's duty only extends to ordinary use by the ordinarily careful road users. Thus, a municipality may be liable for its design and construction of guardrails that provide insufficient protection to the normal cyclist.[137] It is not liable for the configuration of roads that become perilous because a cyclist disregards his or her own safety.[138]

In some provinces such as Saskatchewan, Alberta, and Ontario, municipalities have a special statutory duty to keep roads in repair. In Ontario, for instance, the *Municipal Act* indicates that a municipality having "jurisdiction over a highway or bridge shall keep it in a state of repair that is reasonable in light of all the circumstances, including the character and location of the highway or bridge."[139] A failure to meet this obligation of repair makes a municipality liable for injuries stemming from it, subject to a number of defences. Those defences include ignorance — reasonable in the circumstances — of the disrepair or the making of reasonable efforts to avoid the disrepair. Notably, disrepair may include "any aspect of the road and its environs."[140] It extends to things like design flaws and a failure to post relevant signage warning cyclists of hazards.[141] Thus, the Ontario Court of Appeal has described the municipality's duty as requiring it to keep the road in "such a reasonable state of repair that those requiring to use it may, exercising ordinary care, travel upon it with safety."[142] Inadequate signage indicating hazardous conditions ahead may violate the municipality's duties, as might road maintenance of a sort that causes cyclists to experience "speed wobble" on steep grades.[143]

A city may even be partially responsible where the actual cause of the accident is a driver — in one case, a cyclist was "doored" by a driver exiting his car on a route that was marked (incorrectly) by the city as a bike route. The driver was liable, but so, too, was the city. The court reasoned:

> The designation as a bike route must mean something, some indication that the street is somewhat safer than the unsigned streets. The road, at this location, is not bicycle friendly. It leaves very little room for a cyclist to maneuver, very little margin for error. Sure, a skilled cyclist can pass in safety, but roads should be safe for the ordinary cyclist. At one time, cycling was quite rare in the City, but with the proliferation of bicycles and the City's encouragement for health reasons, reducing congestion, less burning of fossil fuels, the City should have done something more positive about bike safety at this location. The Plaintiff had no choice but to use Queen Street to get to the bike lanes. The City must have known that many cyclists converge in that area to get to the exclusive bike lanes.[144]

These same municipal duty statutes also limit municipal liability. In language largely replicated in Ontario and Alberta,[145] the Saskatchewan statute says that lawsuits cannot be sustained for damages caused "(a) by the presence, absence or type of any wall, fence, guardrail, railing, curb, pavement markings, traffic control device or barrier; or (b) by or on account of any construction, obstruction or erection or any situation, arrangement or disposition of any earth, rock, tree or other material or thing adjacent to or in, along or on a street or road that is not on the travelled portion of the street or road."[146] And so Saskatoon was not liable when a cyclist injured himself, tumbling from an embankment on a street under construction (although the construction company was on the hook).[147]

Recreational Trails and Rural Areas
Public Trails

Government liability for off-road accidents may be governed by different rules. City-maintained recreational pathways, for example, are governed under provincial occupier liability statutes in PEI, Nova Scotia, Ontario, Manitoba, Alberta, and British Columbia.[148] Provincial and federal government property in these provinces is also subject to these rules.[149]

Under these Acts, the standard of care imposed on the government (as "occupier") is quite forgiving. In standard language more or less replicated in other provinces with similar statutes, the Ontario law states that where a person enters a premise, they are deemed to willingly assume all risks if the entry was for the purpose of a recreational activity and no fee was paid for that activity. In these circumstances, the occupier must not deliberately create a danger and not act with reckless disregard to the presence of the person.[150] The occupier is otherwise relieved of their standard duty to act with reasonable care. "Premise" in this context includes both "rural premises" and "recreational trails reasonably marked by notice as such."

Since there will be few, if any, instances in which the occupier will deliberately attempt to create a danger, liability for trail accidents will depend on whether the location of the accident is truly a "recreational trail" attracting the relaxed standard of care, and if so, whether the government has shown "reckless disregard."

Not every pathway will be a "recreational trail." Ontario courts have held, for instance, that a portion of such a trail that allows cars access and egress from a parking lot is not, for instance, a "recreational trail" under the Act.[151] On the other hand, a pathway that bars motor vehicles, follows natural features, is not designed for the efficient movement from one place to another,[152] or is designated as part of a recreational network,[153] is likely a "recreational trail." The relaxed liability standard for recreational trails persist even when cyclists or other users partake in cross-country departures from the marked trails: "Where a person enters a property that is generally used for recreational activity . . . and the property consists in part of a recreational trail reasonably marked as such; and that person leaves the recreational trail but remains on the property while continuously engaged in a recreational activity, then the lower standard of care . . . applies."[154]

As noted, that standard of care is "reckless disregard." This phrase has been interpreted as meaning: "doing or omitting to do something which he or she should recognize as likely to cause damage or injury to [the person] present on his or her premises, not caring whether such damage or injury results."[155] In practice, a failure to inspect and maintain asphalt in a particularly dangerous portion of a trail may violate this standard.[156] Likewise, the placement of a bollard in a location where it is difficult to see without warning signs or efforts to make the obstruction more visible may also constitute reckless disregard.[157]

Private Trails

The same occupier liability statutes generally apply to private facilities. Riding on private recreational trails (and indeed, rural property) is, therefore, covered by the same, relaxed liability standards as described above. In one BC court's words, this rule "encourage[s] the opening up of rural lands to recreational use," and defined "rural" as "in, of, or suggesting the country (opp. URBAN); pastoral or agricultural."[158] The issue of whether land is really rural or not is often contested, since that decision produces very different rules on the standard of care the occupier must meet.[159]

Parking Lots and Private Roads and Sidewalks

Liability rules for parking lots and "private streets" and private sidewalks may be more complex. Unlike trails, parking lots and private sidewalks are generally governed by more demanding occupier standards in occupier liability laws in those provinces that have them, and otherwise by common law rules. And so under occupier liability statutes like that of Manitoba, an occupier "owes a duty to persons entering on the premises and to any person, whether on or off the premises, whose property is on the premises, to take such care as, in all the circumstances of the case, is reasonable to see that the person or property, as the case may be, will be reasonably safe while on the premises."[160] The common law rules in provinces without equivalent statutes now gravitate towards similar rules.[161]

Private roads may be treated differently. Some provincial statutes impose the same "reckless disregard" standard for private roads as for trails and rural areas.[162] Still others preserve a common law approach, which can be more demanding of occupiers. Thus, an Alberta court held that if a private street occupier impliedly or expressly consents to the presence of cyclists, that occupier must "take reasonable care to avoid foreseeable risk of harm from any unusual danger on the occupier's premises of which the occupier has knowledge, or of which he ought to have knowledge because has was aware of the circumstances."[163] And so occupiers may be negligent if they, e.g., construct a speed bump "appropriate only for parking lots and clearly inappropriate for roadways" without posting appropriate warnings useful to cyclists known to frequent the roadway.[164]

A final note: a distinction is often made between those who visit private premises with implied or express permission, and trespassers. In an approach echoed in most other occupier liability statutes, the Alberta law makes an occupier liable only "for damages for death of or injury to the trespasser that results from the occupier's willful or reckless conduct."[165]

accidents outside canada

Many of us take our bikes on our interprovincial and international travels. In fact, living in Ottawa, we both cross a provincial border every time we head out to ride the amazing parkway or trails of Gatineau Park in Quebec. This means accidents may befall us outside of our home province or territory. In that case, the tort rules that arise in any accident will be different than the laws that apply if your accident happened in your home jurisdiction. Canada is a federation, and as our discussion has suggested, the rules governing lawsuits may differ from one Canadian jurisdiction to another. There is little doubt that if your cycling trip takes you outside of Canada, then applicable laws will be different than our own.

The rules determining which laws apply to accidents occurring outside of your home province or territory is called private international law, also known as conflict of laws. This is a complicated area of the law and a full explanation of the basic rules takes Nicole a full semester to explain to her students (and they often still don't get it). So we will try to give you some basics but encourage you to consult a lawyer if you are ever is such a situation.

First, before you cross any border, make sure you have good insurance coverage. Specialized travel insurance exists, as does even more specialized cycling travel insurance. Your home insurer, meanwhile, may offer insurance coverage for such things as liability coverage in the event of an overseas accident. You may be insured for things like medical expenses through an employee plan or because you made your travel arrangements using now commonplace travel-oriented credit cards.

Second, you should appreciate that the rules of the road and their application to cycling may vary from place to place — even within Canada those rules are different, as Chapter 2 suggests. You may wish to research this question before departing.

Third, if you are involved in a collision while riding your bike in another Canadian jurisdiction or a foreign country, you may be able to sue for damages in your home province or territory, but only if you can show that there is a "real and substantial connection" to your provincial or territorial jurisdiction. This generally means more than you simply being a resident — other elements of the tort must have a link to your province. If you cannot make this argument, your lawsuit will have to be submitted to the courts in the other Canadian or foreign jurisdiction.

Fourth, even if you are able to show a real and substantial connection to your province, the court may nevertheless end up applying the law of the foreign jurisdiction to the case (if asked to do so by one of the parties to the lawsuit). This may seem strange, but in fact it is possible for a Canadian court to decide a tort lawsuit using the legal rules of the place where the negligence happened. So it is wise to assess, with the help of a lawyer, what rules are more advantageous to you.

Fifth, if you have to sue in the foreign jurisdiction, and you are successful, your next step will be to enforce the judgment you obtained. If the person responsible for the tort is in another jurisdiction, there will be specific steps you must take to ensure you receive the monetary damages the court awarded you.

Essentially, the best guidance we can give you if you are seriously hurt in an accident in another province or country, is to get some good legal advice about how to proceed if you are seeking compensation for your injuries or losses. And better yet, make sure before you leave that you have adequate insurance protection for such unfortunate eventualities.

conclusion

As this chapter demonstrates, the law governing unfortunate instances of falling off your bike is complicated. If you're lucky, you won't need to understand it. But if you're not, you'll need some understanding of the rules we have outlined in order to properly respond to any criminal or civil liability issues that may arise from a collision or crash.

Advance warning of accident law's content may not help you avoid a mishap. But it is handy to have some appreciation of what happens after a fall, and when legal duties and rights arise. We began this chapter with our chief "takeaways," which may be useful to review. We'll conclude with a final point: read Chapter 2 on the rules of the road again, and teach yourself and your dependents those rules. To be frank, some make little sense – tinkling bells to try to warn off transport trucks, for instance. In all situations, cyclists must exercise judgment. Craig has been known to hop onto sidewalks to avoid city buses stopping abruptly at bus stops, obscured by their bulk. And there is at least one city bridge whose roadway he refuses to ride even though it is marked with bicycle route chevrons. He opts instead for the sidewalk (albeit crossing at least partially dismounted). Tellingly, that bridge has a ghost bike chained at its end, memorializing a cycling fatality.

So the rules are not a perfect foil to an accident. But if you follow them, you become a more predictable road user. That can only be a good thing.

A final, related point: in writing this chapter, we were struck by the number of court cases we read in which the accident was caused, at least in part, by some aberrant action by a cyclist. The human cost of those accidents in terms of pain and suffering was enormous, as was the financial cost when courts concluded that the cyclist was at least in part to blame for his or her misfortune. We encourage you to keep this in mind the next time you hop on your bicycle for your regular commute or weekend recreational ride.

endnotes

1   Bryce Forbes, "Olympian Injured in Confrontation with Motorist While Cycling" *Calgary Herald* (1 October 2012).
2   Canadian Press, "B.C. Cyclist Shot during Race Made Tourniquet out of Pants" *Toronto Star* (29 July 2014).
3   Conal Mullen, "Cyclist Wounds Man in Ride-By Shooting" *Edmonton Journal* (31 October 2003).
4   Sean McKibbon, "Watch Out for Puddles and Potholes, Cyclists Urged in Wake of Accident" *Metro* (11 April 2011).
5   Jeff Hudson, "Burrard Bike Lane Debate Goes On" *Metro* (9 May 2009).
6   Martine Powers, "Bumpy Ride? Give Cyclists a Warning" *Boston Globe* (7 July 2013).
7   "Pothole Suit That Cost Windsor $844,450 Could Happen Here, Cycle Advocate Says" *Ottawa Citizen* (6 June 2007).
8   Ben Spurr, "Streetcar Tracks a Bloody Hazard for Cyclists" *Now* (2–9 August 2012).
9   "Rail Crossing at Porthmadog Is a 'Danger' to Cyclists" *BBC* (14 January 2010).
10 Canadian Institute for Health Information, *Sports and Recreational Injury Hospitalizations in Ontario, 2002–2003* (2004).
11 Transport Canada, *A Quick Look at Fatally Injured Vulnerable Road Users* (June 2010).
12 Transport Canada, *Canadian Motor Vehicle Traffic Collision Statistics 2011* at 2, online: http://www.tc.gc.ca/media/documents/roadsafety/TrafficCollisionStatisitcs_2011.pdf.

13 For a recent summary of this research, see Chris Cavacuiti, *An Overview of Cycling Research: Selected Facts, Statistics, Citations and Quotations* (2012), online: www.sharetheroad.ca/files/Cycling_Safety_Overview___2012_12_05.pdf.

14 See, e.g., Jeroen Johan de Hartog et al, *Do the Health Benefits of Cycling Outweigh the Risk?* (Utrecht: National Institute of Environmental Health Sciences, 2010), online: www.ncbi.nlm.nih.gov/pmc/articles/PMC2920084/. But also see critique in Fred Wegman, Fan Zhang, & Atze Dijkstra, "How to Make More Cycling Good for Road Safety" (2012) 44 Accident Analysis & Prevention 19 at 21.

15 See Malcolm Wardlaw, "Assessing the Actual Risks Faced by Cyclists" *TEC* (December 2002) at 354 for discussion of European evidence for the "safety in numbers" phenomena, online: www.cyclehelmets.org/papers/c2014.pdf; Wegman et al, above note 14 at 20 and 28 ("countries with a lot of bicycle traffic have a relatively low fatality rate while countries where inhabitants do not cycle much (a dozen of kilometres per inhabitant per year only) face relatively high fatality rates," but also suggesting that cycling volume alone is not sufficient and well-designed bicycle friendly road safety features are also required). For a media weighing of cost and benefit, see Julia Belluz, "Do the Health Benefits of Cycling Outweigh the Safety Risks?" *Maclean's* (17 August 2011), online: www.macleans.ca/authors/julia-belluz/do-the-health-benefits-of-cycling-outweigh-the-safety-risks/.

16 Canadian Institute for Health Information, above note 10.

17 Transport Canada, *A Quick Look at Fatally Injured Vulnerable Road Users* (June 2010).

18 Transport Canada, *Canadian Motor Vehicle Traffic Collision Statistics 2011* at 2, online: www.tc.gc.ca/media/documents/roadsafety/TrafficCollisionStatisitcs_2011.pdf.

19 *Ibid.*

20 Meghan Winters et al, "Safe Cycling: How Do Risk Perceptions Compare with Observed Risk?" (2012) 103 (Supp 3) Canadian Journal of Public Health S42.

21 Transport Canada, above note 18 at 2.

22 Statistics Canada, *Commuting to Work*, online: www12.statcan.gc.ca/nhs-enm/2011/as-sa/99-012-x/99-012-x2011003_1-eng.cfm.

23 Lisa Aultmann-Hall & M Georgina Kaltenecker, "Toronto Bicycle Commuter Safety Rates" (1999) 31(6) Accident Analysis & Prevention 675 at 683, computed from table 6. Toronto may be a particularly unfriendly place for cyclists (at least at the time the study was completed). For the same 1999 study, the combined cycling accident rate for Ottawa was 12.9 per 1,000,000 km. The authors attributed this difference to Toronto's more congested environment.

24 This figure was generated from the study's report of 1,196 complete questionnaires, and total commuting distance for the sample of 1,570,000 km. *Ibid* at 678.

25 See, e.g., Melissa Hoffman et al, "Bicycle Commuter Injury Prevention: It is Time to Focus on the Environment" (2010) 69(5) Journal of Trauma Injury, Infection and Critical Care 1112 at 1116 (estimating the rate of "traumatic event" for Portland OR commuters at once every four years).

26 City of Toronto *Bike Plan* at 2–4, online: www1.toronto.ca/city_of_toronto/transportation_services/cycling/files/pdf/chapter02.pdf.

27 Toronto Public Health, *Road to Health: Improving Walking and Cycling in Toronto* (April 2012) at 33, online: www.toronto.ca/health/hphe/pdf/roadtohealth.pdf.

28　Figures computed from Transport Canada, above note 12 at 5.

29　The 2001 figures are drawn from Transport Canada, *Vulnerable Road User Safety: A Global Concern* (March 2004). The 2004–2006 numbers come from Transport Canada, above note 17.

30　Canadian Institute of Health Information, *Ontario Trauma Registry 2009 Report*, at 32, online: www.secure.cihi.ca/free_products/otr_major_injury_ontario_2009_e.pdf.

31　*Ibid* at 31.

32　*Ibid* at 24.

33　*Ibid* at 21–22.

34　Statistics Canada, above note 22.

35　Wegman et al, above note 14 at 22.

36　See, e.g., City of Toronto, *What To Do If You Are Involved in a Collision*, online: www1.toronto.ca/wps/portal/contentonly?vgnextoid=93830995bbbc1410VgnVC-M10000071d60f89RCRD; Greater Victoria Cycling Coalition, *Bike Sense: The British Columbia Bicycle Operator's Manual* (2004), online: www.bikesense.bc.ca/bike-sense-manual.

37　Ontario, Financial Services Commission of Ontario, *What To Do After an Auto Accident*, online: www.fsco.gov.on.ca/en/auto/brochures/pages/brochure_accidents.aspx.

38　British Columbia, *Motor Vehicles Act*, RSBC 1996, c 318, s 183(9) [*BC MVA*].

39　*Ibid*, s 249.

40　See, e.g., *R v Moore*, [1979] 1 SCR 195 (applying BC law, as it then was); see also, e.g., *R v Ramos*, 2010 ONCJ 303 (applying Ontario law).

41　Newfoundland and Labrador, *Highway Traffic Act*, RSNL 1990, c H-3, ss 169 and 170 [*NL HTA*]; Nova Scotia, *Motor Vehicle Act*, RSNS 1989, c 293, s 97 [*NS MVA*]; New Brunswick, *Motor Vehicle Act*, RSNB 1973, c M-17, ss 125–133 [*NB MVA*]; PEI, *Highway Traffic Act*, RSPEI 1988, c H-5, s 232 [*PEI HTA*]; Quebec, *Highway Safety Code*, CQLR c C-24.2, s-s 161.1–79 [*Que HSC*]; Ontario, *Highway Traffic Act*, RSO 1990, c H.8, s-s 199–200 [*Ont HTA*]; Manitoba, *The Highway Traffic Act*, CCSM c H60, s 155 *et seq*; Saskatchewan, *The Traffic Safety Act*, SS 2004, c T-18.1, s 252 *et seq* [*Sask TSA*]; Alberta, *Traffic Safety Act*, RSA 2000, c T-6, ss 69–70 [*Alta TSA*]; *Operator Licensing and Vehicle Control Regulation*, Alta Reg 320/2002, s 145 *et seq*; BC MVA, ss 68 and 183; Yukon, *Motor Vehicles Act*, RSY 2002, c 153, s 94 *et seq* [*YT MVA*]; NWT, *Motor Vehicles Act*, RSNWT 1988, c M-16, s 259 *et seq* [*NWT MVA*]; Nunavut, *Motor Vehicles Act*, RSNWT (Nu) 1988, c M-16, s 259 *et seq.* [*NU MVA*].

42　See, e.g., *NSMVA*, s 85; *NB MVA*, s 176; *PEI HTA*, s 194; *Man HTA*, s 145.

43　*Criminal Code*, RSC 1985, c C-46, s 221.

44　*Ibid*, s 220. See, e.g., *R v Derhak*, [1996] YJ No 8 (SC).

45　*Criminal Code*, s 2.

46　*Ibid*, s 249.

47　*Ibid*, s 2.

48　*Ibid*, s 249.2.

49　*Ibid*, s 249.3.

50　*Ibid*, s 253.

51　*Ibid*, s 252.

52　*Ibid*, s 249.

53　*R v Hundal* (1993), 79 CCC (3d) 97 (SCC); *R v Beatty*, 2008 SCC 5.

54　*R v Song*, 2009 BCCA 470.

55　*R v Robson*, [2004] OTC 25 (SCJ).

56　*R v Richards*, [2003] OJ No 1042 at para 11 (CA); *R v Weldon*, 2008 ONCJ 67 at para 13.

57　*R v MKM*, [1998] OJ No 1606 (CA); *R v Weldon*, above note 56 at para 13.

58　*R v KL*, 2009 ONCA 141.

59　*R v KL, ibid* at paras 19 and 20.

60　2012 ONCJ 690.

61　*Ibid* at paras 43–45.

62　*Ibid* at para 11.

63　*Ibid* at para 49.

64　[2012] OJ No 1475 (SCJ).

65　*Ibid* at para 5.

66　*Ont HTA*, s 165 (the section requires motorists to take "due precautions" before opening the door of a motor vehicle on a highway "to ensure that his or her act will not interfere with the movement of or endanger any other person or vehicle"). In Ontario, the violation comes with two demerit points and a fine: *Demerit Point System*, online: www.mto.gov.on.ca/english/dandv/driver/demerit.shtml.

67　*Ont HTA*, s 130.

68　*R v Beauchamp*, [1952] OJ No 495 at para 19 (CA); *R v Khan*, 2010 ONCJ 265 at para 40 *et seq.*

69　*R v Beauchamp*, above note 68 at para 21.

70　*NL HTA*, s 110; *NS MVA*, s 100; *NB MVA*, s 346; *PEI HTA*, s 176. *Man HTA*, s 188. *Sask TSA*, s 213; *Alta TSA*, s 115; *BC MVA*, s 144. *Que HSC*, s 327 has a closest analogue, but it is phrased quite differently than other statutes in specifying "Any rate of speed or any action that can endanger human life and safety or property is prohibited."

71　*R v Kowalewich*, 2005 BCPC 633 at para 4.

72　*Criminal Code*, s 252.

73　*R v Hansen* (1988), 46 CCC (3d) 504 (BCCA).

74　*R v Robson*, above note 55.

75　*R v Chase*, 2006 BCCA 275.

76　*R v Roche*, [1983] 1 SCR 491; *Criminal Code*, s 252(2).

77　Above note 64.

78　*Ibid* at para 42.

79　*R v JMC*, [2004] OJ No 3049 (SCJ).

80　See *R v Chase*, above note 75.

81　Andrew Nguyen & Marie-Danielle Smith, "Mother Wants Answers after Children Hit by Cyclist" *Ottawa Citizen* (31 July 2014).

82　*R v Ensign*, [2006] AJ No 437 (Prov Ct).

83　Peter Small & Betsy Powell, "Prosecutor: Why Charges against Michael Bryant Were Dropped" *Toronto Star* (25 May 2010).

84　Aileen Donnelly, "Cyclist Charged with Careless Driving after Hitting a Pedestrian" *National Post* (6 July 2011).

85　*Longueuil (City of) v Rodrigue*, 2013 QCCS 6172 at para 2, applying *Que HSC*, s 327.

86   *NL HTA*, s 110; *PEI HTA*, s 176; *Que HSC*, s 327. See *Longueuil (City of) v Rodrigue*, above note 85; *Sask TSA*, s 213; *Alta TSA*, s 115.

87   *NS MVA*, ss 100 and 85. See also *Birch v Eastern Dairyfoods Co-Operative Ltd*, [1986] NSJ No 50 (SC) [*Birch*]. *NB MVA*, ss 176 and 346. *BC MVA*, s 183. See also *Hunstad v Cormier*, 2011 BCSC 1881 at para 66.

88   *Man HTA*, s 188.

89   Alexandra Bosanac, "Cyclist Charged with Leaving Scene after Senior Dies" *National Post* (26 June 2013).

90   Simply by way of example, see City of Edmonton Bylaw 5590, *Traffic Bylaw*, ss 49 and 96.

91   Ontario, *Limitations Act, 2002*, SO 2002, c 24, Schedule B, ss 4–5.

92   Ontario, *Municipal Act, 2001*, SO 2001, c 25, s 44(10) [*Ont MA*].

93   Philip Osborne, *The Law of Torts*, 4th ed (Toronto: Irwin Law, 2011) at 118.

94   *Kempf v Nguyen*, 2013 ONSC 1977 at para 72 [*Kempf*].

95   *Hadden v Lynch*, 2008 BCSC 295 at para 69.

96   *Chiasson (Litigation guardian of) v Baird*, 2005 NBQB 102.

97   *Deol v Veach*, 2011 BCSC 1437.

98   See discussion in *Friedrich (Litigation Guardian of) v Vernon (City)*, 2008 BCSC 1243 at para 45 [*Friedrich*].

99   *Quade v Schwartz*, 2009 BCCA 73. See also *Repic v Hamilton (City)*, [2009] OJ No 4657 (SCJ) [*Repic*].

100 *Evans v Toronto (City)*, [2004] OJ No 5844 at para 25 (SCJ).

101 *Chang v Thandi*, [1987] BCJ No 1200 (SC); *Elliott v Edmonton (City)* (1993), 135 AR 316 (CA).

102 *Deol v Veach*, above note 97 at para 22; *Sivasubramaniam v Franz*, 2008 BCSC 1089 at para 55.

103 *Salaam v Abramovic*, 2010 BCCA 212.

104 See, e.g., *Tubbs v O'Donovan*, [1996] BCJ No 1784 at para 14 (SC).

105 See, e.g., *Miller v Shorsky*, [1987] BCJ No 2122 (SC) (lack of proper headlight in violation of BC law); *Gregus v Belisle*, [1992] BCJ No 696 (SC) (riding on a sidewalk in violation of BC law); *Niitamo v Insurance Corp of British Columbia*, 2003 BCSC 608 (riding across a crosswalk in violation of BC law); *Parent (Litigation guardian of) v Chassé*, [1995] NBJ No 626 (QB) (failing to stop at a stop sign in violation of NB law); *Hartery v Monroe*, [1981] NJ No 185 (Nfld Dist Ct) (riding on the wrong side of the road in violation of Newfoundland law).

106 *Adams (Litigation guardian of) v Zanatta*, 2012 BCSC 952. Likewise, a cyclist turning left and failing to yield to oncoming traffic may be partially to blame for the accident. *Hisco v Stitz*, 2008 MBQB 45.

107 See, e.g., *Kimber v Wong*, 2012 BCSC 783; *Elliott v Edmonton (City)*, [1993] AJ No 117 (CA). See also *MacLaren v Kucharek*, 2010 BCCA 206 (applying BC law and preoccupied by fact that cyclist passed on right in middle of two lanes of traffic).

108 *Birch*, above note 87; *Guimont v Williston and Irving Oil Limited* (1980), 30 NBR (2d) 178 (CA).

109 See, e.g., *NS MVA*, s 114.

110 *Kempf*, above note 94 at paras 102–3.

111 See, e.g., *Dobre v Langley*, 2011 BCSC 1315.

112 *Man TSA*, s 153.

113 *Melnychuk v Moore*, [1989] MJ No 177 (CA).

114 *PEI HTA*, s 286; *Ont HTA*, s 193; *Alta TSA*, s 186.

115 *Senger v Lackman*, 2008 ONCA 323; *Meyer v Neuman*, 2004 ABQB 232 at para 101.

116 *The Manitoba Public Insurance Corporation Act*, CCSM c P215; Quebec, *An Act respecting the Société de l'assurance automobile du Québec*, CQLR c S-11.011; Saskatchewan, *The Automobile Accident Insurance Act*, RSS 1978, c A-35; British Columbia, *Insurance (Vehicle) Act*, RSBC 1996, c 231 [*BC IVA*].

117 Denis Boivin, *Insurance Law* (Toronto: Irwin Law, 2004) at 7.

118 *BC IVA*, ss 20–24.

119 Ontario, *Insurance Act*, RSO 1990, c I.8, s 268(2).

120 *Ibid*, s 265.

121 See Ontario Automobile Policy, s 5.2.1. The OAP provides standard terms for Ontario motor vehicle insurance policies.

122 *Lewis v Economical Insurance Group*, 2010 ONCA 528.

123 *Talbot v GAN General Insurance Co.* (1999), 44 OR (3d) 252 (SCJ).

124 See, e.g., *Jang v Ritchie*, 2013 BCSC 2459.

125 *Jones v Green*, [1993] OJ No 4499 (Gen Div).

126 *Kempf*, above note 94 at para 76.

127 *Ibid* at paras 90 & 91.

128 *Ibid* at para 92.

129 *Ibid* at para 98.

130 For discussion of these difficulties, and especially the so-called policy/operational distinction, see Osborne, above note 93 at 217 *et seq*.

131 See, e.g., *Just v British Columbia*, [1989] 2 SCR 1228.

132 *Civil Code of Quebec*, LRQ c C-1991, art 1457.

133 *Nichols v Warner, Scarborough, Herman & Harvey*, 2007 BCSC 1383 at para 179, aff'd 2009 BCCA 277.

134 See *Martin v St Andrews (Rural Municipality)*, [1997] MJ No 603 at paras 9–10 (QB), aff'd [1998] MJ No 399 (CA).

135 *Friedrich*, above note 98 at para 61; *Holemans v City of St Vital*, [1973] MJ No 47 at para 19 (CA).

136 *Davies v West Vancouver (District)*, [1992] BCJ No 284 (CA).

137 *Aberdeen v Zanatta*, 2008 BCCA 420.

138 *Friedrich*, above note 98 at para 61.

139 *Ont MA*, s 44.

140 *Johnson v Milton (Town)*, [2006] OJ No 3232 at para 77 (SCJ), var'd 2008 ONCA 440, but not on this point [*Johnson*].

141 *Repic*, above note 99; *Yovanovich v Windsor (City)*, [2007] OJ No 2134 (SCJ).

142 *Johnson*, above note 140 at para 35 (CA).

143 *Ibid* at para 72.

144 *Evans v Toronto (City)*, [2004] OJ No 5844 at para 18 (SCJ).

145 *Municipal Government Act*, RSA 2000, c M-26, s 532 [*Alta MGA*].

146 *The Municipalities Act*, SS 2005, c M-36.1, s 345.

147 *Truong v Saskatoon (City of)*, 2001 SKQB 419 at para 77.

148 PEI, *Occupiers' Liability Act*, RSPEI 1988, c O-2 [*PEI OLA*]; Nova Scotia, *Occupiers' Liability Act*, SNS 1996, c 27 [*NS OLA*]; Ontario, *Occupiers Liability Act*, RSO 1990, c O.2 [*Ont OLA*]; Alberta, *Occupiers' Liability Act*, RSA 2000, c O-4 [*Alta OLA*]; British Columbia, *Occupiers Liability Act*, RSBC 1996, c 337 [*BC OLA*]; Manitoba, *The Occupiers' Liability Act*, CCSM c O8 [*Man OLA*].

149 See, e.g., *Cotnam v National Capital Commission*, 2014 ONSC 3614 (Div Ct) (Ontario law); *Jackson v Fisheries and Oceans Canada*, 2006 BCSC 1492 (BC law); *Campbell v Gyurkovits (cob Kootenay Forest Resources)*, [1999] BCJ No 2173 (SC).

150 *Ont OLA*, s 4.

151 *Maloney v Parry Sound* (2000), 184 DLR (4th) 121 (Ont CA).

152 *Dally v London (City)*, [2004] OJ No 3231 at para 44 (SCJ).

153 *Kennedy v London (City)*, [2009] OJ No 1040 at para 33 (SCJ) [*Kennedy*].

154 *Pierce v Hamilton (City)*, 2013 ONSC 6485 at para 34.

155 *Herbert (Litigation guardian of) v Brantford (City)*, 2010 ONSC 2681 at para 18, aff'd 2012 ONCA 98.

156 *Ibid.*

157 *Kennedy*, above note 153.

158 *Hindley v Waterfront Properties Corp*, 2002 BCSC 885 at paras 21 & 22.

159 See, e.g., *Leone v University of Toronto Outing Club et al*, [2006] OJ No 4131 (SCJ); *Crook v LaFarge Canada Inc.*, 2009 NSSC 357.

160 *Man OLA*, s 3. See *Zimmer v Manitoba Housing and Renewal Corp*, 2006 MBQB 269.

161 See, e.g., *Gallant v Labrador City-Schefferville (Diocese of)*, 2001 NFCA 22 at para 27; *Kozmeniuk v Zellers Inc*, 2001 SKQB 114; *McAllister (Litigation guardian of) v Wal-Mart Canada Inc* (2000), 228 NBR (2d) 230 at para 14 (CA).

162 *PEI OLA*, s 4; *NS OLA*, s 6; *Ont OLA*, s 4; *BC OLA*, s 3.

163 *Jetz v Calgary Olympic Development Assn*, 2002 ABQB 887 at para 29.

164 *Ibid.*

165 *Alta OLA*, ss 12 and 13. Provisions with equivalent effect also exist in PEI, Ontario, and British Columbia.

Chapter 4

Breaking Your Bicycle

introduction

As consumers, we are becoming used to the scope of car recalls. Before the year had even ended in 2014, North American automakers had recalled more motor vehicles than in any other year on record. But if you look beyond the automobile industry, you will discover that bicycles and bike equipment are also the subject of recalls for a variety of manufacturing and design defects.

A quick visit to the website BicycleRetailers.com[1] reveals the pace of these recalls. In 2014 alone, a bicycle manufacturer recalled two of its mountain bike models after receiving reports of broken hubs that could cause the disc brakes to fail;[2] a Canadian retail chain recalled bicycle helmets because cracks were reported near the rivets securing the chinstrap;[3] and 125,000 bikes were recalled by well-known bicycles makers because of concerns about suspension forks used on the bikes.[4] Nicole encountered a manufacturing problem when, in her quest to counter the slowing effects of aging, she invested in a very expensive set of aluminium alloy wheels that promised her ride would be lighter, faster, and smoother. Within two months, the rim was cracked on both sides of a spoke. The manufacturer replaced both wheels, as it seemed this was a recurring problem with some of their products.

Given that a top-end bike can be a pricey investment, it is understandable that cyclists fear faulty manufacturing. But more important, given the kinetics of bicycle riding, cyclists need to be secure when riding their bikes: their lives depend on it. Even the cheapest bicycle must be safe from defects that could result in injuries, or even death. A cyclist relies enormously, therefore, on the competence of bicycle and component manufacturers, and on that of the retailers who sell and service these items. Cyclists may also expect (somewhat piously, as it turns out) that governments are regulating safety standards for bicycle and cycling gear, and if not, that the cycling industry is at the very least setting voluntary safety standards that are widely adhered to by manufacturers.

As we will outline in this chapter, the law says quite a bit about the duties of those who make and sell goods to consumers. The three key areas we will focus on are: express contractual warranties; statutory "implied warranties"; and product liability rules. But first, we will say a few words on the regulation of cycling safety standards in Canada.

regulation and safety standards

When you ride a motorcycle or drive a car, you are present in a vehicle whose safety is comprehensively regulated by the Canadian government. All motor vehicles manufactured in Canada for the Canadian market meet Canada Motor Vehicle Safety Standards, through a framework created by the *Motor Vehicle Safety Act*.[5] But as its title suggests, this Act only applies to roadway vehicles "capable of being driven or drawn on roads by any means other than muscular power exclusively."[6] It does not extend, in other words, to bicycles.

Both the United States and the United Kingdom developed mandatory bicycle safety standards, and one 1995 study concluded that these rules were associated with decreased bicycle accident rates.[7]

Canada does not, however, have mandatory bicycle or bicycle component-specific safety standards. Indeed, there does not even appear to be robust voluntary industry standards in place — the Canadian Standards Association (CSA) had a bicycle standard introduced in 1980, but appears to have withdrawn it.[8] (That said, there are bicycle and bicycle-component standards established by standard setting bodies in key manufacturing countries, such as China and Japan.)

However, the CSA does have important safety standards for bicycle helmets,[9] and these (along with their US counterparts) are often invoked in provincial regulations governing bicycle helmet use, discussed in Chapter 2. For instance, bicycle helmets are mandatory in British Columbia, and must meet the CSA (or alternative international) standards.[10]

Another aspect of bicycle and bicycle equipment safety that may be mandatory involves recalls. As discussed further below, manufacturers are strongly motivated by their liability exposure to issue recalls and warnings of defects. Most manufacturers voluntarily undertake recalls. However, under federal law, the government can compel a recall if persuaded on reasonable grounds that a consumer product is dangerous to human health or safety. Consumer goods manufacturers, importers, and sellers also must report "incidents" to Health Canada, including occurrences or defects that may result in death or serious adverse effects on health.[11]

Finally, we should note that particularly egregious business practices are also closely regulated by the state. Provincial and territorial consumer protection law often prohibits deceptive practices that mislead consumers into thinking products have features or are of a quality that they are not.[12] Criminal fraud, meanwhile, reaches defrauding someone out of, among other things, money through "deceit, falsehood or other fraudulent means."[13]

contract law and safety

While these government measures are obviously important, Canadian product safety still mostly depends on private law rules, including those under the law of contract. Every time you buy something you enter into a contract, whether it's for a bicycle, the services of a mechanic at a bike store, or a bike fitting from a certified professional. The key elements of such contracts are that the seller has offered to sell something, and you have accepted that offer. In addition, there must be what is called "consideration" in common law provinces, and "lawful cause" under Quebec civil law. While there are technical differences between these two concepts, both essentially require that each party take on obligations. For instance, the purchaser agrees to pay a set price for a product, and the seller agrees to surrender the item. It is not necessary that the goods or services be exchanged at the time of the purchase. You could negotiate to pay for your custom built frame only once it is delivered to you.

When it comes to manufacturing defects, the existence of a contract is the key requirement to any claims you may make for defective parts or services. In the retail industry, contracts often include a "warranty" that consist of a promise that the manufacturer makes regarding the good condition of the product, and a guarantee that they will repair or replace the goods should they be defective within a certain period of time. The contract may also include disclaimers which limit the scope of the warranty. Finally, the contract, including the warranty and any disclaimers, is generally the basis for any contractual remedy a consumer may pursue in relation to faulty products or poor services.

We will now discuss the type of warranties that often attach to purchases of bicycles, components and cycling gear.

warranties

Regular Warranties
Content

Bicycle equipment often comes with express warranties. Even the most basic of bikes seem to come with one of these. The website of a retailer whose bikes are probably pedalled by a great number of Canadian kids reports basic warranties on defective frames (the duration of which is dependent on whether the frame is steel or aluminum) and a shorter warranty on at least some parts.

Craig looked up the warranties for his road, time trial, cyclocross, and mountain bikes. The road bike manufacturer's warranty provided that the frame was warranted "against defects in workmanship and materials for as long as the frame is owned by the original owner, excluding paint and decals. . . . This warranty is expressly limited to either the repair or replacement of the defective frame . . . and no other remedies are available under the warranty." The warranty did not extend to "damage caused by normal wear and tear, improper assembly, improper maintenance, or installation of parts or accessories not originally intended for use with or compatible with the frame or bicycle sold," nor did it reach "damage or failure of . . . bicycle frames caused by accident, misuse, abuse or neglect. Any modification of the frame or its components shall void this warranty." The warranty also admonished that, to be valid, the bike had to be purchased through an authorized retailer.

Other bike manufacturers replicate these guarantees, although the duration of the warranty varies. Craig's time trial bike frame, for instance, was warranted against manufacturing defects for three years, for the original purchasers, so long as purchased from an authorized dealer. As with the road bike warranty, this guarantee did not cover accidents, or defects resulting from severe winter climate and salted roads, an important consideration for many Canadians.

Enforceability

Curiously, there is some doubt in many jurisdictions as to whether these express warranties to consumers are (legally) worth the paper they are written on, at least when they are issued by manufacturers as opposed to the retailer. Most bicycle buyers tend to purchase bikes from their local bike stores or large retailers, not directly from manufacturers. Moreover, these retailers are often, although not always, completely separate companies from manufacturers. This means that buyers have "privity of contract" with retailers, not manufacturers. "Privity of contract" basically means a *direct* relationship between a seller and buyer. Privity does not generally exist "up the chain" from seller to manufacturer. Privity is important because a contract cannot generally confer any rights or impose any obligations to a person who is not a party to it, and as discussed above, a warranty is essentially a contract (or part of a contract). That means the warranty that matters is the one given by the retailer to the buyer. The principle of "privity of contract" applies in most provinces and territories. Quebec has different rules. There, the law provides that it is not necessary to establish privity of contract. A purchaser can sue every participant up the distribution chain.[14] Likewise, in Saskatchewan, a manufacturer of a consumer product is liable for breach of warranties that it has given consumers. The express warranty is enforceable by the original consumer and any person who acquires this product from the consumer.[15]

But even in other jurisdictions, courts may find ways to make manufacturer warranties meaningful. For one thing, privity may exist between buyer and manufacturer when a retailer acts as an "agent" of the manufacturer.[16] We are not in a position to know what the relationship is between bike stores in Canada and the manufacturers of the bikes and gear that they sell. However, the fact that many bike manufacturers insist in their warranties that bikes are purchased from authorized retailers suggests that an agency relationship may exist between the two. If that is the case, manufacturer warranties would then probably flow down to buyers through their agent sellers.

A buyer might also be induced into a purchase by the existence of the warranty, in which case a "collateral" contract between manufacturer and buyer may come into existence.[17] Again, courts would then enforce the warranty.

Also, some manufacturers promise benefits — like an extended warranty — when buyers register their purchase with the manufacturer. Here, you could argue that a separate contract now exists between buyer and manufacturer incorporating the express warranties.

In other instances, however, there may be doubt that a manufacturer's warranty is legally enforceable.[18] Of course, dismissing warranty claims on this sort of technicality is not likely to enhance a bike manufacturer's reputation. It is difficult to imagine, therefore, that an unprincipled manufacturer would persist in business very long. More than that, even if the warranty cannot be enforced, the company's misleading warranty practices would probably violate consumer "deceptive practices" prohibitions in many provinces.[19] This sort of behaviour can result in fines and imprisonment.

Implied Warranties from Bike Stores
Content

A second protection for consumers is the "implied warranty" found in provincial and territorial sale of goods and (in some instances) consumer protection laws. Whatever express warranties might say, provincial and territorial sale of goods statutes impose implied warranties that a product is fit for the purpose for which a consumer buys it.

In standard language replicated across the common law jurisdictions (that is, the provinces and territories except Quebec, which is dealt with later on), if a buyer (either expressly or impliedly) notifies the seller in the business of supplying a particular good of the purpose for which the goods are required and shows that he or she depends on the seller's skill or judgment, there is an implied condition that the good is reasonably fit for that purpose.[20]

Put another way, when you buy a bicycle from a bike store in a manner that communicates the purpose to which you wish to put the bike (e.g., riding it) and you rely on the store employee's judgment, the contract between you and the bike store includes an implied guarantee that the bike is reasonably fit for that purpose. If the bike is not reasonably fit, the bike store is in breach of its contract, and is "strictly liable." That is, it is not necessary to prove the seller acted negligently or with an intention to sell a faulty product. The seller's liability for breach of the warranty reaches all "consequential damages" — basically, everything that a reasonable person would foresee as flowing from that breach,[21] subject to the limitations imposed by "privity of contract" in common law provinces.

Enforceability

As we mentioned previously, in common law provinces, privity of contract is all about the immediacy of the relationship between buyer and seller. In the context of implied warranties, this means that the bike store is only liable to the original purchaser. Let's take a concrete example: a bike buyer has privity of contract with the seller from whom they purchase the product, but the friend who rides the bike does not become party to the contract. Others who may use the bike (or may be injured by some failure with it) do not enjoy any proximity to the contract — they are too far removed from the original sale and cannot rely on the implied warranty.[22] This "privity" rule can make implied warranties next to useless for young riders — these are the people injured by a defect, but are rarely the people who bought the bike.[23] Privity exists between the parent and the seller, not the child and the seller.

Likewise, as we have already noted, when a consumer buys goods from a bike store, they have privity of contract with that store, but unless that store is also the manufacturer, they usually will not have privity of contract with a manufacturer. While provinces like Saskatchewan and Quebec do not apply (or at least create exceptions to) this privity rule for implied warranties in consumer sales, other jurisdictions do continue to follow it.[24] Of course, there may be instances in which a consumer buys bicycle equipment directly from a manufacturer, without going through a retailer. In that instance, the privity of contract between manufacturer and buyer clearly exists.

Note also that the "reasonably fit" standard established by the implied warranty does not reach every conceivable circumstance in which a bike might be used, or more importantly, abused. Canadian law "does not require manufacturers to create products that are fool-proof or incapable of causing injury."[25] Implied warranties do not amount to insurance for anyone who might be injured using a product.[26] In a bicycle context, this has meant that there is no requirement that a bicycle be equipped with a light or reflectors, even if to ride the bike at night without this equipment is both unsafe and contrary to the rules of the road. The retailer does not violate the implied warranty by failing to include lighting features to pre-empt unlawful use of the bicycle — the bike remained reasonably fit for riding purposes, so long as it was operated lawfully.[27] And so the implied warranty is honoured.

Recall that statutory implied warranties in common law jurisdictions rest on the consumer's decision to rely on the seller's skill and judgment when making their purchase. Where there is no reliance, there is no implied warranty.[28] So implied warranties are not likely to apply when a cyclist arrives with firm and set views on the bicycle or cycling equipment he or she wants, and who simply plumps down a credit card to purchase the desired product.

Finally, the application of implied warranties may, at least theoretically, be excluded by terms contained in the contract between the purchaser and seller or manufacturer. Such contractual exclusions are, however, strictly construed by the courts — and indeed are invalid if not brought to the attention of the purchaser prior to sale.[29] Moreover, consumer protection laws often limit the use of exclusions to deny statutory warranties. Thus, in several provinces, consumers (i.e., non-business buyers) cannot be denied implied warranties through contractual exclusions.[30]

A quick review of bicycle manufacturer websites suggests that companies do try to exclude liability for "consequential damages," promising only to replace or repair the bicycle. But assuming that privity of contract exists between purchaser and manufacturer in those provinces where that matters, consumer protection law may make these attempts to limit liability ineffective, something that manufacturers recognize in their warranty descriptions.

Up to now, we have described statutory warranties adopted in common law jurisdictions. Quebec contract law follows a civil law tradition. The law does, however, cover much of the same ground, with some differences. The *Quebec Civil Code* creates what is called a "legal warranty" that arises at the time of sale and protects the consumer against latent defects making the product unsuitable for its intended use, or so diminished in quality that the purchaser would not have paid the requested price had they known of the defect.[31] This concept can reach both manufacturing and design defects, concepts discussed further below. Quebec does not require privity of contract, meaning that both original and second-hand purchasers can sue up the distribution chain.[32] This approach makes Quebec's contractual rules more sweeping than their common law counterparts. Contractual rules (and not the extra-contractual, tort style claims discussed below) are the primary means by which Quebec consumers are compensated for defects in the products they buy. The Quebec *Consumer Protection Act*[33] says, moreover, that goods that are part of a consumer contract "must be fit for the purposes for which goods of that kind are ordinarily used" and "durable in normal use for a reasonable length of time, having regard to their price, the terms of the contract and the conditions of their use." These rights also exist for subsequent (as in second-hand purchaser consumers) as against the manufacturer, but probably are not available to mere users who are not themselves the purchasers of the product.[34]

negligent manufacture or design

As the discussion above makes clear, warranties are a species of contract law, and they often suffer from the limitations of contract law principles, especially privity of contract in common law jurisdictions. But in some large measure, consumer protection through contract law has been superseded by developments in tort law. In this section, we cover the basics of a vast area of tort law known as products liability, as it has developed in common law jurisdictions. Quebec law in this area is generally similar to the common law rules.[35] However, because Quebec's contractual warranty rules are broader than those in common law provinces (and do not depend on privity), extra-contractual liability is less important in that province. Where it may be most important is with users who are not purchasers (and thus have no contractual relationships) and with "safety defects" in which purchasers are not sufficiently warned. We discuss the latter issue further below.

Products liability is, at its core, a subset of negligence law, discussed also in Chapter 3. Here, though, our focus is on two different issues: products liability for defects in manufacture and products liability for defects in design.

negligent manufacture

The classic court case for negligent manufacture is one of the first cases many common law students read in their introductory torts class: *Donoghue v Stevenson*.[36] Most of those who read it remember little about the principle of law it establishes and more about its colourful facts. In this golden oldie, Ms Donoghue "drank a bottle of ginger beer, manufactured by [Stevenson], which a friend had bought from a retailer and given to her. The bottle contained the decomposed remains of a snail which were not and could not be detected until the greater part of the contents of the bottle had been consumed. As a result she . . . suffered from shock and severe gastro enteritis." Cutting to the chase, the court concluded that Ms Donaghue had a legitimate legal claim for compensation (even though there was no "privity of contract"), and the most famous passage in that decision reads:

> . . . a manufacturer of products, which he sells in such a form as to show that he intends them to reach the ultimate consumer in the form in which they left him with no reasonable possibility of intermediate examination, and with the knowledge that the absence of reasonable care in the preparation or putting up of the products will result in an injury to the consumer's life or property, owes a duty to the consumer to take that reasonable care.[37]

Put in simpler language, manufacturers must "take reasonable care that their products are manufactured in compliance with their intended specifications and design and that they are not dangerously defective."[38] This obligation exists for manufacturers of component parts, those who assemble the product and those who repair it, and is owed to all those who may be foreseeably injured by the product's defects[39] — that is, basically anyone who could reasonably be expected to use it, or be around it.

Manufacturing defects involve the presence of something in the product that should not be present, or conversely the absence of something that should be present. Put another way, "[s]omething goes wrong in the manufacturing process itself, or the handling of the product, which produces a product which is below the standard set by the manufacturer."[40] Negligence may be inferred from proof of the presence of the defect and its link to the injury.

Not surprisingly, sporting good manufacturers have been sued for defectively produced goods. In a relatively recent case, a boy suffering head injuries after been flung from a mountain bike recovered $3.5 million in damages from the bike's manufacturer and affiliates and the retailer. The bike had been recalled for defects, but was not repaired because replacement parts were not in stock.[41]

Another classic case involving "a 10-speed racer bicycle" is *Goldsworthy v Catalina Agencies & CCM Ltd*, a decision from Newfoundland.[42] Here, fourteen-year-old Michael Goldsworthy purchased a pre-assembled "C.C.M. FORMULA II Racer" from the defendant's store for use by himself and his brother. The bike was used lightly by the boys and remained in working order, although at one point it went over a wharf into a harbour. Short immersion of bicycles in salt water was apparently a frequent occurrence in the region. The court observed, judicial tongue in cheek, "that most red-blooded boys residing in outport Newfoundland have on at least one occasion seen their bicycle go over the wharf to be retrieved by the well-established method of using a jigger without there being any damage to the vehicle but often serious damage to the pride of the cyclist."[43]

Then two weeks after the purchase, the young Goldsworthy — brother of Michael — rode up a steep local hill, with his seven-year-old nephew astride the front crossbar. As the fifteen-year-old boy pedalled the incline, the front wheel detached, the forks dropped and dug in to the pavement, and young Goldsworthy pitched over the bike, suffering severe head injuries.

The errant wheel had been attached to the forks with two butterfly nuts, on the inside of which were serrated washers. Notably, there were no tab (or "lock") washers — described as a "lip that bridges the bottom of the fork so that when the front wheel becomes slack, it will wobble back and forth but will not come off immediately." Tab washers came with at least some other bicycle models manufactured by the same company, as well as other 10-speed bicycles. Indeed, the owner's manual accompanying the bike seemed to endorse the presence of tab washers, even though these features were not included with the bike. The court concluded:

> The evidence satisfies me that C.C.M., by failing to provide tab washers, and substituting therefor a butterfly nut with a serrated washer attached, placed in the hands of the first defendant [the store], for sale to the general public, a bicycle which was inherently dangerous and defective. I am equally satisfied that if C.C.M. had, in the interest of customer safety, supplied tab washers, the plaintiff would have had adequate warning that the front wheel of his bicycle had developed a dangerous condition and would have taken the necessary remedial action to avoid the accident. C.C.M. knew or should have known of the danger to users of the bicycle, which could arise, as the result of its failure to provide tab washers and the kind

of injuries sustained by the plaintiff, under the circumstances of this case, were predictable and should have been foreseen by C.C.M. Such wanton disregard by C.C.M. of the safety of those who would use its high speed racer bicycles constituted negligence towards such prospective users and whilst not culpable, was most reprehensible.[44]

The store meanwhile, had not properly assembled a safe bicycle before selling it: "the bicycle was received by the first defendant, who had or should have received instructions regarding the assembly of same. If the bicycle was not defective when it left the factory and if it was assembled properly by the first defendant, then the accident would not have occurred."[45] In the result, each of the defendants was equally to blame, and the court declined to apportion blame between them.

negligent design

On top of manufacturing defects, product producers may be liable for design defects. The latter sort of "actions involve the claim that the product, although conforming to the design chosen by the manufacturer, nevertheless, does not satisfy the manufacturer's duty to make reasonable efforts to reduce any risk to life and limb that may be inherent in the product design."[46] That means "manufacturers must design their products so as to minimize the losses that may result from reasonably foreseeable mishaps involving their products."[47]

Manufacturing defect may be a contested issue in sports equipment cases, especially when a standard setting body certifies the equipment. In one BC lawsuit, the plaintiff suffered a significant head injury during a hockey game, even while wearing a hockey helmet certified as meeting the relevant CSA standard. He sued both the manufacturer and the CSA, claiming negligent manufacture and design and negligence on the part of the CSA for failing to adopt more demanding standards.[48]

On the facts, the helmet was designed for one sort of blow, while the plaintiff had been injured by quite another sequence of forces. The injury was not reasonably foreseeable, and indeed was very rare. Moreover, the CSA sticker affixed to the helmet warned that injuries were still possible, despite the protection offered by the headgear. The plaintiff's case was dismissed on these bases. Moreover, the Court of Appeal held that the CSA owed no duty of care to users of its certified helmets: "the threat of legal action creates the very real risk that CSA could not continue to operate, which would result in harm not only to wearers of hockey helmets, but to manufacturers, and ultimately, consumers of goods that now benefit from the establishment and certification of minimum standards."[49] This same logic could well extend to claims about CSA certified bicycle helmets.

warning customers

As the discussion of warning labels suggests, the legal rules on defects create corollary obligations to warn customers about things that may go amiss. In *Goldsworthy*, the store had failed to apprise its customer of the issues associated with the bike and its existing assembly and did not provide instructions or parts for proper assembly. Indeed, the Goldsworthys never received the owner's manual at the time of purchase. This was a violation of the store's duties.

Put simply, retailers and "[m]anufacturers are subject to a duty to warn customers and others who may reasonably be affected about any dangerous properties of their product whether they are 'inherent dangers' or 'dangers attendant on the use'."[50] The duty to warn is ongoing — those who deal in the product must not only warn of known defects and dangers, but also those that are suspected.[51]

In Quebec, as noted, manufacture and design defects are often addressed through contractual rules. However, since these contractual rules may not reach failures to warn, extra-contractual liability under the *Quebec Civil Code* becomes quite relevant in this area. Actionable safety defects in Quebec include "lack of sufficient indications as to the risks and dangers [the product] involved or as to the means to avoid them."[52] This means that manufacturers and those who sell the product must give adequate warnings concerning dangers and risks associated with their products and must also provide adequate safety instructions.[53] These common law and Quebec warning rules constitute one reason why there are recalls on defective products. In addition to the examples cited in the introduction to this chapter, bicycle recalls include one initiated in 1997 by a bicycle component manufacturer that constitutes the largest North American bicycle-part recall in history, recalling more than one million defective cranks installed on 200 models of bikes built between 1994 and 1996.[54] In 2014, a major upscale bicycle manufacturer recalled several of its models, on the basis that the "steer tube on the bicycle fork can break and cause the rider to lose control."[55]

Indeed, at the time of this writing, the Canadian government website[56] that compiles recalls was reporting notices for: twenty-five types of bicycle;

twelve types of forks; seven type of brakes; seven types of handlebars or stems; five types of child bicycle trailers or child seats; two types of frame; two types of helmets; two types of car-mounted bike carrier; one type of wheel; one type of derailleur; one type of cranks; one type of pedals; one type of chains; one type of tires; and one type of bike pannier rack. Not surprisingly, we both checked the list. Craig was distressed to discover his type and model of time trial bike on the list, but fortunately not for his bike's model year. Nicole saw that her mountain bike manufacturer was recalling several models, but not the one she rides.

conclusion

To summarize some key points from this chapter: If you take your hybrid commuting bike off a jump on a mountain trail and wipe out when the front wheel smashes, don't count on being able to hold the manufacturer or bike shop liable. Neither contract nor products liability laws insure you against damage stemming from unreasonable use of your bicycle. On the other hand, if you instead go off that jump astride a mountain bike designed for the rigours of downhill racing and the frame splinters, you may have grounds for compensation in both contract and tort law.

Be attentive to the express warranties offered by retailers and manufacturers. Register your bike, as many warranties suggest. Seek the advice of knowledgeable staff at reputable bike stores in making your purchase, both because that's wise and to trigger implied warranties. If worse comes to worst, and your bike shatters in circumstances where it truly shouldn't, contractual warranties may cover some of the material and personal injuries, and if they don't, products liability rules probably do.

endnotes

1   Bicycle Retailers and Industry News, Recalls, online: www.bicycleretailer.com/recalls-0.

2   *Ibid*, online: www.bicycleretailer.com/recalls/2014/07/17/csg-recalls-150-gt-fury-bikes-us-and-canada#.U_YadaMZk1J.

3   *Ibid*, online: www.bicycleretailer.com/recalls/2014/07/30/canadian-retailer-fgl-sports-recalling-bike-and-skateboard-helmets#.U_YeE6MZk1I.

4   *Ibid*, online: www.bicycleretailer.com/recalls/2014/06/26/fork-recall#.U_YfW6MZk1I.

5   SC 1993, c 16 [*Can MVSA*].

6   *Ibid*, s 1.

7   Wesley Magat & Michael Moore, *Consumer Product Safety Regulation in the United States and the United Kingdom: The Case of Bicycles*, Working Paper No 5157 (Cambridge MA: National Bureau of Economic Research, 1995).

8   CSA Standard CAN/CSA-3, D113.1-M, Bicycles — its status as "withdrawn" is listed at https://scc.ca/en/standardsdb/standards/2529.

9   CSA Standard CAN/CSA D113.2-M89 (R2009), Cycling Helmets.

10 British Columbia, *Motor Vehicle Act*, RSBC 1996, c 318, s 184 [*BC MVA*]; *Bicycle Safety Helmet Standards Regulation*, BC Reg 234/96, s 1.

11 *Canada Consumer Product Safety Act*, SC 2010, c 21, ss 14 and 31.

12 See, e.g., British Columbia, *Business Practices and Consumer Protection Act*, SBC 2004, c 4, s 4 [*BC BPCPA*]; Ontario, *Consumer Protection Act, 2002*, SO 2002, c 30, Schedule A, s 14 [*Ont CPA*].

13 *Criminal Code*, RSC 1985, c C-46, s 380.

14 Borden Ladner Gervais, *Canadian Product Liability Handbook* (2013) at 5 [BLG Handbook].

15 Saskatchewan, *The Consumer Protection Act*, SS 1996, c C-30.1, ss 41 and 50 [*Sask CPA*].

16 *Millar v General Motors of Canada Ltd*, [2002] OJ No 2769 at para 39 (SCJ).

17 *Murray v Sperry Rand Corp*, [1979] OJ No 4088 (HCJ). See the discussion in *Arora v Whirlpool Canada LP*, 2012 ONSC 4642 at para 174 *et seq*, aff'd on this point 2013 ONCA 657 [*Arora*].

18 *Schick v Boehringer Ingelheim (Canada) Ltd*, 2011 ONSC 1942 at para 23. But see also *Arora*, above note 17 at para 176.

19 See, e.g., *BC BPCPA*, s 4. Note that privity of contact is irrelevant to this issue. *Ibid*, s 1 (definition of "supplier").

20 See, e.g., BC, *Sale of Goods Act*, RSBC 1996, c 410, s 18 [*BC SGA*]; Ontario, *Sale of Goods Act*, RSO 1990, c S.1, s 15 [*Ont SGA*].

21 BLG Handbook, above note 14 at 7.

22 *Resch v Canadian Tire Corp*, [2006] OJ No 1505 (SCJ).

23 By way of example, see *ibid*.

24 *Arora*, above note 17 at para 32 (CA) (discussing Ontario law); *Clare v IJ Manufacturing Ltd*, 2003 BCSC 856 at para 20 (discussing BC law).

25 Jamie Cassels & Craig Jones, *The Law of Large-Scale Claims* (Toronto: Irwin Law, 2005) at 72.

26 *Baker v Suzuki Motor Co* (1993), 12 Alta LR (3d) 193 at para 77 (QB) [*Baker*].

27 *Claudio v Claudio*, [1986] BCJ No 825 (SC).

28 *Baker*, above note 26 at para 140.

29 BLG Handbook, above note 14 at 8–9.

30 Nova Scotia, *Consumer Protection Act*, RSNS 1989, c 92, s 26 [*NS CPA*]; New Brunswick, *Consumer Product Warranty and Liability Act*, SNB 1978, c C-18.1, s 24 [*NB CPWLA*]; *Ont CPA*, s 9; Manitoba, *Consumer Protection Act*, CCSM c 200, s 58 [*Man CPA*]; *Sask CPA*, s 77.16.

31 *Civil Code of Quebec*, LRQ c C-1991, arts 1442 and 1726. See discussion in Dominique Gibbens, *Overview of Quebec Product Liability Law: Basic Principles under the Quebec Civil Code and Consumer Protection Act*, online: www.fasken.com/files/Publication/ddbc666d-d8a2-4b6e-9fc4-3886505ab6e4/Presentation/Publication-

Attachment/30b2dea4-73c3-411c-a507-da3a7308ef8c/OVERVIEW_OF_QUEBEC_
PRODUCT_LIABILITY_LAW.PDF.

32 *Civil Code of Quebec*, art 1730. BLG Handbook, above note 14 at 5.

33 CQLR c P-40.1, s 37 and s 38 [*Que CPA*]. See Gibbens, above note 31 at 38–39.

34 *Que CPA*, s 54.

35 See discussion in Gibbens, above note 31.

36 [1932] AC 562 (HL).

37 *Ibid* at 599, Lord Atkin.

38 Philip Osborne, *The Law of Torts*, 4th ed (Toronto: Irwin Law, 2011) at 140–41.

39 *Ibid* at 141.

40 *Rowe (Guardian ad litem of) v Sears Canada*, 2005 NLCA 65 at para 19.

41 "Bicycle Accident Nets Victim $3.5M" *Edmonton Journal* (4 March 2006).

42 (1982), 142 DLR (3d) 281 (Nfld SCTD).

43 *Ibid* at para 10.

44 *Ibid* at para 25.

45 *Ibid* at para 43.

46 Halsbury's Laws of Canada, *Torts* (Markham, ON: LexisNexis Canada, 2012 Reissue)
    at HTO-101.

47 *Ibid*.

48 *More v Bauer Nike Hockey*, 2011 BCCA 419.

49 *Ibid* at para 60.

50 Halsbury's Laws of Canada, *Torts*, above note 46 at HTO-104.

51 BLG Handbook, above note 14 at 16.

52 *Civil Code of Quebec*, art 1469.

53 Gibbens, above note 31 at 27.

54 "Recall Fails to Stir Local Cyclists" *Windsor Star* (1 Aug 1997).

55 Government of Canada, *Felt Bicycles Recalls Triathlon Bicycles* (24 April 2014), online:
    healthycanadians.gc.ca/recall-alert-rappel-avis/hc-sc/2014/39155r-eng.php.

56 This website is online: healthycanadians.gc.ca/recall-alert-rappel-avis/index-eng.php.

Chapter 5

Losing Your Bicycle

introduction

For persons of our vintage, the comedic troupe Kids in the Hall's 1991 skit on bicycle theft remains a classic. Characterized as an "open letter to the guy who stole his bike wheel," comedian Bruce McCulloch speaks from stage under his suspended, and now incomplete, bicycle: "Well, why did you do it? Are you some sort of jerk or something? It's *my* front wheel! What did you think, that I'd — drive home and not notice it was stolen? . . . What would you do with just my front wheel anyway? What good would just one wheel be? You human loser! Well, why didn't you buy your own wheel if you wanted one so badly. That's what I did."[1]

The comedy skit captures well how we all feel when confronted with the theft of a bicycle or bicycle part. If you search Google for "bicycle theft" and "statistics" for Canada, you will quickly discover that many people have reason to repeat McCulloch's rant, probably using more colourful language. Bicycle theft is depressingly commonplace — a 2012 Montreal study concluded that over 50 percent of the study's survey participants "were subjected to a bicycle theft in their life time as active cyclists."[2] Nicole and her partner had a brand new mountain bike stolen within twenty-four hours of its purchase, and to get at it, thieves had to smash the windows of a locked car. Moreover, she has had just about every possible part stolen from her not-so fancy commuter bike over the last few decades: wheels, seats, lights, bar extensions (but they always leave the bell that she would gladly give up).

In this chapter, we discuss the problem of the disappearing bike, examining briefly current academic research on the phenomena. We will introduce

this chapter's takeaways

» Bike theft is commonplace, and recovery rates are low. There are steps you should take, nevertheless, to improve your prospects of keeping your bike (or getting it back).

» If you leave your bike with someone else, they probably owe you a duty of care, but not necessarily much of a duty.

» If you lock up your bike on someone else's property without permission, that is trespass, and your bike could end up being removed.

» If you lock your bike up on someone else's property with permission, that is usually a licence that lets you lock the bike up, but does not impose any duties on the occupier. That said, occupier liability law could impose a duty of care on the occupier to take reasonable precautions with your bicycle.

» If someone else takes possession of your bike, say in a lock room they control, they owe you duties to take care of that bike, subject to whatever waivers of liability you enter into with them.

» If your bike is stolen, the thief is a criminal and also can be sued in tort . . . if you can find them.

» You do have a power of "citizens arrest" if you catch the thief in the act, or soon after, but this is a limited right available when police intervention is implausible, you use only reasonable force to detain, and you call the police right away.

» Your bike may be insured, but you need to confirm that you have this coverage, and also decide if it is worth making a claim.

» If you're the jerk who buys a stolen bike from the jerk who stole it, you do not have ownership rights any better than those of the thief, in most provinces and territories.

» If you pay a deposit on that new bike, and the bike store closes, you're just another creditor, but you may have remedies through your credit card plan.

» If the airline loses your bike, be aware they have probably limited their liability in their contract of carriage. If you haven't paid an extra fee to lift this limitation, you will need to be attentive to whatever private loss insurance you might have.

you to some basic principles about property law, and then present a number of different scenarios in which your bike goes missing, and the legal questions that arise in each situation. Most of this focus is on bike theft. We also consider, however, other circumstances in which your bike disappears.

the scale and scope of jerkiness

It is quite difficult to measure the scope and nature of bike or bike component thefts. International research suggests that bicycle theft numbers are poorly reflected in police records. Data drawn from seventeen countries in 2000 suggested "on average only 56 percent of bicycle thefts were reported to police."[3] Indeed, United States estimates point to a rate of bike theft four times higher than the number reported to police.[4] A common reason for underreporting is a belief by those victimized that police are either disinterested or helpless in terms of apprehending thieves and returning bicycles.[5] Bike theft has been described as a "low police priority."[6]

The 2012 Montreal study mentioned in the introduction found that "around 36% of participants claimed that they did report the crime to the police. Of the participants who did not report their theft, the majority reported that they did not think it was worth the effort."[7] There is some basis for this belief — only 2.4 percent of stolen bicycles were recovered, although, within this overall number, bikes were more often recovered if victims reported the theft to police.[8] It was also the case that some victims sometimes resorted to self-help, and were able to themselves find their stolen bikes.[9]

Whether reported or not, clearly bikes are stolen, and stolen often. One 2012 estimate places the number of bikes reported stolen annually in Canada at 100,000, and the number actually stolen at 200,000.[10] A 2014 CBC report placed the number of stolen bikes in Montreal at 20,000 per year, of which only 1,856 were reported to police in 2012.[11] The following statistics on reported bicycle thefts illustrate the problem in several Canadian municipalities: 3,456 bikes in Toronto in 2012;[12] 1,700 bikes in Vancouver in 2008;[13] 1,052 bikes in Calgary in 2010;[14] 1,007 bikes in Ottawa in 2010;[15] 433 bikes in Victoria in 2012;[16] and an estimated 3,000 bikes actually stolen in Winnipeg in 2012.[17]

Only a small number of these bicycles are ever recovered. This may indeed reflect the low priority police generally give to bicycle theft, and the problems in actually solving such crimes. But it also stems from the problem of matching a recovered bicycle with its lawful owner. Stolen bikes may often be stripped of their parts and components, or rebuilt into new bicycles.[18] More importantly, many cyclists never register their bicycles or record serial numbers, and many others simply cannot provide evidence of ownership, such as a receipt.[19]

Registering and documenting your bicycle ownership is wise, but it is not foolproof. The 2012 Montreal study on bike theft concluded that

Photographing and registering bicycles . . . appear to have some positive effect, although the numbers involved are too low to make a strong claim. It is interesting that a third of recovered bicycles were not reported stolen: perhaps respondents recovered them on their own. Most compelling, however, is the evidence that, while measures such as reporting, photographing, and registering bicycles might improve chances of recovery, they offer little assurance that a bicycle will be returned. While only 22 stolen bicycles (2.3% of most recent thefts) were reported stolen, registered, and photographed, indicating substantial room for improvement on the part of owners, not one of these bicycles had been recovered at the time of the survey, suggesting currently insufficient police attention to bicycle theft that is echoed in 24% of written comments.[20]

The study also included instructive data on the nature of bike theft:

» Nearly half of bike thefts occurred when bikes were "fly-parked" — that is, secured to street furniture not designed for bicycle parking. This underscores the importance of adequate bike parking facilities, especially ones that are well lit and secure.
» New bicycles valued between $150 and $500 were the most frequently stolen. This is not to say, of course, that thieves pass on more expensive bikes. Instead, it most likely reflects the fact that owners of more expensive machines employ better security.
» The most common theft techniques are simply snatching an unsecured bicycle or picking it up and lifting it off whatever it is locked to. Thieves will also use bolt cutters, hacksaws and crowbars to cut through many types of locking devices.
» Bikes were most often stolen in the summer, even though ridership levels remain even through the May to September period.
» Bicycles are most frequently stolen at night. The next highest theft period is the afternoon, followed by the evening, and then the morning.

Taken together, these results suggest steps bicycle owners can take to minimize the risk of losing their bicycle. Clearly, the first step is to get a good lock and use it, preferably by locking your bike to a bike parking rack. Better yet, take advantage of the increasing number of secure bicycle parking facilities that are appearing on campuses and workplaces. Don't leave your bike out overnight and be particularly cautious in the summer. It is very important to document the ownership of your bicycle: note down the serial number; register the bike with an online registry[21] and the manufacturer (something many high end bike producers encourage); photograph it; and generally keep any documents that prove your ownership, like the purchase receipt. It is worth supporting efforts to get municipalities and other institutions such as schools, universities, hospitals, and private employers to invest in adequate and secure bike parking facilities.

All that said, we know that bikes will be stolen despite the best precautions. In the balance of this chapter we look at various scenarios in which a bike goes missing, and the legal questions those scenarios raise. But first, we will outline some basic principles about property law in Canada.

property law primer

Property law regulates the ways in which all kinds of property may be disposed of and acquired. It is the body of law that essentially establishes the rights individuals have over property, and the duties owed them by others in relation to that property. In our system, property includes "real property," in the form of land and buildings. It also includes "personal property" (also called "chattels" in common law jurisdictions and movable property in Quebec) that consists basically of everything that is not fixed in place as real estate. Bicycles, components and cycling gear, are thus considered personal property under our laws (although we suspect that some of the ancient and apparently abandoned bike frames locked to bike racks around our university campus may be slowly morphing into real estate fixtures).

Transfer of ownership of personal property is typically governed by provincial and territorial legislation, such as provincial sale of goods acts discussed in Chapter 4. Moreover, in all provinces and territories except Quebec, common law property rules are largely still in force. In Quebec, property law is rooted in civil law principles and the *Quebec Civil Code* contains the rules applicable to private persons and ownership of their movable property.

In common law provinces and territories, there are generally two types of personal property interests. The first is ownership, which usually means that a person has the ability to control property — for instance to destroy it — and to exclude others from such control. The second property interest is possession, a clearly important component of ownership. But possession can also give rise to legal rights and duties in situations known as "bailment"; that is, when an owner transfers possession of some property to another for a fixed period of time, without transferring ownership rights. Quebec law includes a similar concept of "deposit."[22]

In this chapter, we will examine situations when individuals are deprived of their property rights and the legal remedies that are available in such circumstances. For the purpose of the following discussion, and as way of examples, we will generally refer to the legal rules that apply in common law jurisdictions in Canada.

missing bicycle scenarios

dashing into the store while your friends look after your bike

Imagine, first, that you leave your bicycle with your cycling club companions as you dart into the bakery during the group ride rest break. Upon your return, you discover your companions have been debating the penalty imposed in the latest cycling doping scandal, and your bicycle has gone missing. As discussed below, the thief has committed a crime, but what responsibilities do your cycling companions have?

In common law provinces, at issue is a "bailment," namely the delivery of possession of personal property from one person to another in expectation that the property will be returned once the bailment has ended.[23]

Traditionally, there are different types of bailment reflecting, essentially, whether the bailment was done as a favour or for some sort of payment. Depending on the type of bailment, and the jurisdiction where the incident took place, there are different expectations as to how carefully the person looking after the property has to be. Without belabouring all the nuances, someone who is being paid to look after your bicycle must act with due care and diligence in looking after your property. On the other hand, in some provinces, a person minding your property as a favour is traditionally only liable for damage or loss to the property if "grossly negligent."[24] Put another way, the person looking after your property has to be extremely careless in order for you to be compensated for your loss.

Whether your cycling companions transgressed the appropriate standard is a question of fact, and something to mull over as you call home for a rescue ride from the bake shop.

locking up your bike on campus (or anyone else's property)

Let's now imagine a second scenario. You have carefully chained your bicycle to a fence on your local university campus, and you return to find your bicycle missing. After voicing your own "open letter to the jerk who stole your bicycle," you wonder if the occupier (in this case, the university) might have some obligation to compensate you.

Bailment and Licence

Here, you are unlikely to be in a bailment relationship with the university. In *Baker v Toronto Board of Education*, Baker locked his bike to a parking lot fence. He did this after asking an attendant where he could safely leave his bike and receiving assurances that his chosen spot was safe. When Baker returned, his bike was gone (except for the front wheel, requiring a small adjustment to the Kids in the Hall "open letter to the jerk" skit). The court concluded that there was no bailment — the garage did not have possession or control over the bicycle. Instead, the garage offered a licence to Baker. A licence is simply a revocable permission to do what would otherwise be trespass. Trespass to property is a common law tort arising where a person intentionally intrudes onto another's land without permission. The licence permitted Baker's presence. But because it issued a mere licence, the garage was not liable for the loss of the bicycle.[25]

The same reasoning applies to our university scenario: in chaining your bicycle up on campus, you are at best exercising a licence to use the university's property. The situation could be a little different if you use special university bicycle parking. At our campus, there are many bike racks, most of which are open to the public, and tragically festooned with stripped down, but still-locked bicycle frames. There are also, however, controlled access and gated bicycle lock-ups. In order to use these facilities, one needs to register with university security and obtain an access swipe card. In offering this service, might the university come close to a bailment relationship? Probably not, as you continue to have access and there has been no delivery of possession and control of the bicycle to the university. If they padlock the secure bicycle parking facility and deny you access, the situation might be quite different. But even then, to obtain the access card you need to sign an agreement that includes a waiver and release of liability, acknowledging the university bears no responsibility for anything that might befall the bicycles. This contractual provision offered in return for use of the secure parking almost certainly binds you.

Occupier Liability

Bailments and licences are not, however, the only relevant legal principles. In language similar to that of other provinces with equivalent laws, the

Ontario *Occupiers' Liability Act* requires occupiers to "take such care as in all the circumstances of the case is reasonable to see that persons entering on the premises, and the property brought on the premises by those persons are reasonably safe while on the premises."[26] In *Boire v Eagle Lake Enterprises*,[27] a Saskatchewan plaintiff stored her property in the defendant's building. There was no bailment because the plaintiff retained control over the storage area — she had the key. Nevertheless, the defendants still owed a duty of care as an occupier; that is, to take reasonable steps to ensure that property stored on the premises was safe.[28]

This duty of care may, however, be modified by contract. Thus, in our university scenario, the duty is likely inapplicable to those using the secure bicycle parking facilities because of the agreement (and waiver) they signed to obtain the access card. On the other hand, those chaining their bicycles up elsewhere on campus have not entered into an equivalent agreement. Certainly, the web-archived university's parking rules purport to exclude university liability for lost or damaged bicycles, and there may be signs so posted around campus. However, as discussed more in Chapter 6, the enforceability of this sort of attempted waiver depends on there being a contractual relationship, something that seems unlikely to exist simply because a cyclist comes to campus and locks his or her bike to a bike rack. Moreover, to be valid, a waiver's terms must be brought to the attention of the party at the time the contract was formed.

Of course, even without the waiver, the university's occupier duties do not amount to insurance — they need only provide reasonable care. We suspect the reasonable care a court would expect a university to take in relation to bicycles locked up around campus would be met by periodic patrols by the university's security service. Moreover, some provincial occupiers' liability statutes exclude liability for loss of or damage to property stemming from acts of a third party (e.g., a thief).[29]

your bicycle is impounded

Let us assume, however, that it turns out the missing bicycle has not been stolen, but instead has been removed by the university. Our university has a rule declaring that all bicycles "not parked at a bike rack . . . are considered illegally parked." Illegally parked bicycles are to receive a warning. For instance, Craig was particularly incensed to receive an officious notice that because of the parking rules, he could no longer keep his bicycle in his office where it was safely stowed and did absolutely no harm. He was instructed to park his bicycle outside. After inspection of the stripped down frames chained to the bike racks closest to his office, he engaged in civil disobedience (and is hoping the relevant university officials don't read this book). Once a warning has been issued against an illegally parked bicycle, the university may remove and store the bicycle, after which bike owners need to pay a fee and provide proof of ownership to recover their two-wheeled vehicle.

Municipalities and other property occupiers may have equivalent rules. For instance, Toronto bylaws indicate

> no person shall, without prior authorization from the General Manager, chain, lock or otherwise attach any article or thing to a waste receptacle, streetlight, parking meter, utility pole, transit shelter, fence, tree or any other municipal property or authorized encroachment that is located in a street, and any article or thing that remains attached for more than 24 consecutive hours may be removed by the General Manager and disposed of [in accordance with other rules].[30]

A proviso was added, however, in 2012: the rule does "not prohibit the chaining, locking or attaching of a bicycle that, in the General Manager's opinion, is in good operating condition and is not chained, locked or attached so as to damage or interfere with the use of municipal property or an authorized encroachment."[31]

The university and any other property occupier are, of course, within their rights to exercise this sort of control over their premises. Chaining a bicycle onto private property without permission from the occupier would amount to trespass.[32]

Still, this does not mean that the occupier may do what they wish with the bicycle, whether it is illegally parked or not. The university still has its obligations to exercise some care under the occupiers' liability statute.

At any rate, once the bike is seized by the university and stored in its facility, without access by the bike owner, we now have a bailment, on top of the occupier due care standard. In *Robertson v Stang*,[33] a cooperative apartment's manager placed many of the items from Ms Robertson's seriously overcrowded apartment into the building's storage facility. The goods were then stolen from this storage area, to which Ms Robertson did not have a key. The court concluded that a bailment existed, and indeed that the manager had breached the duty by placing the property in a storage unit that was, in fact, quite insecure. An "exclusion clause" waiver in the lease did not save the defendant. The waiver deemed all use of storage in the facility to be a licence, but the court held it inapplicable because it was the defendant who moved the goods into storage.

In our university scenario, it seems unlikely that any waivers would apply to seized bicycles for exactly the same reason: the bailment is involuntary from the perspective of the bicyclist. Likewise, occupiers' liability may "not be restricted or excluded by any contract to which the person to whom the duty is owed is not a party, whether or not the occupier is bound by the contract to permit such person to enter or use the premises."[34] As we have already suggested, whatever may be said on the university's parking web page about the university's liability limitations, this website proviso is not part of a contract into which the cyclist merely chaining their bike up entered.

your bike is stolen

First Steps

Sadly, it turns out that the university does not have your bicycle — it has been stolen. Before turning to the legal details, there are steps you should probably take promptly:[35] contact the police and supply your bike serial number, photos, and other identifying information; if you have registered your bike with an online registry, list it as stolen and trigger whatever processes they have (such as automated social media alerts); if you are insured, contact your insurer; determine whether your lock company offers its own anti-theft compensation guarantees; keep your eye on resale websites such as Kijiji, Craigslist, eBay, etc.; and get the word out yourself to the local community and local bike shops and pawn stores so many watchful eyes can be enlisted.

Lawsuits

Turning to the law, the theft of your bike is both a tort and a crime. The tort of conversion involves "a wrongful interference with the goods of another, such as taking, using or destroying these goods in a manner inconsistent with the owner's right of possession."[36] It includes, in other words, stealing your bicycle. Assuming you could ever find the thief who has dismantled your bike and sold it on the black market, you could sue him or her for damages. This is not a likely prospect, although there may be occasional circumstances where the concept is relevant. As we wrote this chapter, there were reports of a Toronto shopping mall management company ordering its security firm to seize bicycles from city property adjoining the mall.[37] Conversion and bailment are the most relevant legal issues in such a scenario.

Prosecutions

But rather than suing, your more likely response in a true theft situation is to enlist the assistance of the state. In criminal law, "theft" means "fraudulently and without colour of right" taking or "converting" to the thief's use anything with intent, among other things, of depriving the owner of it (permanently or temporarily) or dealing "with it in such a manner that it cannot be restored in the condition in which it was at the time it was taken or converted."[38] Upon conviction, the offender is liable to imprisonment for up to ten years when the property is worth more than $5,000, and up to two years when it is worth less than $5,000.[39]

Recovery

There is little more to say — there are not many shades of gray when it comes to someone snatching your bicycle. This is an indisputable wrong by someone who really does intend to take your bike. The real difficulty when it comes to bike theft is not idiosyncratic law. Instead, it is collaring the jerk that snatches your bike. As already suggested, that does not happen very often: bikes are rarely recovered, despite an occasional large-scale bike theft bust.[40]

Police Powers

Police do have the power to seize without warrant any thing that the officer believes on reasonable grounds has been obtained via a violation of criminal law.[41]

Calgary police used this power in 2013. News reports describe police chatting up "countless people riding or walking with bicycles."[42] Those who did not identify themselves as owners persuasively had their bikes seized, and then had to show proof of ownership to recover their bicycles. The tactic apparently relied on what sounds like "bike rider profiling": "We certainly weren't stopping couriers or people commuting or things like that," the police spokesperson said. "It was people who were walking around, pushing a bike, perhaps didn't look like they were cyclists. So, as a result, we'd stop and chat with them. And, you know, nine times out of 10 people were rightful owners."

The blitz recovered fifty bikes and police made seventeen arrests, but the police methods ignited controversy. As one lawyer observed, in our view correctly: "It's highly unorthodox and very problematic for the police to be stopping somebody and then asking them to essentially prove ownership of property."

Pawnshops and Second-hand Sales

Sometimes, stolen bicycles are discovered in pawnshops. In 2004, for example, police recovered 103 bicycles in two London, Ontario area pawnshops.[43] They were aided by the Ontario *Pawnbrokers Act* requiring pawn shops to be licensed and record (and supply to police) details of each pawned item, including biographical and physical description details concerning the person delivering an item for pawn. The pawnbroker is also obliged to report items to the police that he or she reasonably suspects to be stolen.[44] Elsewhere in Canada, a number of municipalities have similar pawn-related rules, and Saskatchewan has a modernized pawn law in which information on the pawn transaction is transmitted electronically to police.[45]

It is also worth noting that Nova Scotia[46] and Manitoba statutes prohibit defacing serial numbers on bicycles. Manitoba law also says that no one shall buy or sell a bicycle that is so defaced. Police are to impound bicycles with such defacement, and the person in whose possession the bicycle is found must come to court and show why the bicycle shouldn't be confiscated.[47] Manitoba law also imposes special rules on second-hand bicycle dealers: they must keep records on bicycles and parts in which they deal and file them according to rules set out by regulations.[48]

Hot Pursuit

There are also instances where the bike owner nabs the thief in the act, or pursues the fleeing thief. The *Criminal Code* has a new provision that allows someone to act reasonably to prevent a thief from unlawfully taking his or her property.[49] There are also new, so-called "citizen's arrest provisions."[50] But this form of private detention is a relatively narrow concept. For one thing, you need to be the property owner, in lawful possession of the property, or have been authorized by the owner or lawful possessor. The concept is also narrowly time-limited: you may detain someone you find committing the crime or stop the person within a reasonable period of time after the crime, in circumstances where it is not feasible for a peace officer to make the arrest. You must also call police promptly — a citizen's arrest is not authorization to detain the thief for prolonged periods. Moreover, the force you use must be reasonable in the circumstances.[51] If you act excessively, you are criminally culpable. For instance, in *R v Neyland*, the defendant chased a thief in an effort to recover stolen tools. After a verbal altercation, the defendant struck the thief with a baseball bat. The court concluded "the accused used excessive force to assert his will with a trespasser.

He had other less violent options open to him that included restraining the complainant while waiting for the police to respond."[52]

Self-Help

There may also be instances where, weeks later, you spot your bike being ridden down the street. These sorts of fortuitous encounters do occur, sometimes engineered by the victim responding to sales ads for the bike posted online by the thief.[53] But whatever the poetic justice of scamming the jerk, you are advised to call the police in this sort of case. There are obviously safety issues. Moreover, police involvement may mean that a thief gets collared, other bikes are recovered, and future crimes pre-empted. And because of their immediacy timing requirements, the *Criminal Code* citizen's arrest provisions are likely unavailable. Indeed, weeks later, you may no longer be the owner of the bicycle — if you filed an insurance claim, ownership may have been transferred to the insurance company in return for the payout.

Insurance

In this last respect, bicycles may or may not be covered by homeowner insurance. Readers should verify their policies. It may also be possible to buy separate, special bicycle insurance, or "schedule" high value bikes separately in home ownership policies in return for an extra premium. In deciding whether to make an insurance claim if you do have coverage, you will need to consider a number of things. For instance, your deductible may be high, making it uneconomical to claim on insurance. Bicycle insurance coverage may have caps on payouts. Moreover, there may be costs over the long run, as insurance premiums go up.[54]

Finally, the proof of loss that insurers usually require you to sign may transfer ownership to the insurance company in return for a payout. Craig's insurer, for instance, specifies that "[a]ll right, title and interest in any salvage is hereby assigned to the Insurer." This may not matter much, since your bike most likely will not be recovered. But if it is, it is no longer yours.

you naively buy a stolen bike

Final word in this section goes to all those who fuel the black market in stolen bikes by buying stolen two-wheeled vehicles. The bottom line in most provinces is that you never really own the bicycle. We have already described Manitoba's law disallowing sales of bikes with defaced serial numbers. More than this, provincial sale of goods statutes specify that goods sold by a non-owner give no better rights to the buyer than the seller had in the first place. So if a thief sold you a bike, you have no better rights to the bike than did the thief.[55] Quebec is something of an exception on this point. There, a good faith purchaser acquires rights to the goods after the passage of enough time.[56]

If you find yourself out of pocket because you "bought" someone else's bike, you could, of course, sue the thief for selling you something they had no rights to sell. But you would need to find that person first, and if you did, they probably have larger problems. See above about the criminal law.

you buy a new bike and it never appears

With the insurance payout, you place a deposit on a new bicycle from your local bike store. After paying for the bike, you leave the bicycle with the store for the customary mechanical adjustments. The next week, you return to pick up and pay the balance on your new machine, only to discover that the doors are locked and the store is bankrupt. Do you get your deposit back? Not easily. In Canadian bankruptcy law at present, there is no such thing as a "consumer lien" giving consumers priority over other creditors of the bankrupt store.[57] This means you become another unsecured creditor waiting in line hoping for reimbursement. But if you paid by credit card, check your card agreement to see if it includes "chargeback" or other purchase protection provisions covering situations when goods are not delivered.

Credit card protection measures may also be the best solution for an online purchase that goes amiss. For instance, when you purchase that Shimano Dura-Ace Di2 component grouppo online for $99, you have probably been scammed and the goods are unlikely to be delivered. Consumer protection standards have been violated and you have been deceived. There may also be the elements of criminal fraud. But these are all theoretical considerations, since your purchase was made in response to an unsolicited email to your Hotmail account from the son-in-law of a deposed dictator, now running Bikes R Us Nigeria. In order to facilitate online transactions (ideally wiser than this one), Craig's credit card company promises to reverse a charge to his card if the goods are never received and he has been unable to resolve the dispute with the online merchant.

your bike is lost in transit

Happily, your troubles have now been resolved, and you are the proud owner of a new $7,000 bicycle purchased (in person) from the other local bike store. Fortunately, this purchase came just in time for your travels to Mallorca for a spring riding spree. Sadly, upon arriving in Mallorca via Air Budget, you discover that your bicycle has not arrived with you. All this, despite the significant baggage premium you paid to fly with your machine.

A quick review of cycling and triathlon discussion forums reveals often colourful reports of such mishaps — sometimes outright loss and sometimes damage. And the usual result is that the airline has limited liability to a very modest amount in the conditions of carriage contract to which you agreed when you purchased your ticket. In some cases, this contract allows you to declare especially valuable baggage at check-in, and pay an additional fee to lift the liability limit. This may be a worthwhile investment.

But at the end of the day, if the amount the airline is prepared to compensate you is inadequate, you may find yourself composing a sardonic song and posting it as a YouTube video. Alternatively (or in addition) it is wise to ensure that you have insured your bicycle for just this sort of travel mishap.

conclusion

In sum, thieves steal bikes. Most are not caught, and few bikes are recovered. In stealing bikes, they commit both a crime and a civil wrong. You do have some limited ability to resist those who try to steal your bike, if you catch them in the act or very soon after. But thereafter, you need to rely on the police. And in most instances, you need to consider whether to make an insurance claim, assuming you have coverage.

Where you park your bike is, therefore, important in retaining possession of that bike. Depending on where you place that bike, and who has charge over it, there may be responsibilities that premise occupiers (or those with charge of your bike) owe you. Those duties vary quite dramatically depending on the circumstances. Bottom line: leave your bike only with people who are reliable, and lock it well in places where you are allowed to lock it.

When you buy a new bike, realize that deposits just make you another creditor if the store goes under. And if you travel with your machine, you're wise to consider insurance.

endnotes

1   *The Kids in the Hall*, Season 3, Episode #3.5 (1991).

2   Dea van Lierop, Michael Grimsrud, & Ahmed El-Geneidy (accepted), "Breaking into Bicycle Theft: Insights from Montreal, Canada" International Journal of Sustainable Transportation (posted online April 2014) at 21, online: tram.mcgill.ca/Research/Publications/Cycling_theft.pdf.

3   *Ibid.*

4   *Ibid.*

5   *Ibid.*

6   Shane Johnson, Aiden Sidebottom, & Adam Thorpe, *Bicycle Theft*, Guide No 52 (2008), online: Center for Problem-Oriented Policing www.popcenter.org/problems/bicycle_theft/.

7   Van Lierop et al, above note 2 at 16.

8   *Ibid* at 19.

9   For media reporting of just such an occurrence, see "Woman Sees Her Stolen Bike for Sale on Craigslist, Makes an Appointment To Buy It, Then Rides Away and Never Looks Back" *Daily Mail* (26 August 2013).

10 Gordon Sinclair Jr, "Why Police Didn't Bust Bike Thieves" *Winnipeg Free Press* (14 June 2012).

11 CBC News, "Where Do Montreal's Stolen Bikes End Up?" (26 February 2014).

12 Toronto Police Service, *2012 Annual Statistical Report* at 12, online: www.torontopolice. on.ca/publications/files/reports/2012statsreport.pdf.

13 Michael McCarthy, "Bike Theft a Growing Industry" *Vancouver Sun* (4 June 2013).

14 Bike Calgary, *Bicycle Theft*, online: www.bikecalgary.org/theft.

15 Larissa Cahute, "Bike Theft a Big Problem" *Ottawa Sun* (14 July 2011).

16 Derek Spalding, "Reported Bike Thefts in Capital Region Spike 20% in Year" *Times Colonist* (11 February 2013).

17 Sinclair, above note 10.

18 "Bike Thefts 'Very Common' in Guelph, Police Say" *Guelph Mercury* (14 April 2014).

19 See discussion in Johnson et al, above note 6.

20 *Ibid* at 20–21.

21 One such service is bikerevolution.ca, which describes itself as the sole national bicycle registration system in Canada. The company sells ID tags with (apparently hard to remove) scannable barcodes that can be used to establish a bike's ownership.

22 *Civil Code of Quebec*, LRQ c C-1991, art 2280.

23 See, e.g., *Punch v Savoy's Jewellers Ltd* (1986), 26 DLR (4th) 546 at 552 (Ont CA).

24 See discussion in *Chiaravalloti v Leading Edge Auto Collision*, 2012 ONSC 4554. Provinces like British Columbia have abandoned this concept and simply ask what behaviour was reasonable in the circumstances. See *Smith v British Columbia*, 2011 BCSC 298.

25 *Baker v Toronto Board of Education*, [1999] OJ No 299 (Gen Div).

26 Ontario, *Occupiers' Liability Act*, RSO 1990, c O.2, s 3 [*Ont OLA*].

27 2009 SKPC 84.

28 *Campbell v 0698900 BC Ltd (cob Soup's Welding)*, 2010 BCPC 136 at para 31.

29 Alberta, *Occupiers Liability Act*, RSA 2000, c O-4, s 14.

30 *City of Toronto By-laws*, s 743-9P.

31 *Ibid*, s 743-9Q.

32 See, e.g., *Trespass to Property Act*, RSO 1990, c T.21.

33 *Robertson v Stang*, 1997 CanLII 2122 (BCSC).

34 *Ont OLA*, s 5.

35 This list is drawn from that proposed by www.bikerevolution.ca.

36 *Boma Manufacturing Ltd v Canadian Imperial Bank of Commerce*, 1996 CanLII 149 at para 31 (SCC).

37 Katrina Clark, "Toronto Property Company Stops Cutting Locks and Seizing Bikes after Cyclist Complains" *National Post* (16 August 2014).

38 *Criminal Code*, RSC 1985, c C-46, s 322.

39 *Ibid*, s 334.

40 Ian Robertson, "Toronto Man Busted in Stolen Bikes Sting" *Toronto Sun* (23 October 2012).

41 *Criminal Code*, s 489.

42 Robson Fletcher, "Calgary Police Blitz Nets 50 Stolen Bikes, 17 Arrests, and Questions about Tactics" *Metro* (12 December 2013).

43 Paul Mayne, "Bike Theft Ring Smashed" *Western News* (26 November 2004).

44 RSO 1990, c P.6, ss 9 and 11.

45 *Pawned Property (Recording) Act*, SS 2003, c P-4.2; *Pawned Property (Recording) Regulations*, RRS c P-4.2 Reg 1.

46 Nova Scotia, *Motor Vehicle Act*, RSNS 1989, c 293, s 50.

47 Manitoba, *The Highway Traffic Act*, CCSM c H60, s 151.

48 *Ibid*, s 152.

49 *Criminal Code*, s 35.

50 *Ibid*, s 494.

51 Justice Canada, *What You Need to Know About Making a Citizen's Arrest*, online: www.justice.gc.ca/eng/rp-pr/other-autre/wyntk.html.

52 *R v Neyland*, 2008 ONCJ 303 at para 24.

53 See above note 9.

54 See discussion TD Insurance, *A Stolen Bike – To Claim or not to Claim*, online: www.tdinsurance.com/products-services/home-insurance/shop-and-buy/stol.jsp.

55 See, e.g., *Wekan Holdings v Insurance Corp of British Columbia*, 2002 BCPC 716; *Jen-Zam Enterprises Inc v Mehrabian*, 2006 CanLII 17753 (Ont SCJ).

56 *Civil Code of Quebec*, arts 927 and 2919. *Compagnie d'assurance Guardian de Canada c Robinson*, 1992 CanLII 3953 (Que CA).

57 Industry Canada, *Statutory Review of the Bankruptcy and Insolvency Act and Companies' Creditors Arrangement Act* (2014) at 10.

Chapter 6

Running Your Bicycle Club

introduction

Cycling is not just a sport and a mode of transportation. It is also a social activity, and nowhere is this truer than with the classic "club ride." In many parts of the country, cyclists assemble on weekend mornings from spring to late fall to pedal the country's back roads with other club members. We have both enjoyed numerous cycling outings with our club, both weekly rides and organized tours. It is a great way to stay fit, to hone group riding skills, and to establish friendships with like-minded individuals. In fact, our local club is the oldest in Canada and one of the largest in the country as well. In addition to weekly rides, most clubs including ours offer different levels of programming and activities, ranging from recreational to high performance cycling, and geared to novice and experienced riders. But an obvious prerequisite to the club ride and all other club activities is the existence of such sporting organizations.

In this chapter, we briefly describe legal issues associated with the creation and operation of a bicycle club, including liability and how to minimize it. We also look at sports coaching and the legal obligations associated with it. We end with a basic primer on insurance law for bicycle clubs.

organizing your bicycle club

to incorporate or not, that is the question

There are "clubs" and then there are "Clubs Inc." A club can be nothing more than an informal association of like-minded individuals, coming

this chapter's takeaways

» If your riding activities are becoming organized, consider whether you should form a club, and decide whether to incorporate. Incorporation requires paperwork, which never really ends. On the other hand, a company can own property, and shield its members from personal liability.

» If you decide to incorporate, expect a number of administrative steps to complete the process, and be ready for the expectations that come with corporate status. These vary from province to province — there are many guides to which you can refer. But basically, you will be incorporating a not-for-profit corporation. In almost all instances, your club will not qualify for charitable status, so don't worry about that too much.

» Once you incorporate, you need to follow certain steps to comply with corporate law. Again, follow the rules applicable to your jurisdiction.

» In running your affairs, be attentive to various areas of the law that apply to your operations. This includes human rights laws and privacy law. Non-profit sporting clubs may be exempted from privacy laws, or they may not be. Be attentive to your provincial rules.

» Once you start doing bike club things — like organizing rides and events — you need to worry about people hurting themselves. Make sure you understand your liability exposure. Once you have coaches training athletes, make sure you and they understand everyone's full range of legal obligations. Above all, make sure you use proper liability waivers.

» Affiliate with provincial cycling associations and take advantage of the insurance policies that come with membership.

together to enjoy a shared activity. We suspect that many Canadian bicycle clubs are just loose associations of people with shared interests and a mailing list, rather than formally structured organizations.

At some point, however, an association may reach a higher level of organization and even begin acquiring property, at which point the club may wish to incorporate. Incorporation has obvious virtues: an incorporated entity has "separate legal personality," meaning that it is a person in law. One corollary of this concept is that liability is generally limited to the corporation itself, and does not extend to its members or, to a lesser degree, its directors and officers. This may become a very important consideration as the club's activities become more sophisticated, and its liability exposure increases apace. We will have more to say about liability further below.

A corporation may also be the legal owner of property; it may enter into contracts and leases; and it can sue (and be sued) in its own name. A corporation also endures indefinitely, until dissolved, and so its persistence does not depend on that of its founders and members.[1] It is also the case that charities are almost always corporations — but more on sporting bodies and charities below.

The disadvantage of incorporation is red tape. There are all sorts of regulatory and paperwork requirements that corporations must meet. There are also requirements relating to governance structures and accountability that must be observed.

The balance of this section assumes that a bike club has made the decision to incorporate and therefore we outline the basic legal considerations that arise in those circumstances. A word of warning: this chapter is not intended as a definitive guide to the process, not least because of the number of provincial and territorial jurisdictions in which a club can be incorporated which have slightly different rules and procedures. In practice, it is useful to seek the assistance of a lawyer to help finalize this process — perhaps even a member of the club willing to do the incorporation for free or at reduced cost.

basic law of not-for-profit corporations

Where to Incorporate
A bicycle club, like other community sports organizations, is almost certainly a not-for-profit (NFP) enterprise. Not-for-profit status does not mean that the club cannot earn revenue — any operation will almost certainly need to raise money to finance its operations. It does mean, however, that the enterprise is not operated for the financial gain of its directors and members, but instead for some community benefit. Thus, if an NFP generates a return on some club activity that exceeds the costs associated with that undertaking, this "profit" may be reinvested back into the organization's activities. The company may not, however, redistribute its income to the NFP's directors and members.

Organizers can incorporate NFPs in Canada at either the federal or provincial level. At the time of writing, the law governing this process was in a state of transition in some jurisdictions. Saskatchewan has a specific not-for-profit corporations statute.[2] Other provinces, such as British Columbia[3] and Alberta,[4] have "society" acts that cover associations incorporated for non-profit "sporting" purposes, among other things. In 2011, a new federal statute governing NFPs came into force.[5] Ontario's legislature has also passed a new law.[6] It was not in force at the time of writing, but it may be by the time you read this.

Federal incorporation has benefits for an entity with a national reach. It would mean for instance that the company has a nationwide monopoly over its approved name and may operate in all the provinces and territories (subject to possible filing requirements in those places). National sporting organizations such as the Canadian Cycling Association (originally incorporated in 1935) or Triathlon Canada (incorporated in 1990) are both federal NFPs. So too is at least one international cycling-related sporting group: the International Triathlon Union (incorporated in 1994).

It seems likely, however, that most bicycle clubs that choose to incorporate do so under their relevant provincial laws. Most of these clubs are local in their operations and there likely is no virtue in federal incorporation — the latter is mostly a benefit to companies that may want to move their corporate activities from place to place in Canada. There may even be a disadvantage — federal annual filing requirements may be more demanding than those of at least some provinces.

How to Incorporate

The precise mechanics and requirements of incorporation vary slightly from jurisdiction to jurisdiction, and readers should be attentive to those differences. In this section, we summarize commonplace key steps, and comment on some provincial variations.

Charitable Status

Speaking generally, a first consideration is whether the NFP will also apply for charitable status from the Canada Revenue Agency (CRA). It is important not to confuse NFP status with charitable status. They are two different legal statuses — to be a charity, the NFP has to be accepted as such by the CRA. The latter will only do so in limited circumstances.

Under Canadian tax law, a NFP that has as its primary purpose and function the promotion of amateur athletics in Canada on a nation-wide level enjoy some of the tax advantages of a charity, as we outline in Chapter 7.[7] Other, more local organizations do not qualify for this status, and must instead satisfy the rather indefinite test for being a charity. Since a bicycle club in unlikely to be engaged in the relief of poverty, or the advancement of religion or education, it must qualify, if at all, on the basis that its purpose is something else "beneficial to the community."[8] Promoting a sport or physical activity does not meet this test, even if there are certain positive community by-products.

Put another way, a bicycle club that wishes also to be a charity must have as its *main* objective a more squarely charitable objective, such as providing services to children with disabilities or those living in poverty.[9] The basic, run-of-the-mill bicycle club would not meet this test, and for such an entity, charitable status is simply unavailable. That means two things: first, a basic bike club that seeks charitable status is wasting its time. Second, because most bicycle clubs are not charities, they cannot issue charitable tax credits for things like donations.

Choosing a Name

Practically speaking, the first step towards incorporation is picking an acceptable name. This seems obvious, but under the law, it means much more than simply choosing a name the club's founders like. A corporate name has to be distinct — that is, it cannot be "deceptively" similar to that of another, existing business name. It must not mislead or befuddle the public as to the identity of the corporation, the nature of its activities or its relationship with other businesses. Some provincial and territorial laws prohibit the use of a name that is the same as the name of an existing association if its use would be likely to deceive. In *Re Ontario Bicycle Moto Cross Association*,[10] the Ontario Cycling Association successfully challenged a group that had adopted a name that the OCA argued would confuse the public as to which of the two associations was the governing body for BMX bicycle racing.

So for these reasons, the name will generally have a "distinctive" component, as well as descriptive and legal elements. To be distinctive, the name can use an invented word, or a regular word used in an unusual way. The descriptive element identifies the company's main activity. The legal aspect recognizes the incorporated nature of the enterprise. The Ontario government's primer on NFPs includes a topical example: Canvelo Cycling Club Inc (with "Canvelo" constituting the distinctive element, while "Cycling Club" and "Inc" reflect the descriptive and legal aspects of the name, respectively).[11] Some provinces require other legally-distinctive nomenclature, such as use of the term "society" or "club."[12]

At the same time, the name must not be too general — general names likely overlap too much with existing names. Excessively general names often lack distinctive or descriptive components. For instance, "Canvelo Inc" lacks a descriptive element, and is too general.[13]

There are a host of other limitations on names — for instance, references to "royal" or the use of a geographic name alone. Perhaps of greater concern for a local bicycle club, names must not imply a link to government or a government agency. A name like 'Toronto Bicycle Committee,' for instance, might suggest such an official linkage. Incorporators will need to parse closely the regulations of the jurisdiction in which they are incorporating to confirm whether their proposed name offends any restrictions.

Once the club settles on a name, it must conduct, and obtain a report of, a name search of other similar business names and trade-marks. A NUANS Name Search Report may be the easiest way of proceeding, as you can conduct for a fee a search of a databank of names registered everywhere in Canada, other than Quebec.[14] A Quebec search, if it is required, is an extra step involving the Registraire des entreprises, Quebec.[15]

Filing the Initial Paperwork

The precise filing requirements and fee for incorporation vary from jurisdiction to jurisdiction. That paperwork will, however, generally require "articles of incorporation" or the equivalent. This is a document establishing the basic parameters of the new organization. Incorporation rules often require the club to identify its name, a head office (within the province, if it is a provincially incorporated NFP) and identity of the incorporators. The club will also need to specify the objects for which it is incorporated.

A head office does not need to be a business premises — it can be a residential address of one of the club members, for instance. But it is the place where corporate records are kept and at which the corporation can be contacted.

The jurisdiction's rules may also require that the incorporation application name initial directors. Unlike those who follow them, the directors named in the application are not elected, but simply named in the application documents. That said, they have the same duties and liabilities of any other director, a matter discussed below. Directors must also generally be members of the corporation.

The required statement of objects is best kept short and broad, but not to the point of ambiguity. For example, the Ottawa Bicycle Club has the following as its objects:

> » to conduct, encourage, and promote cycle racing, cycle touring, and recreational touring;

- » to assist the community at large in the promotion, encouragement, and understanding of all aspects of cycling and related activities;
- » to ascertain, defend, and pursue the rights of cyclists;
- » to carry on the above objectives in affiliation with the Canadian Cycling Association and Ontario Cycling Association; and
- » to promote amateur youth sport (bicycling).[16]

Care should be taken in framing these objects — they do serve as the outer limits of what the NFP can do.

Managing Your Bicycle Club

Once the paperwork is completed and filed, the fee paid, and the incorporation accomplished, the real business of organizing the new 'Bicycle Club Inc' begins.

The classic first step is for the founding directors to convene an organizational meeting, or sign organizing resolutions, to approve the initial policies that will permit the new corporation to conduct its affairs. At this first meeting, they approve bylaws, appoint officers and an interim public accountant, establish banking arrangements, and issue memberships, among other things.[17]

Bylaws allow the incorporated club to structure its affairs and operations. The bylaws thus deal with matters not governed by the NFP statute under which the corporation was created, or they modify some of the default rules that would otherwise apply under that law (assuming the statute allows departures of this sort). Examples include: establishing the NFP's financial year; procedures for banking; requirements for membership; the manner of appointing officers; the process of calling and running directors' and members' meetings; and, the manner of amending bylaws.

Members

Rules establishing exactly who is a member of the club are imperative — members will be participating in governance activities and so clarity as to who is a member is very important. Some jurisdictions permit different categories of members, including members with non-voting status.[18] NFP statutes generally require that the bylaws establish the conditions for membership in each member class or group, the manner of withdrawing from a class or group or transferring between them; and, the conditions on which membership expires.

For example, the Regina-based Wascana Freewheelers Bicycle Touring Club Inc, incorporated under the Saskatchewan NFP Act, includes only one class of member, within which there are two categories: individual and family. Any person with a family membership has the same rights and privileges as an individual member. Any person may become a member of the Club upon application and payment of the membership fees, and membership endures from January 1st or the date at which the application is received, whichever is later, until December 31st, or the conclusion of the Annual General Meeting, whichever is later. Members may resign, but are not entitled to a refund for so doing.[19]

The bylaws should also describe the basis for expelling a member, a matter discussed further below in director duties to members.

Board of Directors

The directors are the governing minds of the company. They manage the corporation, and hold ultimate responsibility for overseeing any staff, and developing and implementing policies. Because of their pivotal role, the law imposes a number of duties and responsibilities on board members. It also imposes liabilities for failing to exercise these duties and responsibilities properly. As discussed at the end of this chapter, it may be advisable for clubs to purchase director and officer liability insurance, to encourage people to take on the sometimes thankless duties and risks of being on the board of a not-for-profit corporation.

There are a number of useful resources describing how to be an effective NFP director.[20] In this book, we just highlight some of the principal legal issues.

The cardinal obligation of a director is to exercise his or her functions with competence and diligence in the "best interests" of the corporation. The law calls this requirement to act in the best interests of the NFP a "fiduciary obligation." A director who violates her fiduciary duties may be legally liable and the corporation can sue him or her for damages. A director's fiduciary duty has two key components. Moreover, directors of a non-profit also owe duties to members.

DUTY OF CARE

First, the director must meet a "duty of care." This means that the director must act with sufficient competence or skill, meeting what is known as the "standard of care." Exactly what this "standard of care" includes can be variable. Speaking generally, the director must exercise a degree of skill and diligence associated with the reasonable care an ordinary person would demonstrate if acting for him or herself. The law traditionally may permit, however, a "subjective" application of this approach — there is no expectation that the person have a greater level of skill than what would be true for a person with a similar degree of knowledge and experience. As a result, the level of expertise expected of directors will vary according to their background and education.

In other instances, legislation may impose a truly "objective standard" — that is, a standard indexed to what a reasonably prudent person would do. The objective standard does not vary according to the background of the director.

In practice, these duty of care expectations boil down to directors acting with due diligence — a director should inform him or herself of the corporation's affairs, and make decisions with the fullest information possible. This means informing oneself of the corporation's operations. It may also mean taking advice from professionals where necessary. The director should also be regular in meeting attendance, be attentive to corporate documents, such as financial reports and meeting minutes, exercise diligent control over staff, and exercise decision-making authority on a reasoned basis, among other things.

DUTY OF LOYALTY

Second, the director must meet a "duty of loyalty." Put simply, this means that directors must act honestly and in good faith — they may not profit from their activities or place themselves in positions where the duty to the corporation conflicts with their own interests. This means, for instance, that the director should not have a personal stake in any contract into which the corporation enters. It also means, more generally, that the directors must avoid all other circumstances where there is both a real and an appearance of conflict between the corporation's best interest and a personal interest of the director. The director is also obliged to be truthful in her dealing with the corporation and must avoid misleading or inadequate disclosures or representations. That means declaring any conflicts that might arise, and then recusing oneself from the decision-making process that creates that conflict.

DUTY TO MEMBERS

The company's constituting documents (such as articles of incorporation) and bylaws are analogous to a contract between the corporation and its members. Directors must make significant efforts to ensure that the corporation's activities comply with those instruments.

In their relationship with members, directors must treat all members equally, unless the best interests of the corporation demand otherwise. In disciplining members by, for instance, expelling them, directors should ensure that the bylaws allow them to do so and that any procedural requirements required by those bylaws are met. At the very least, the member should be given notice and an opportunity to be heard by open-minded directors before being disciplined.

The 1999 constitution of the Ottawa Bicycle Club, for instance, states that the directors "may expel a member on reasonable grounds relating to conduct. In such cases the individual is to be advised in writing stating the reasons for expulsion. The Board may consider reinstatement if the reasons for expulsion are corrected." The OBC board of directors concluded (quite plausibly) in 2010 that this bylaw was insufficiently detailed. Moreover, a rule permitting comments from the affected member only after expulsion likely does not meet basic procedural requirements for fairness.

The rule change presented by the OBC directors to the club's 2011 AGM preserved the directors' ability to expel a member by resolution "provided that such expulsion is done in good faith and in a fair and reasonable manner." and defined "fair and reasonable" as giving the member fifteen days notice of the expulsion, with reasons, and an opportunity to be heard (in writing or orally) not less than five days before the expulsion takes effect.

A final point on expulsions goes to process: directors should be wary of the statements they make about the member — comments that sully the person's reputation may be defamatory and expose the directors to personal liability.

DIRECTOR QUALIFICATIONS

Most NFP corporations will wish to establish baseline qualifications for becoming a director. Of course, as noted in more detail below, the essential requirement is that the director ultimately be elected to the post by the membership. The law under which the club is incorporated may impose other requirements. For instance, under the federal law, the director must be eighteen years old, be an individual (as opposed to another corporation), not be bankrupt and not be legally incompetent (as declared by a court). Beyond that, there may be additional qualities the NFP may wish to prescribe in its bylaws. The Ottawa Bicycle Club requires, for instance, that a director be a member and not be a current employee of the OBC.

Officers and Executive Committees

It is common for the NFP to have officers — a president, one or more vice-presidents, a treasurer, and a secretary. The corporate law of the jurisdiction in which the NFP incorporates may require some of these positions. In other instances, bylaws may create these offices and assign roles to them.

The jurisdiction's corporate law may also authorize the creation of a management or executive committee of directors to exercise the powers of the board of directors, subject to certain limitations.

Directors' Meetings

As noted, directors are expected to meet regularly, in order to govern the company and meet expectations tied to their fiduciary duties. But there is generally no fixed schedule for these meetings in corporate law; these are matters that may instead be prescribed by the club's bylaws.

Quorum for these meetings may also be prescribed in the corporation's articles of incorporation or its bylaws, although here corporate law may create some default requirements depending on the jurisdiction in question. By way of example, the Wascana Freewheelers Bicycle Touring Club director quorum rules provide, simply, that a quorum exists upon "the presence of a minimum of three Board members consisting of 1) the President, 2) one other member of the Executive, and 3) any other Board member."

Members and Annual Meetings

One of the first tasks of the new NFP once the original directors have met is to convene a members meeting. This meeting must be conducted within a certain period of time of the incorporation; e.g., within eighteen months, depending on the statute under which the corporation is created. Among other things, members elect directors at the meeting, ratify, modify, or reject the bylaws drafted by the original directors, and appoint an accountant.

Thereafter, subsequent general meetings of members must be held annually, and no later than a fixed period after the immediately prior meeting; e.g., within fifteen months in some jurisdictions. At these annual meetings, directors are elected by a majority of member votes cast, although NFP law generally allows directors to be elected on rotation for staggered terms; that is, only a portion of the directors are up for election every year.

Record-Keeping and Filing Obligations

In choosing to incorporate, a bicycle club also takes on a number of important record-keeping and filing obligations. These obligations vary between jurisdictions, but generally, an NFP will be required to maintain: articles of incorporation; bylaws; minutes (and any resolutions) of member and director meetings; a director, officer, and member registry with contact information for everyone in those three categories. Directors have access to these documents, and members may be entitled to see at least some of them.

Corporate law also requires a NFP to create and maintain adequate financial records, including financial statements. It may also impose detailed reporting requirements such as obliging the transmission of financial statements to members prior to annual general meetings.

Generally, there are also obligations to file certain documents with the relevant government bodies on an annual or occasional basis. There may be an annual corporate return that NFPs must file. Companies may also need to file updated documents where there are changes in registered office addresses, the names of directors, and the content of articles of incorporation and bylaws.

privacy law 101 for bicycle clubs

The federal *Personal Information Protection and Electronic Documents Act* (*PIPEDA*)[21] has completely changed privacy law in Canada. As of January 2004, the *PIPEDA* applies to all organizations collecting, using or disclosing "personal" information in the course of "commercial" activities. In the absence of equivalent provincial laws, the *PIPEDA* rules apply even to organizations not otherwise regulated by federal law under the Canadian constitution.

It should not be assumed that NFP associations — incorporated or otherwise — are exempt from *PIPEDA* because they do not engage in "commercial" activities. The Act defines a commercial activity as ". . . any particular transaction, act or conduct or any regular course of conduct that is of a commercial character, including the selling, bartering or leasing of donor, membership or other fundraising lists."[22] It is true that the federal Privacy Commissioner considers that "collecting membership fees, organizing club activities, compiling a list of members' names and addresses, and mailing out newsletters are not considered commercial activities. Similarly, fundraising is not a commercial activity."[23] However, "selling, bartering or leasing a membership list or a list of donors would be considered a commercial activity. As a result, consent is required for the disclosure of this information."[24]

Moreover, there are now also provincial laws that expressly extend privacy rules to non-profit organizations. British Columbia[25] is a case in point. A bicycle club operating in these jurisdictions must meet important privacy standards. Even if provincial or territorial law does not impose such disclosure duties, some clubs have nevertheless chosen to introduce privacy policies. The Ottawa Bicycle Club, for instance, has a detailed privacy policy posted on its website.

Speaking generally, privacy law is about consent. Subject to certain exceptions, personal information can only be collected, used or disclosed with notice and consent of the individual to which this information related. A club must therefore set up a mechanism for seeking, obtaining, and recording this consent. Personal information typically includes such things as age, name, ID numbers, opinions, evaluations, comments, credit records, and the like. The federal Privacy Commissioner defines personal information as "any factual or subjective information, recorded or not, about an identifiable individual."[26] The BC law speaks of "information about an identifiable individual."[27] Put another way, the concept of personal information is sweeping.

Another aspect of privacy law is proper protection of personal information in the organization's possession. That means ensuring that the information is only used and disclosed for the purposes for which it is collected (e.g., to communicate with and maintain a roster of club members). The personal information must also be destroyed when the purpose for which it was collected comes to an end, in a manner that prevents improper access to that information; for instance through shredding paper records. And where that personal information is retained, it must be held securely to avoid unauthorized access, inadvertent disclosure, or the like.

The organization's policies on these and related matters should be transparent, accessible, and easily understood, and there should be someone within the organization designated with the responsibility of ensuring compliance with privacy rules.

human rights law 101 for bike clubs

Human rights legislation exists in every province, territory, and at the federal level, and these laws protect people against discrimination based on race, age, sex, sexual orientation, and several other grounds. Such human rights legislation prohibits discriminatory practices in both the private and public sectors by individuals or organizations, businesses or government bodies. Since bicycle clubs and cycling associations offer services to the public, their activities and programs are subject to the jurisdiction of human rights legislation. This means that bicycle clubs must avoid discriminating on prohibited grounds when offering their services or conducting their activities.

As explained in more detail in Chapter 7, not all types of distinctions or acts of discrimination are illegal. Human rights legislation does recognize that the general rule prohibiting discrimination does not apply if the discrimination is reasonable and justifiable. It may therefore be legal to discriminate and segregate in organized sport, if the decision to discriminate can be reasonably justified, for instance, to ensure fair competition, the safety of participants, or to account for the physical differences in strength, stamina, and physique of the athletes. In cycling, the following distinctions and restrictions are entrenched in the sport: single-sex competitions; restrictions based on disability; and restrictions based on age.

Human rights laws and statutes at the federal and provincial/territorial levels also make provision for 'special programs,' also known as employment equity or affirmative action programs. These programs are intended to correct the negative effects of historic or systemic patterns of discrimination that have worked to disadvantage certain groups of people. Such programs are not considered to contravene human rights legislation. So a cycling activity geared to women, or to disabled cyclists, might meet the requirements of an affirmative action program.

bicycle club events and liability

We have discussed basic liability concepts in Chapter 3. These rules are very important for bike clubs that do what they are designed to do: get people riding bikes. To summarize: an occupier may be liable for injuries that occur on the land they occupy, although the standard of care expected of such an occupier is generally low where users voluntarily assume risk in, e.g., recreational activities. More generally, a person may be liable to another in negligence where his or her activities create foreseeable risk to that other person, and she or he did not take reasonable care in conducting those activities.

occupier liability

We have discussed occupier liability on several occasions in this book — particularly in Chapters 3 and 5. Occupier liability rules are inapplicable to most bike clubs, since the organization would generally not be operating activities on lands it occupies. It is, however, conceivable that a mountain bike club may own land on which it operates a trail network, or a cross-country ski club switches over to trail riding on its network in the summer. In some cases, a sporting group may occupy a velodrome, or it may operate an indoor facility where athletes use stationary bikes, trainers, or rollers. It may also be the case that a club shares liability with an occupier who has failed to maintain a premise: in one skating club case, the club and its coaches violated their duty of care by failing to inspect the ice of an arena prior to a skating lesson, when it knew that the ice was likely pocked.[28]

In all of these circumstances, occupier liability law is relevant. We offer up one case as an example of how the occupier liability rules apply in a sporting context. In *Roscoe v Halifax (Regional Municipality)*,[29] a badminton player at a municipal recreational facility stumbled over a piece of duct tape affixed to the gym floor, injuring her knee. The gym was owned and operated by the municipality of Halifax. The city was, therefore, the occupier during the relevant period of time, and had a duty of care to keep the premises reasonably safe under Nova Scotia's occupier liability statute. The court held "[p]eople renting a gymnasium to play badminton reasonably expect the floor to be uniform and clear of foreign substances and objects. Badminton involves rapid and multidirectional foot movement. In my view, it is reasonable to expect that the occupiers of a gymnasium being used to play badminton will offer some protection against foreign substances and objects on the floor."[30] Moreover, the city had not cleaned the gym on the day of the incident. In the final analysis, the city was liable for $30,289.48. Thus, bike clubs who occupy lands are expected to maintain the facilities in a way to ensure a reasonable level of safety.

negligence

While occupier liability issues only arise where the club runs a premise, negligence law is important to all clubs. It is also important to the coaches and event organizers that the club may employ.

Clubs should be attentive to several basic rules in negligence law. As explained in Chapter 3, a key issue in negligence law is the "standard of care"

clubs must meet in relation to those to whom they owed a "duty of care" (that is, those who may be foreseeably injured). Reasonableness (measured according to an objective standard, and not the defendant's actual state of being) is the usual litmus test for the standard of care, but there are wrinkles. For instance, someone who holds themselves out as particularly expert and having special skills will be scrutinized against a higher standard than the norm.[31] Moreover, generally accepted "industry" practices may be important in deciding what is objectively reasonable.[32] A bike club organizing an event that departs, for instance, from guidance provided by a sporting federation may have trouble defending itself in a negligence case. The Ontario Cycling Association publishes, for example, a "Provincial Ride Guidelines" document and "[c]lubs are asked to take a look at this general document and consider the various points when having their club activities."[33]

Relatively few negligence cases go to trial, as most litigants settle their cases outside of the courtroom. But if you are involved in running a bicycle club, it is important to understand some basic negligence law. We will illustrate those principles with two cases involving sporting organizations, one in which the plaintiff won and the other in which the defendants succeeded.

In *Parker v Ingalls (cob Pure Self Defence Studios)*,[34] a BC karate studio's proprietor injured an adult karate student during a demonstration on the student of a martial arts move. The court concluded the proprietor owed an obvious duty to the student to take reasonable care. That duty was breached where, in using a student to perform a demonstration, the instructor inflicted physical harm. Moreover, a liability waiver did not protect the studio. While there was waiver language in the student enrollment agreement, that language was not specifically brought to the student's attention, and it amounted to a very small part of the agreement. Moreover, the waiver appeared "in extremely small print with no emphasis to direct the reader to its importance or to the fact that he or she is giving up all rights to sue the Studio. It does not refer to negligence. There is a space for the student to place his or her signature. There is no provision that draws the student's attention to the fact that by signing, he or she is waiving any legal rights."[35] The studio was liable for damages totalling $150,000.[36]

The second case is from Utah. In the United States, the law on negligence is essentially identical to that of Canada, at least at the level of detail set out in this book. In *Milne v USA Cycling*,[37] a cyclist was injured and another killed in a mountain bike race organized, promoted, and conducted by the defendant organizations. The race was an "open course" event in which riders shared the course with vehicles. The two cyclists were struck by a truck/trailer. The defendants had posted signs advising road users of the event, and marshalls and parking attendants were positioned at the race start. Race officials cautioned the participants about the open course, and at least one person was on the course for traffic control purposes. The riders also signed a waiver that repeated warnings about the open course. In the end, the defendants prevailed because of the waiver.

Both of these cases illustrate the importance of good liability waivers, the subject of the next section. But we conclude this section with a final point: liability is not limited to those participating in sporting events. There are cases in which spectators injured by sporting events have sued in negligence.[38] Waivers are inapplicable to these types of injuries — people don't sign a release before they stroll down to see the local criterium race. Instead, this is an instance where insurance is vital. We discuss insurance at the end of this chapter.

waivers

Waivers of liability are essential for any organization that conducts activities in which someone may get hurt — which is another way of saying, any cycling club. Liability waivers for recreational sporting activities are controversial in some quarters,[39] but they remain the principal means of legal risk transfer — from event sponsors, organizers, and managers to participants who willingly assume risk.

A proper waiver is a recognized defence for both occupier liability claims and tort negligence actions. Voluntary assumption of risk may apply in very limited circumstances even without the existence of a waiver,[40] but proper waivers are the gold standard. The emphasis is on "proper" waiver. As the *Parker* case discussed above shows, courts will strictly construe waivers in favour of those injured. That is, the courts will give a waiver the narrowest possible reading in terms of its scope, and they will also be vigilant in considering whether those supposedly bound by waivers were given reasonable notice of its terms.[41]

In *Crocker v Sundance Northwest Resorts*,[42] Crocker and a friend entered a tubing race down a ski hill. They paid their race fee and signed an entry and waiver form, but Crocker did not read the form and did not realize it was a waiver. On race day, Crocker and his friend consumed substantial quantities of alcohol and went racing. During the race, they tumbled from the tube and Crocker was cut. Nevertheless, the visibly drunk Crocker continued in the event, and was not stopped by the competition organizers, who in fact provided a replacement tube after the first mishap. Subsequently, Crocker and his friend crashed on a mogul, and Crocker was rendered a quadriplegic, the second competitor of the day to suffer serious injury. The Supreme Court of Canada concluded that the resort, which had organized the event, had a duty of care to Crocker and had failed to meet its standard of care — not least it had not prevented the inebriated plaintiff from competing.

Much turned, therefore, on whether the waiver exonerated the defendant resort. The Court concluded that it did not, as Crocker's attention had not been drawn to the waiver's language, he did not read it and did not know of its existence. He thought he was just signing an entry form.

Crocker is a lesson in contract formation. A waiver is, in essence, a contractual release on tort liability. Its validity depends therefore on a contract being formed. This in turn means that the plaintiff must agree to its terms. That is why courts focus on reasonable notice: would a reasonable person know that a waiver was part of the contract? The facts, therefore, matter: what font was used for the waiver; was the wording bolded; was there truly an opportunity to read the waiver; how clear was the language; etc.[43] Additional issues are significant, such as the education, experience, and sophistication of the waiver signer.[44]

What constitutes reasonable notice is particularly complex with unsigned waivers — disclaimers on tickets or signs, for example. Here again, the facts of the case are key, and the same sorts of questions arise as with signed waivers — font, language, location of the sign, etc.[45] Timing may also matter: did the plaintiff have notice at the time the contract was formed? For instance, "[i]f a waiver is found on a sign at the top of the ski-hill it will be seen as an attempt to unilaterally impose a term into a contract that was made when the consumer entered the premises and paid for a ski ticket at the foot of the hill. The notice is too late."[46]

By way of example, Craig is an avid participant in running and triathlon races. When he registers online for these events, he usually reaches a screen that asks him to read and acknowledge a waiver of liability. In his experience, Ironman events are the most detailed in relation to these waivers, as befits their quasi-insane nature. When he registers for Ironman online, he is asked to read, and then click to acknowledge, four different waivers and agreements. If he fails to do so he cannot proceed with registration. Two of the documents have language on assumption of risk in bolded and sometimes CAPITAL LETTERS. The language includes notice of the necessary risks of participating in Ironman endurance events and that roads may be open to traffic and that weather and other conditions are unpredictable and potentially risky. One of the waivers then enumerates risks associated with triathlon's three disciplines (e.g., "being submerged underwater, hitting bottom or drowning"). Other specifically enumerated risks include:

» Risks in any competitive or athletic activity;
» Risks present in an outdoor environment;
» Risks involved in decision making and conduct;
» Personal health and participation risks;
» Risks connected with location;
» Risks associated with premises;
» Equipment risks;
» Supervision and activities risks;
» Risks regarding conduct.

The waiver then lists all the horrible things that these risks might do to Craig's body (e.g., "colliding . . . with the bottom of a lake or other water body"). Participants then are told that they are participating voluntarily with knowledge of the risks, and IN CAPITALS and occasionally **BOLD** surrender their, their heirs, assigns, and beneficiaries or anyone else's right to sue for any injuries, damage, death, or other loss suffered. Moreover, disputes must be submitted to mandatory dispute resolution through arbitration, governed (in the case of Craig's races) by Quebec law. Put another way, participants are not in a position to rush to the courts in case of accident or serious injury.

The document goes on for several pages in a similar vein. Participants must then enter an "electronic signature" before proceeding with the registration.

In a "belts and suspenders" approach, there is then an extra step: in picking up their race kits the day before the event, all participants are funnelled through a process that includes signing (and checking off boxes to indicate that they have read and understood) another detailed waiver. This entire, very considered process presumably is designed to make it much more difficult for potential plaintiffs to argue, subsequently, they had no idea that they were surrendering their legal rights to sue. It may be that, like Craig, most participants give the document a mere quick glance in practice. But it is difficult to see how else the organizers could reasonably bring the waiver to the attention of participants in a mass participation event like a triathlon, and courts are unlikely to reward Craig's delinquent scan as he rushes to get his race t-shirt, especially given his legal training.

Of course, there may be some issue of timing here, at least with the second waiver: the supplemental waiver is signed well after registration, on the eve of the race. There may be some doubt as to whether it amounts to a unilateral condition superimposed on participants, something on which courts may frown. On the other hand, this argument has not found much traction where the contract originally entered by a plaintiff signals that a liability waiver must also be signed before participating in an activity.[47]

Moreover, some courts see waivers as separate contracts. In *Loychuk v Cougar Mountain Adventures Ltd*,[48] two plaintiffs were injured ziplining in British Columbia and sued the zipline operator. The latter's website included a list of policies, including a requirement that guests sign a liability waiver. The plaintiffs made reservations via credit card, and later claimed that this was the point at which a contract was formed. In their view the waiver they signed upon reaching the mountain came too late to be part of the contract. The BC Court of Appeal concluded, however, that the waiver was a pre-condition for the ziplining activity. Signing the waiver was the "consideration" for continuing with the activity, creating a self-standing contract between the plaintiffs and the operator.

The supplemental Ironman release described above probably falls into the same category: unless Craig signs the supplemental waiver, he doesn't get to line up on the beach at race day. This is made even clearer by the lengthy Ironman online waiver that Craig is supposed to read (and must acknowledge) when he registers. It specifies, among its many other things, that participants understand and agree "my final acceptance and participation in the Event is contingent upon WEC's receipt and review of all required information and forms, including this Agreement." Arguably, this would reach the supplemental waiver signed at the time of the race kit pickup.

Sometimes Nicole crosses out portions of liability waivers, and she initials the changes, usually where they purport to exclude liability for all types of negligence. She operates on the theory that she is countering the "offer" made by the event organizer — if she then participates in the event, she can argue either that the organizer accepted her counter-offer or that there was no true meeting of the minds on the nature of her involvement, and the waiver is not part of a binding contract. Electronic registrations make this sort of modification impossible. But where paper waivers are still used, attentive event organizers will check to see if language has been crossed out prior to permitting the person to participate.

As a final point on the validity of waivers, sometimes contracts are invalidated by courts as unconscionable and against public policy because of the nature of the power imbalance between contracting parties. This concept is of marginal importance in waivers for recreational events. In *Loychuk*, the BC court held "there is no power-imbalance where a person wishes to engage in an inherently risky recreational activity that is controlled or operated by another. Equally important, . . . it is not unfair for the operator to require a release or waiver as a condition of participating."[49]

However, one area in which courts may invalidate a waiver is with minors. Craig regularly signs waivers when he registers his child for her sporting activities. Where these waivers purport to promise that the child and her representatives refuse to sue, they may be unenforceable. At least this is widely assumed in legal circles,[50] although the matter appears not to be entirely settled.[51] In British Columbia at least, the *Infants Act* bars parents or guardians from unilaterally binding a minor to a waiver that denies a right to sue in tort.[52]

One solution to the problem of binding minors is to have parents sign waivers in which they agree to indemnify clubs or event organizers for any judgments obtained by the child. This shifts the loss back to the parents of suing children, obviously deterring such lawsuits. It is not certain, however, that such indemnity agreements are themselves valid, exactly because of these pernicious consequences.[53]

Bottom line: liability waivers are important for cycling clubs. But preparing proper waivers can be a complicated, lawyerly task. Provincial cycling associations may help local clubs with these matters. For instance, the Ontario Cycling Association posts both youth and adult waivers that affiliated clubs are instructed to use before letting anyone participate in club activities.[54] In fact, it is interesting to note that, in keeping with comments above, the youth waiver specifies that the parent or guardian "indemnify and hold harmless the Organization from any and all damages or losses of any kind" stemming from the child's participation in club activities. The OCA also warns "Failure to obtain waivers from all members of the club will place the clubs insurance coverage at risk."[55] We will further discuss insurance issues at the end of this chapter.

coaches and coaching

Some bicycle clubs and teams have coaches. These coaches have legal duties, as do the organizations that hire them.

safe coaches

Craig coaches children for his local cross-country ski club. In order to coach, he needed to supply a police records check, and he was strongly encouraged to complete coaching courses.

Requiring coaches to take coaching courses is an obvious way to exercise due diligence for any club concerned about legal exposure. It is both common sense and legally advisable not to let loose unqualified people on vulnerable populations, especially children.

Police records checks are now commonplace for all organizations whose volunteers or employees may work with children or other vulnerable groups. Again, this is a precaution tied both to common sense and negligence law: those who are coached are at foreseeable risk of harm from coaches, especially because of the relationship of trust typically associated with coaches and those under their supervision. An organization that retains coaches must act reasonably to avoid this harm: it must "take reasonable steps to screen employees and volunteers."[56] In British Columbia, this screening may be mandatory, depending on the activities of the bike club. Here, employers must ensure that every employee working with children or vulnerable adults undergoes a criminal record check or verification.[57] "Employer" in this context generally means a government body or agency, but also extends to anyone else who receives operating funds from the government. Likewise, non-profit organizations can voluntarily register under the Act, after which they have an obligation to police screen their volunteers working with children or vulnerable adults.[58] In other provinces where the legal obligation to screen may be less stringent, it is still a good idea, for the reasons noted.

Exactly when and what sort of screening organizations should do is a question a general book like this cannot address, but is a matter on which expert advice should be sought.[59]

safe coaching

When someone does coach, they have both ethical and legal responsibilities. Here, we discuss some of the legal obligations of coaching staff.

Civil Liability Issues

In negligence law, coaches have important duties of care to those they coach. As already noted, coaches may be liable where they fail unreasonably to ensure safe premises. Moreover, coaches have a duty to ensure that equipment is reasonably safe and suitable to its intended purpose and that the activity is safely organized.[60] The coach is "under a duty to exercise reasonable care in the control and supervision of activities, anticipate and warn against dangers and prevent participants from embarking on unreasonably dangerous activities."[61] These duties of care flow naturally from the foreseeable risk a coach's conduct poses to an athlete's health.

The standard of care question can be more complex. As a BC court put it in *Hamstra v BC Rugby Union*, the standard requires coaches to act in "accordance with the ordinary skill and care of a selector/coach in the circumstances in which he found himself."[62] As this passage suggests, the application of the standard may hinge in practice on "the setting, the nature of the activity, age of the participants, their skill level, and other factors."[63] Also relevant is whether a coach meets the standards of the sport. In *Hamstra*, the court concluded that so long as the coach "acted in accordance with the Laws of the Game as promulgated by the [sporting federation], and the instructions, notes and guidelines accompanying those Laws, he has met that test and cannot be found negligent." In *Lam v University of Windsor*, the court found that a judo instructor acted negligently in leaving a class and allowing participants to continue to spar. Such conduct was negligent in the face of "overwhelming preponderance of evidence from those with many, many years of experience in the sport of judo was that it was inappropriate for this class to have been left on its own to practice."[64]

The expertise of the coach may also be critical. In *Hamstra*, the court was prepared to relax the standard of care for a volunteer coach, even one who had significant expertise.[65] This is, however, far from a universal view. Other courts have rejected the idea that non-profit clubs or volunteers benefit from a lower standard of care, at least on the facts before them.[66] Indeed, courts have often required a heightened standard of care from coaches, certainly in the school context. In one Ontario case, the court concluded that coaches in a school board program had to meet the standard of a careful and prudent parent, adjusted upwards to reflect that coaches may have expertise above and beyond that of parents.[67] The leading British Columbia case also imposed the standard of care of a reasonable and careful parent, modified by the "supraparental expertise" of the teacher coach, but also taking into account the larger-than-family size of a physical education class.[68] The court also referenced considerations coaches should contemplate in deciding whether to let a child participate in a sport. A coach should ask "(a) if it is suitable to his age and condition (mental and physical); (b) if he is progressively trained and coached to do it properly and avoid the danger; (c) if the equipment is adequate and suitably arranged; and (d) if the performance, having regard to its inherently dangerous nature, is properly supervised."[69] In that case, the injured child had not attended prior sessions and had not developed the progressive building blocks. The coach who allowed the child to play therefore breached her standard of care.

Putting all these guiding principles into operation can be complicated for a coach. But lists of precautionary steps exist. For instance, the Sport and Law Strategy Group recommends coaches adopt a "personal risk management plan" with the following ten elements:

"1. Be familiar with and adhere to applicable standards, both written and unwritten, as well as internal policies and rules governing the facility, the sport and your program.

2. Monitor your participants fitness and skill levels and teach new skills in a progressive fashion suitable to the age and skills of your participants. Never leave participants unsupervised!

3. If you do not have access to medical personnel or a qualified trainer, keep adequate first aid supplies on hand: ideally, you should be trained in administering first aid.

4. Develop an Emergency Action Plan for the facility or site where you regularly practice or compete. Carry with you at all times emergency contact numbers and participants personal and medical information.

5. Inspect facilities and equipment before every practice and game and take steps to ensure deficiencies are corrected immediately. If they cannot be corrected immediately, adjust your activities accordingly to avoid the risk.

6. Work with your employer or sport organization to use appropriately worded assumption of risk agreements in your programs, and where appropriate in settings involving adult participants, waiver of liability agreements.

7. You should be covered by the liability insurance policy of your employer (if you are a paid coach) or your organization (if you are a volunteer coach). Confirm that this is the case. If it is not, obtain your own insurance.

8. Do not be afraid to stop or withdraw from any activity that poses unreasonable risks, including stopping a practice or removing your team or your athletes from a competition.

9. Trust your common sense and intuition!

10. Lastly, actively pursue your own training, professional development and coaching certification."[70]

The British Columbia law firm Dolden Wallice Folick LLP proposes its own list:

"1. provide competent and informed instruction in how to perform the activity;

2. assign drills and exercises that are suitable to the age, ability, fitness level or stage of advancement of the group;

3. progressively train and prepare the participants for the activity according to an acceptable standard of practice;

4. clearly explain to participants the risks involved in the activity;

5. group participants according to size, weight, skill or fitness to avoid potentially dangerous mismatching;

6. inquire about illness or injury and prohibit participation where necessary;

7. in the event of a medical emergency, provide suitable first aid; and

8. where possible, keep written records of attendance, screening, training and teaching methods in order to provide evidence of efficient control."[71]

Following the items on both of these lists is a sensible strategy for coaches. And clubs that retain coaches should take all reasonable efforts to have coaches follow this sensible strategy. Clubs who employ coaches may be vicariously liable — that is, liability may flow up automatically to the club — if their coaches are negligent.[72] In other instances, a club that fails to supervise adequately activities that take place on its premises may be liable under occupier liability rules.[73]

Treatment of Athletes by Coaches and Clubs

Clubs and coaches need also to be aware of rules that affect their interpersonal interactions with athletes.

Harassment and Discrimination

Harassment and discrimination in sport is an unfortunate practice that has drawn the attention of sports authorities for decades now.[74] Harassment and discrimination are certainly ethics issues. Harassment can also be a violation of human rights law, although the latter generally focus on employment relationships. That said, as mentioned above, human rights law is certainly engaged where there is discrimination on the basis of a protected ground (such as sex, colour, race, etc.) in denying persons a service otherwise available to the public.[75]

Some cases suggest the emergence of a tort of harassment, in which a defendant's extreme conduct creates extreme emotional distress in the plaintiff.[76] There is definitely a tort of intentional infliction of mental suffering, where there is "(i) flagrant or outrageous conduct; (ii) calculated to produce harm; and (iii) resulting in a visible and provable illness."[77]

Finally, extreme forms of harassment are criminal matters. Unwanted touching can be assault.[78] More generally, it is criminal harassment to knowingly or recklessly harass another person by following, communicating with, watching, or engaging in threatening conduct towards them, causing them to have reasonable fear for their safety or that of persons known to them.[79] The *Criminal Code* also includes sex crimes, including sexual exploitation by a person of trust or authority towards a young person.[80]

Again, clubs should take reasonable steps both to ensure their coaches understand their responsibilities, and to protect against abuse. The club itself may be negligent if it does not.

Procedural Fairness

Athletes may also be entitled to "procedural fairness," a form of due process in decision making that generally requires that a person affected by a decision is entitled to be heard by an impartial decision maker. While procedural fairness (also called "natural justice") is usually a concept applicable to public bodies, some courts have extended it to decision making by private sports bodies, at least where those body's rules are silent on whether due process standards apply or not. For instance, in *Farren v Pacific Coast Amateur Hockey Association*, a BC court held that a hockey association had to apply procedural fairness in a decision regarding the registration of the applicant's children. Summarizing the applicable standards, the court concluded:

failure to abide by the rules of natural justice can lead (and has led) to intervention by the court in the affairs of voluntary organizations or domestic tribunals. However, if the organization's bylaws expressly authorize/require the breach of natural justice, there appears to be no basis for intervention . . . . Which procedural safeguards are required is determined by the nature of the organization and the seriousness of the decision. A suspension from a minor hockey association, which is somewhat similar to the facts at hand, requires at least (1) that the decision-makers act in good faith and with an open mind, (2) that the affected person have notice of the hearing, and (3) that the affected person be given a right to respond . . . . Whether procedural deficiencies amount to a denial of natural justice can be assessed by asking if, "although imperfect, the process was fundamentally fair?" In the event that it was not fundamentally fair, the Court can still decline to order a remedy if it is convinced the remedy would be ineffectual. But the decision-makers would be obliged to approach a new hearing in good faith and with open minds.[81]

insurance law 101 for bike clubs

As should be clear to anyone who has reached this point in the chapter, running a bike club and its activities can be a complicated affair. Issues like director liability, occupier liability, negligence, police checks, coaching training, and coaching obligations, increase the complexity of operating a club and create much legal risk.

In life, where there is risk, there is often insurance. As one expert body notes liability "waivers do not guarantee the protection that providers seek and prudent providers likely continue to carry liability insurance."[82] In other words, it is very advisable for any bike club to consider its insurance needs, and indeed the national and provincial cycling associations often fill an important niche in that respect. Cycling Canada organizes a general liability insurance policy in which all provincial cycling associations outside of Quebec participate, while the Fédération québécoise des sports cyclistes participates in a different insurance package.

As of 2014, the Cycling Canada policy covers key liability exposure for "[a]ll employees, volunteers, officers, directors, coaches, managers, instructors, officials, affiliated clubs, and or teams, members. Also municipalities, government departments, sponsors and organizers but only as it relates to their involvement in a sanctioned event."[83] This insurance program is a benefit for clubs affiliating with provincial cycling associations. For instance, the Alberta Bicycle Association includes the following as a benefit of membership: "All members in good standing of the Alberta Bicycle Association (ABA) with coverage under any federal or provincial hospital or medical plan are covered under this insurance policy. This policy covers all members who are either directly on their way to or from, or are at, an event sponsored by the ABA or ABA affiliated club."[84]

As suggested in Part B above, director and officer liability insurance may also be advisable. Bodies like the Ontario Cycling Association make it possible for bicycle clubs to purchase director and officer liability insurance, protecting these people from circumstances in which they are directly liable for their conduct.

conclusion

Most people who have completed this chapter may decide not to form a club, or if they are members of club, not to become a director. And if they are participating in a club activity, they may choose to never read waivers put in front of them. Such reactions are, of course, cynical responses to how our sometimes overly complex law apportions responsibility for risk. Truth be told, we were unable to find many cases in Canada (or at least cases that went to trial) involving bicycling clubs or activities. Indeed, we found relatively few cases involving recreational activities, and most of these involved thrill activities or contact sports.

In the final analysis, this chapter is not intended to deter. Rather, it provides pointers on which dots should be connected, so that bike club organizers and coaches have time to get out and ride their bikes, rather than sitting in stuffy rooms with court reporters typing depositions.

endnotes

1   Resources discussing the advantages and disadvantages of incorporation include: Government of Ontario, *Not-for-Profit Incorporator's Handbook*, online: www.attorneygeneral.jus.gov.on.ca/english/family/pgt/nfpinc/Default.asp [Ontario Handbook].

2   Saskatchewan, *The Non-profit Corporations Act*, 1995, SS 1995, c N-4.2.

3   RSBC 1996, c 433.

4   RSA 2000, c S-14.

5   *Canada Not-for-Profit Corporations Act*, SC 2009, c 23.

6   *Not-for-Profit Corporations Act, 2010*, SO 2010, c 15, s 48 [*Ont NPCA*] (not yet in force at time of this writing).

7   *Income Tax Act*, RSC 1985, c 1 (5th Supp), s 248(1) ("registered Canadian amateur athletic association"). See also ss 110.1(1)(a)(ii), 118.1(1)(b), and 149(1)(l).

8   See *AYSA Amateur Youth Soccer Association v Canada (Revenue Agency)*, 2007 SCC 42 at para 26.

9   See discussion in *ibid* at para 42.

10 (1986), 11 CPR (3d) 335 (Companies Branch, Ministry of Consumer and Commercial Relations, Ontario).

11 Ontario Handbook, above note 1.

12 *Societies Regulation*, Alta Reg 122/2000, s 7.

13 Ontario Handbook, above note 1.

14 See, online: www.nuans.com/nuansinfo_en/home-accueil_en.cgi.

15 See, online: www.registreenrreprises.gouv.qc.ca/en/services_ligne/demande-de-services/S00436.aspx?source=menu-droite.

16 See Ottawa Bicycle Club Constitution (2011), online: www.ottawabicycleclub.ca/constitution.

17 See Industry Canada, *Next Step Following Incorporation*, online: www.ic.gc.ca/eic/site/cd-dgc.nsf/eng/cs04993.html.

18 See, e.g., *Ont NPCA*, s 48 (not yet in force at time of this writing).

19 Wascana Freewheelers Bicycle Touring Club Inc Bylaws (16 January 2005), online: wascanafreewheelers.ca/wp-content/uploads/2013/04/Bylaws.pdf.

20 See, e.g., Industry Canada, *Primer for Directors of Not-for-Profit Corporations* (2002), online: www.ic.gc.ca/eic/site/cilp-pdci.nsf/eng/h_cl00688.html.

21 SC 2000, c 5.

22 *Ibid*, s 2.

23 Office of the Privacy Commissioner of Canada, *Fact Sheets: The Application of the Personal Information Protection and Electronic Documents Act to Charitable and Non-Profit Organizations*, online: www.priv.gc.ca/fs-fi/02_05_d_19_e.cfm.

24 *Ibid*.

25 *Personal Information Protection Act*, SBC 2003, c 63, s 1 (definition of "organization") [BC PIPA].

26 Office of the Privacy Commissioner of Canada, *An Overview of the Personal Information Protection and Electronic Documents Act for Businesses and Organizations*, online: www.priv.gc.ca/resource/tool-outil/ekit/pp_01_01_e.asp.

27 BC PIPA, s 1 (definition of "personal information").

28 *Blondeau (Litigation guardian of) v Peterborough*, [1998] OJ No 3428 at para 63 (Gen Div).

29 2011 NSSC 485.

30 *Ibid* at para 60.

31 Dolden Wallace Folock LLP, *A Guide for Amateur Sports Organizers and their Insurers* (2012) at 4–5, online: www.dolden.com/content/files/1348766055151-sport-liability-law-september-2012.pdf.

32 *Ibid* at 6.

33 See, online: www.ontariocycling.org/clubsteams/general-and-oca-club-forms/.

34 2006 BCSC 942.

35 *Ibid* at para 71.

36 2007 BCSC 1763.

37 489 F Supp 2d 1283 (D Utah 2007), aff'd 575 F3d 1120 (10th Cir 2009).

38 See, e.g., *Fisher v West Colchester Recreation Assn*, 2010 NSSC 358.

39 See, e.g., Manitoba Law Reform Commission, *Waivers of Liability for Sporting and Recreational Injuries* (2009), online: www.manitobalawreform.ca/pubs/pdf/120-full_report.pdf.

40 Philip Osborne, *The Law of Torts*, 4th ed (Toronto: Irwin Law, 2011) at 112 *et seq.*

41 *Ibid* at 115.

42 [1988] 1 SCR 1186.

43 Manitoba Law Reform Commission, above note 39 at 8.

44 *Ibid* at 11.

45 *Ibid* at 8.

46 *Ibid*.

47 See, e.g., *Mayer v Big White Ski Resort*, 1998 CanLII 5114 at para 15 (BCCA).

48 2012 BCCA 122.

49 *Ibid* at para 33.

50 Manitoba Law Reform Commission, above note 39 at 14.

51 See discussion in *Wong (Litigation guardian of) v Lok's Martial Arts Centre Inc*, 2009 BCSC 1385 (raising doubts about the unenforceability of parent-signed waivers against children at common law).

52 *Ibid*.

53 *Stevens v Howitt*, [1969] 1 OR 761 (HCJ); Manitoba Law Reform Commission, above note 39 at 14; Law Reform Commission of British Columbia, *Report on Recreational Injuries: Liability and Waivers in Commercial Leisure Activities* (October 1994) at 52, online: www.bcli.org/sites/default/files/LRC140-Recreational_Injuries.pdf.

54 Ontario Cycling Association, General and OCA Club Forms, online: www.ontariocycling.org/clubsteams/general-and-oca-club-forms/.

55 Ontario Cycling Association, 2014 Club Affiliation Package, online: www.ontariocycling.org/clubsteams/general-and-oca-club-forms/.

56 Volunteer Canada, *Provincial Laws and Screening* (2003) at 3, online: www.sportlaw.ca/2003/04/provincial-laws-and-screening/. See also Hilary Findlay, "The Most Recent Buzz about Police Records Checks" (10 December 2010), online: Sport Law & Strategy Group www.sportlaw.ca/2010/12/the-most-recent-buzz-about-police-records-checks/.

57 *Criminal Records Review Act*, RSBC 1996, c 86, s 7.

58 *Ibid*, s 24.1.

59 Some more detailed guidance may be found in Findlay, above note 56.

60 Dolden Wallace Folock LLP, above note 31 at 15.

61 *Ibid*.

62 *Hamstra (Guardian ad litem of) v British Columbia Rugby Union*, [1989] BCJ No 1521, rev'd on other grounds [1995] BCJ No 633 (CA) which was in turn rev'd on those other grounds, [1997] 1 SCR 1092.

63 "Coaches Duty of Care Revisited," Sports Law & Strategy Group (3 January 2010), online: www.sportlaw.ca/2010/01/coaches-duty-of-care-revisited/.

64 *Lam v University of Windsor*, [2001] OJ No 865 at para 38 (SCJ) [*Lam*].

65   *Hamstra*, above note 62.

66   See, e.g., *Oppedisano v Agustinoat*, [1997] OJ No 790 at para 19 (Gen Div); *Blondeau (Litigation guardian of) v Peterborough*, [1998] OJ No 3428 at para 63 (Gen Div).

67   *Thomas v Hamilton Board of Education*, [1994] OJ No 2444 at para 24 *et seq* (CA).

68   *Hussack v Chilliwack School District No 33*, 2011 BCCA 258 at para 35.

69   *Ibid.*

70   Centre for Sport and Law, *Information Package on Legal Issues for Coaches* (2003) at 4–5, online: www.sportlaw.ca/wp-content/uploads/2011/03/a-General-Information-Package-on-Legal-Issues-for-Coaches.pdf.

71   Dolden Wallace Folock LLP, above note 31 at 17.

72   See, e.g., *Dunn v University of Ottawa*, [1995] OJ No 2856 at para 19 (Gen Div).

73   *Lam*, above note 64.

74   See, e.g., various resources form the Sport Law & Strategy Group, such as Rachel Corbett, "Harassment: Some Definitions and Guidelines for Coaches and Athletes" (10 April 2009), online: Sport Law & Strategy Group www.sportlaw.ca/2009/04/harassment-some-definitions-and-guidelines-for-coaches-and-athletes/.

75   See, e.g., British Columbia, *Human Rights Code*, RSBC 1996, c 210; Ontario, *Human Rights Code*, RSO 1990, c H.19, s 1.

76   See, e.g., *Savino v Shelestowsky*, 2013 ONSC 4394 at para 15.

77   *Ibid* at para 21.

78   *Criminal Code*, RSC 1985, c C-46, s 265.

79   *Ibid*, s 264.

80   *Ibid*, s 153.

81   *Farren v Pacific Coast Amateur Hockey Assn*, 2013 BCSC 498 at para 25 *et seq*. For another example of a court applying procedural fairness principles to a sporting organization, see *Rankin v Alberta Curling Federation Appeals Committee*, 2005 ABQB 938.

82   Manitoba Law Reform Commission, above note 39 at 20.

83   Cycling Canada, 2014 Insurance Program Summary, online: www.cyclinginsurance.ca/forms/2014%20CC%20Insurance%20Summary.pdf.

84   Alberta Bicycle Association, Membership Benefits, online: www.albertabicycle.ab.ca/membership-benefits.

Chapter 7

Racing Your Bicycle

introduction

In the 1890s, a cycling craze swept the world with the advent of the 'safety bicycle.' This was a new device characterized by a steerable front wheel, a chain, a sprocket drive, and two equally sized wheels — innovative features that remain the foundation of bicycle design to this day. Because the safety bicycle was faster, and more stable and comfortable than existing cycles, cycling took off in popularity all around the world. In Canada, bicycles began to be widely used for leisure, work, exercise, and athletic competition.

In 1894, at the height of the cycling boom, a bicycle race took place in Toronto. Five clubs entered the event to compete for the honour of winning the 'Challenge Cup.' The course consisted of several loops around the Woodbine racetrack and down several roads: in all, a distance of just over 32 km. The result of the race was to be decided according to the points scored by each competing club. After the race, two clubs disputed the outcome, arguing over whether a cyclist from the Athanaeum Bicycle Club had properly rounded the barrel at a turn. Before the race organizers made any decision, the Royal Canadian Bicycle Club made an application to the Ontario High Court of Justice for an injunction to restrain the trustees of the Challenge Cup from handing the award over to the Athanaeum Bicycle Club.[1] The court rejected the application, deciding that the Challenge Cup trustees were first required to determine for themselves who had officially won the bicycle race before the courts could adjudicate a request for an injunction.

The case may be the earliest reported Canadian court decision involving competitive cycling. The facts are remarkably revealing of some of the basic

this chapter's takeaways

» Bicycle racing is a privatized activity, but one that is strongly affected by federal, provincial, and municipal laws.

» International, federal, and provincial cycling associations have manifold rules that determine who can race and how races are run, and these tend to operate through a complex set of legal contracts entered into by associations and international organizations, between federal and provincial associations, between associations and bicycle clubs and race organizers, and between associations and athletes.

» Athletes' behaviour is subject not only to these rules, but also special standards on performance enhancing drugs and the more general laws of the land such as tort and criminal law.

» Disputes stemming from bicycle races are generally resolved through alternative dispute resolution — especially arbitration — and not often the courts.

features that continue to characterize the legal and regulatory environment of competitive sports in Canada.

First, the rules governing participation in sports are generally established by private sport-governing bodies, like the trustees of the Challenge Cup in the example above, rather than by statute or the common law.

Second, it is also true that the activities of private sports associations are ultimately subject to judicial oversight; the Royal Canadian Bicycle Club sought such a judicial remedy, in the form of an injunction, in 1894. Indeed, courts can review the decisions of private sporting bodies, for instance when an association has exceeded its powers or contravened principles of natural justice.

Finally, while it was not yet the case in 1894, governments eventually took an interest in regulating some aspects of amateur and professional sports. Federal, provincial, and territorial statutes, as well as municipal bylaws, now prescribe additional rules for the conduct of competitive sporting activities, including for the sport of cycling.

It is thus the case that competitive cycling in Canada is governed by a body of regulations that straddle private and public law. A network of private, self-regulating international and national associations set most of the rules. They oversee participation in cycling as a sport, and set administrative and disciplinary rules, as well as rules of play. While the regulations adopted by private cycling associations make up the bulk of the rules governing the sport, Canadian statutory law and judicial authorities are also involved in regulating some aspects of the sport of cycling.

This chapter will provide an overview of the private as well as the state-created regulations that govern the sport of cycling in Canada. We will start by describing the domain of autonomous self-regulation of cycling by national and international sport associations. We will then outline some of the ways Canada's laws and judicial system have an impact on competitive cyclists and their sport.

sport and cycling governing bodies

To understand the complex labyrinth of regulations that governs organized cycling, it is essential to first describe the organizations involved in setting the rules, and the source and boundaries of their authority over the sport.

Organized cycling in Canada, along with many other sports, is governed by non-profit agencies at the international, national, provincial/territorial, and local levels. For the most part, cycling governing bodies are private and self-regulating. They are generally not created by statute, but are incorporated as not-for-profit organizations under national, provincial, or territorial laws. We discuss incorporation in Chapter 6.

At the top of the field are international organizations and federations, which have developed a regulatory monopoly over cycling. At the national level, the Canadian-organized cycling system is made up of a number of associations that develop and administer services and programs of competition, and provide regulatory oversight of the sport across the country and in each province and territory.

international organizations

There are a number of international non-governmental organizations that regulate different aspects of organized cycling.

International Cycling Union (UCI)

Founded in 1900, the International Cycling Union (generally referred to by its French-language acronym UCI) is the international governing body for all cycling sports. Headquartered in Switzerland, the UCI is registered as a not-for-profit and non-governmental organization under Swiss law. Its members are the national cycling federations in each Member State who are required to comply with the constitution and regulations of the UCI.

The UCI's main mandate is "to direct, develop, regulate, control and discipline cycling under all forms worldwide."[2] The UCI is therefore responsible for establishing the rules of the sport at a global level in eight cycling disciplines: road, track, mountain bike, BMX, para-cycling, cyclocross, trials, and indoor cycling.

The most important activities of the UCI include organizing the UCI World Championships and World Cup events, and planning, in collaboration with the International Olympic Committee and the International Paralympic Committee, the cycling events at the Olympic and Paralympic Games. The UCI also sets the international racing calendar, manages cycling referees (known as 'commissaires'), sets technical rules for the use of equipment, and adopts anti-doping regulations. The regulations that govern national cycling federations, athletes, coaches, commissaires, teams, and bicycle manufacturers are found in the UCI Constitution[3] and in a number of general and discipline-specific regulations.[4]

World Anti-Doping Agency (WADA)

The World Anti-Doping Agency was established in 1999 and is headquartered in Montreal. It is an independent foundation charged with coordinating the fight against doping in sport at the international level. Its main mandate is to harmonize anti-doping regulations across all sports and countries. It achieves this goal by implementing uniform anti-doping rules and maintaining a list of prohibited substances and methods. In effecting anti-doping measures, the WADA works with intergovernmental organizations, governments, public authorities, and other public and private sports bodies such as the UCI.

Cycling Anti-Doping Foundation (CADF)

The UCI created the Cycling Anti-Doping Foundation in 2008 to manage its anti-doping program. The UCI sets the CADF's priorities through a contract of services, but the CADF is a separate entity under Swiss law. In fact, as of September 2013, the Foundation operates independently from the cycling governing body, as the Board of Directors no longer includes any members of the UCI senior management.

The CADF is responsible for conducting doping controls, creating testing pools, managing sample collections, and implementing anti-doping educational programs. It also is responsible for the Athletes' Biological

Passport Program, an anti-doping practice that monitors selected biological variables of individual athletes over time, rather than attempting to directly detect the doping substance or method itself.[5]

Court of Arbitration for Sport (CAS)

The Court of Arbitration for Sport settles sports-related legal disputes through arbitration or mediation. It is based in Lausanne, Switzerland, and has two permanent branches in Sydney, Australia, and New York, United States. The CAS operates independently of sports organizations or governments. Athletes, sports associations, or commercial entities may bring a case before the CAS, but the parties must agree to do so in writing. The majority of international sporting federations, including the UCI, have included in their statutes an arbitration clause referring disputes to the CAS.[6]

national organizations

In Canada, cycling is regulated by both multi sports organizations and sport specific associations.

Multi Sports Organizations

Multi-sport organizations are generally responsible for setting sport policy, providing support programs and services, or organizing various aspects of international and national multi sports games. They are not typically responsible for the governance of specific sports like cycling, but their activities often have a direct or indirect impact on numerous aspects of organized sports in Canada.

Sport Canada

Sport Canada is a branch of the federal government's Department of Canadian Heritage. It is responsible for developing Canada's sport policy. Sport Canada also provides financial assistance to national sport organizations, including Cycling Canada, and to major multi-sport games like the Canada Games. It further assists high performance athletes by working with national sporting organizations to develop the criteria for financial assistance and to identify qualified athletes. For instance, the Sport Canada Athlete Assistance Program — also known as the carding system — provides direct funding to cyclists who have achieved international results to help with living, training, and tuition costs. For instance, in 2014, seventy-two track, road, mountain bike, and BMX cyclists and para-cyclists received financial support from the Sport Canada Athlete Assistance Program.[7]

Sport Canada does not have the authority to regulate directly a national sporting body or a particular sport. It is through funding agreements that Sport Canada persuades national sporting bodies to implement government policies. Recipient organizations and athletes are required to sign contribution agreements which outline their contractual obligations, including mandatory obligations regarding anti-doping programs, dispute resolution mechanisms, and official languages services.

Canadian Olympic Committee (COC)

The Olympic Games have featured cycling since the birth of the modern Olympic movement. The Summer Olympic Games have included men's events since 1896, while women's cycling entered the Olympic program at the 1984 Summer Olympics.

The Canadian Olympic Committee is a national, private, not-for-profit organization responsible for all aspects of Canada's involvement in the Olympic summer and winter games. As such, it is bound by the *Olympic Charter*[8] and decisions of the International Olympic Committee (IOC). The COC is responsible for the selection of the cycling teams that represent Canada at three major multi-sport games: the Olympic, Youth Olympic, and Pan American Games.

In actuality, the COC works with the national cycling federation to select the athletes who will participate in these three international sporting events. The COC also provides financial support and rewards high performance athletes, including cyclists, through its Athlete Excellence Fund. Finally, part of the COC's role is to take action against the use of performance-enhancing substances and methods.[9]

Canadian Paralympic Committee (CPC)

The Canadian Paralympic Committee promotes the Paralympic movement in Canada, a sporting movement dedicated to athletes with a physical or sensory handicap. Para-cycling was first introduced as a Paralympic sport in Seoul in 1988: blind and partially sighted athletes competed with sighted athletes using tandem bicycles. Today, para-cycling also includes events for athletes with cerebral palsy, amputations and other physical impairments. Athletes race on bicycles, tricycles, tandem, or hand cycles, based on their impairment.

Para-cycling is now fully integrated into the governance structures of the UCI and Canada's national cycling federation. Para-cycling has, therefore, become a separate discipline within cycling organizations, enjoying the same services as other cycling disciplines. For its part, the CPC is responsible for sending Canada's team to the Paralympic Games and provides services and programs to Paralympic team members.

Commonwealth Games Association of Canada (CGC)

The Commonwealth Games is a multi-sport event where athletes represent countries that are members of the Commonwealth. This latter is an intergovernmental organization of fifty-three independent member states that are, for the most part, former colonies or protectorates of the British colonial empire. In Canada, the Commonwealth Games are promoted by Commonwealth Games Canada, a not-for-profit organization led by a volunteer Board.

The program of events at the Commonwealth Games is comparable to the Summer Olympics and it has included the sport of cycling for men since 1934. Women's events were added in 1990, while para-cycling track events were part of the program in 2014. The CGC funds athletes, including cyclists, to represent Canada at the Commonwealth Games.

Canada Games Council

The Canada Games Council is the governing body for the country's foremost multi-sport sporting event. It is responsible for selecting the host communities for both winter and summer games, and for providing technical and organizational support. The Canada Council works with national and provincial sport organizations in planning the competitive programming of the games. The summer games, held every four years, generally include several cycling disciplines. In fact, the national athletic gathering is often the first opportunity for promising young Canadian cyclists to compete at a multi-sport event.

Canadian Centre for Ethics in Sport (CCES)

The Canadian Centre for Ethics in Sport is a private, not-for-profit organization that is responsible for implementing the rules that govern doping controls in Canada. In addition to its efforts to deter the use of banned substances, the CCES offers ethics education and doping control services to event organizers, sport organizations, and clubs. The CCES operates independently from sport organizations and governments.

Sport Dispute Resolution Centre of Canada

Contrary to the majority of sport organizations, the Sport Dispute Resolution Centre of Canada was established by a federal statute, namely the 2003 *Physical Activity and Sport Act.*[10] It is not, however, a government agency or Crown corporation; it is an independent not-for-profit corporation. According to the Act, one of the mandates of the Centre is to provide to the sport community "a national alternative dispute resolution service for sport disputes."[11] The Centre has also been given jurisdiction by the Canadian Centre for Ethics in Sport to rule on doping-related disputes under the Canadian Anti-Doping Program in Sport.[12]

Cycling Organizations

In addition to multi-sport-governing bodies, there are a number of associations that are exclusively devoted to promoting the sport of cycling in Canada.

Cycling Canada Cyclisme (Cycling Canada)

Cycling Canada Cyclisme is cycling's national sport organization. It is one of Canada's oldest sport-governing bodies, having been founded in 1882 as the Canadian Wheelmen's Association.[13] In 1968, it was officially incorporated under the name 'Canadian Cycling Association,' but today it actually does business under the brand name of 'Cycling Canada Cyclisme.'[14]

Cycling Canada is incorporated as a not-for-profit organization under federal law[15] and serves as an umbrella organization for provincial and territorial cycling associations. Cycling Canada is directly affiliated with the UCI as Canada's national cycling federation. As such, the association is required to comply with the constitution and regulations of the UCI in regulating and promoting the sport of cycling in Canada.

Cycling Canada's main mandate is to promote cycling in six disciplines: road, track, mountain bike, BMX, para-cycling, and cyclocross. It establishes the rules and regulations that govern cycling events at the national level, and organizes national competitions. It also manages national teams and provides coaching for cyclists under its jurisdiction.

Cycling Canada's responsibilities include submitting to the Canadian Olympic Committee the names of athletes it proposes for inclusion on Canada's Olympic team. It also selects cyclists for the Commonwealth Games, the Pan Am Games, and the Jeux de la Francophonie, an international event that included cycling for the first time in 2013. It also recommends a list of athletes to Sports Canada for funding under the Sport Canada Athlete Assistance Program. Since the association is responsible for most aspects of national and international cycling programs in Canada, it is eligible to receive federal government sport funding.

Provincial and Territorial Cycling Associations

Because Canada is a federation, there are sport-governing bodies not only at the federal level, but also at the provincial and territorial levels. Provincial and territorial sport associations are not-for-profit organizations responsible for the overall development of their sport, from grassroots to high performance, within their jurisdiction. They may receive government grants to assist with the operation, administration, and promotion of their sport in their province or territory.

There are eleven provincial and territorial associations affiliated with Cycling Canada.[16] They are the link between local clubs and the national cycling federation. They provide various resources for athletes and clubs, in addition to professional development opportunities for coaches and commissaires. They sanction competitions within the province or territory, usually in partnership with Cycling Canada. In some provinces, the sport bodies may administer provincial funding programs for athletes, especially for cyclists destined to represent the province or territory at the Canada Games. Finally, as discussed in Chapter 6, provincial and territorial cycling organizations adopt rules that are binding on their members. For instance, the Ontario Cycling Association requires that cyclists wear safety helmets at all times when participating in club and OCA activities.[17]

Local Cycling Clubs

As discussed in detail in Chapter 6, clubs that deal with the sport at the local level are frequently an athlete's first entry into cycling. For the most part, local cycling organizations are private, not-for-profit clubs that may be incorporated under provincial or territorial laws. Clubs are run by their members and offer different levels of programming and activities, ranging from recreational to high performance, and for novice to experienced riders. Cycling clubs may focus exclusively on recreational cycling activities, offer racing programs, or campaign for improved facilities for cyclists.

Cycling clubs are usually affiliated with their provincial or territorial sport-governing bodies. Once affiliated, they are required to adopt policies and by-laws that are consistent with the rules adopted by their provincial or territorial governing body. Membership status with a cycling club allows individuals to compete for a club, though it is also true that independent cyclists may be permitted to participate in races.

Trade Teams

In addition to (or instead of) being a member of a cycling club, a competitive cyclist may belong to a trade team. A trade team is a private organization, very often owned by a for-profit corporation, whose purpose is generally to promote itself through sport cycling events. A trade team is run by its corporate owners, in contrast to cycling clubs that are run by their members.

Cyclists who compete for a trade team are normally under a contractual agreement that provides them with some form of compensation, ranging from the provision of equipment, such as bicycles and clothing, to performance stipends or salaries. Trade teams are generally composed of elite athletes, both at the junior and senior levels, and must be affiliated with the UCI, Cycling Canada, or a provincial or territorial association.

private regulations

Most of the policies, rules, and regulations that govern organized cycling are established not by public authorities, but by the private associations we have just described. The main function of these private sport-governing bodies is to set the rules of play for cycling sports and to organize competitions in which participating cyclists are required to observe such rules. International and national associations also establish disciplinary proceedings to enforce the rules and to impose sanctions on athletes, coaches, and officials who infringe them. Accordingly, cycling governing bodies have created an extensive private regulatory framework to govern the sport of cycling. Each level and area of governance establishes its own rules and regulations; at the same time, each association is required to comply with the rules set by other governing bodies in the greater regulatory network.

There are benefits to the private regulation of sport. It ensures that the same rules are followed worldwide and applied uniformly on all member associations and their athletes. Other benefits of private self-regulation include reducing the regulatory and judicial burden of governments and entrusting decision-making powers in the hands of individuals with sport expertise. At the same time, because the model is one of private self-regulation, the binding nature of the rules, the enforcement mechanisms, and the avenues of redress are different that those associated with rules emanating from statutes or judicial authorities.

legal nature of the rules

As described above, the vast majority of sport organizations are privately constituted bodies that are autonomous and self-governing. They derive their power from their governing documents — constitution, letters patents, bylaws — which establish the legal basis for the organization to write rules and make decisions that affect its members. In addition, to oversee and administer a sport beyond the boundaries of their own organizations and members, sports governing bodies resort to contractual agreements.

Indeed, contract is the principal way sport and cycling associations exert regulatory control over the sport, their members, officials, coaches, and athletes. Sports contracts include membership agreements, funding arrangements, employment contracts, athlete contracts, team selection agreements, event management contracts, sponsorship agreements, and broadcasting deals. Contracts may certainly involve the transfer of money or goods, but in the sports world, they often set out the rights and obligations of athletes, coaches, referees, and officials; establish standards of behaviour or play; and outline and delimit the punitive jurisdiction exercised by disciplinary bodies.

It is also true that contractual agreements are what link sport and cycling governing bodies to each other. In the hierarchy of sport governance, a chain of contracts ensures that national levels comply with the regulations of their international counterparts, and provincial/territorial bodies and local groups incorporate the rules and policies of their national bodies. At the lowermost level of the cycling pyramid, membership contracts exist between cyclists and the local clubs or trade teams of which they are members. This network of legal agreements explains how a cyclist or coach may be subject to the disciplinary jurisdiction of a sporting body with which he or she is not in a direct contractual relationship.

Because sport regulations stem primarily from contractual agreements, private contract law governs the form, substance, and enforcement of those agreements. Contract law in all Canadian jurisdictions generally follows similar rules. A contract is defined as a legally binding agreement or promise between two or more parties. Individuals or organizations have a right to enter into whatever type of legally binding agreement they wish with few legal limitations, except those imposed by Canadian law. Failure to comply with the terms of a contract without a valid reason recognized by law is considered a breach of the contract. In that case, the aggrieved party may turn to the courts either to force the defaulting party to carry out its promise, or to demand compensation in the form of monetary payments, called damages.

As we will explain later in this chapter, sports organizations have tried to keep contractual disputes from reaching the courts by setting up alternative dispute resolution mechanisms, chiefly arbitration, which are less expensive and less formal forms of resolving conflicts.

We will now describe some of the rules that apply to competitive cycling.

participation rules

An important mandate of sport and cycling associations is to formulate and apply the rules that govern participation in cycling competitions.

Racing Licences

The right to take part in cycling competitions depends on the possession of a 'licence,' an official document issued by a recognized cycling body. According to the *UCI Cycling Regulations*, a licence "is an identity document confirming that its holder undertakes to respect the constitution and regulations and which authorize him to participate in cycling events."[18] The licence is thus proof that a cyclist has agreed to follow the regulations of the sport, to be subject to the relevant disciplinary and anti-doping measures, and to participate in cycling events in a sporting and fair manner.[19] A licence also identifies a cyclist as a member of a national cycling federation affiliated with the UCI, and most importantly, it confers a right to participate in races in the categories and disciplines listed on the licence. Essentially, a licence is a contractual agreement that delineates the rights of access of the holder to cycling competitions and his or her corresponding duties.

In Canada, licences are issued and sold by provincial and territorial cycling associations affiliated with Cycling Canada. They are mandatory to enter a cycling competition in the following disciplines: road, track, mountain bike, BMX, para-cycling and cyclocross. According to UCI regulations, a person who does not hold the requisite licence may not participate in a cycling event organized or supervised by the UCI, UCI member federations, or their affiliates.[20] Cyclists must present their licences at the check-in of every race. This allows race organizers to verify the identity of the cyclist. If a cyclist fails to produce their licence, they may be denied entry to the race.

Cyclists are not the only persons involved in the competitive aspects of cycling who must take out a licence. At sanctioned races, licences are required for persons occupying different roles at the event. For instance, race organizers, commissaires, coaches, medical staff, team managers, mechanics, pacers and vehicle drivers are all required to take out specific licences.[21]

The licensing process is important for another reason; it is the main way by which cycling associations, race organizers, commissaires, and cyclists gain access to insurance coverage for their participation in an organized cycling event. As discussed also in Chapter 6, many provincial and territorial cycling associations have arranged for dedicated cycling insurance for their members.[22] Such policies generally cover liabilities and sports injuries associated with club events and racing. They are also in line with UCI regulations that require national federations to ensure that licence holders are adequately insured against injury to person or property in every country where they compete.[23]

Within each cycling discipline, there are licences tailored to all skills and abilities, and to different levels of competition. According to the licence they hold, a cyclist can compete at the club level, provincial level, and the national and international levels. There are generally four types of licences issued by provincial and territorial cycling associations.

UCI International Licence

Cyclists who wish to compete in sanctioned races anywhere in Canada or the world must obtain a UCI International Licence. These licences are issued by provincial and territorial cycling associations on behalf of Cycling Canada and the UCI. This means that Canadians who wish to compete in races at the national level and outside of the country must obtain a UCI international licence. It is also true that foreign cyclists who wish to compete in Canada must hold a UCI international licence issued by their national cycling federation. Without a valid UCI International Licence, a foreign national is not permitted to compete in races in Canada and may not purchase a single-event licence, in part because the Cycling Canada insurance associated with a day-licence does not provide medical coverage for non-residents.

Citizen Licence

A Citizen Licence allows cyclists to enter some designated provincial, territorial, and regional level races. It is not a UCI or Cycling Canada licence and as a result, it does not permit a cyclist to race nationally or internationally. It is intended to allow novice cyclists to gain more racing experience. It can also be used to enter club-level races.

Single Event Licence

A Single Event Licence, also known as a day-licence, is sold onsite during race registration and is valid only for the event for which it is purchased.

This licence is intended for people who aren't members of provincial or territorial cycling associations and who do not have a UCI International Licence or Citizen Licence.

Club Membership

Individuals belonging to a club affiliated with their provincial or territorial cycling associations can participate in club-level races. Club members are not actually licensed, but their membership in an affiliated club provides them with the required sport injury and liability insurance coverage to participate in club races. If club members wish to participate in provincial or regional level races, or races held by other clubs, they must purchase one of the licence types described above.

Team Selection Rules

The process by which high performance cyclists are selected to represent Canada or their province or territory at sanctioned cycling events is very complex. It is beyond the scope of this book to provide readers with a comprehensive description of each selection process. However, since team selection accounts for a large number of the disputes between athletes and sport organizations,[24] it is important to briefly sketch out the way in which cyclists may be named to high performance teams. We shall therefore describe the selection process for the cycling squad that represents Canada at the Summer Olympics.

The selection process for the Olympic cycling team is established by the complex interplay of agreements between the IOC, the UCI, the COC, and Cycling Canada. The IOC decides which cycling events will be included in the Summer Olympics. It then delegates to the UCI the responsibility to craft a qualification process that will determine how many spots a country will have for different cycling disciplines and events. The actual selection of a Canadian Olympic cycling team is then done collaboratively by the COC and Cycling Canada. Through a selection agreement, Cycling Canada sets up an internal procedure that yields nominations of qualified athletes to the COC.

First, athletes are selected by Cycling Canada for what is called the 'Olympic Selection Pool' based on their performances at UCI qualification events. It is from this shortlist of athletes that the High Performance Advisory Committee of Cycling Canada then selects the individuals to be nominated to the COC to represent Canada at the next Olympic Games. Once the COC accepts the athletes nominated by Cycling Canada, it publicly communicates the names of the team members, at which point the Olympic cycling team is considered to be official.

The selection process for members of other national, provincial, and territorial cycling teams is similar, in accordance with selection agreements between the relevant multisport and cycling associations.

rules of play

Cycling governing bodies are responsible for setting the rules of play for all cycling disciplines. In Canada, race organizers follow Cycling Canada and the UCI competition rules, as well as additional modifications provincial or territorial associations may have introduced. There are general rules that apply to all bicycle races, and others that are specific to each discipline. The regulations not only outline the format of each cycling event, but also the procedures required to create a safe, fair, and inclusive environment for all participants on and off the road, trail, or track. Indeed, the *UCI Cycling Regulations* outline races procedures, safety measures, expected standards of behaviour, technical and equipment criteria, and complaint processes.

In terms of conduct, the rules state that everyone is expected to participate in racing events in a sporting and fair manner.[25] Cyclists must be properly dressed and refrain from behaviour that may "harm the reputation or question the honour of other licence holders, officials, sponsors, federations, the UCI or cycling in general."[26] The UCI code of behaviour also prohibits the harassment and bullying of others, the uttering of threats or insults, or any other improper or violent behaviour.[27] Naturally, any collusion or behaviour likely to falsify the results of a race is forbidden.[28]

In terms of safety, the rules state that cyclists must ride with utmost caution, and avoid putting other persons in danger.[29] Cyclists must at all times obey the instructions of race commissaires and observe the legislation of the country where the race takes place.[30] The rules further mandate the wearing of safety helmets,[31] and forbid the use of glass containers,[32] mobile phones, and radios[33] during a cycling race.

Finally, the rules specify mandatory standards for the equipment used by cyclists during a race.[34] For instance, the UCI Technical Regulations include a definition of what constitutes a 'bicycle' and specifies the equipment components and wheel sizes required for each discipline.[35] Some rules apply to specific categories of cyclists: for example, the UCI has set specific limits on the gears used by young riders in road events.[36]

Participants are expected to obey the rules; otherwise, they may be subject to penalties such as verbal or written warnings, monetary fines, disqualification, or suspension. The onus is on the participants to know the rules of competition and to use the proper equipment.

Commissaires

While cycling associations set the rules, race referees ensure that the competition is carried out in accordance with the regulations and in the spirit of fair play. In the sport of cycling, race officials are called 'commissaires,' a French term for 'referee,' and they are empowered to interpret and enforce the rules. They are responsible for briefing participants, checking the equipment compliance, starting the race, monitoring the behaviour of participants, overseeing the conduct and safety of the race, and disciplining participants who have committed infractions. Commissaires also track and certify the results of the race. The Chief Commissaire has ultimate authority over a cycling event.

Participants can lodge protests with race commissaires related to foul or dangerous riding, the order of the finish, or the regularity of race entries, category classifications, and equipment. The rules generally specify a very short time delay during which a protest can be lodged after the end of the race or after the announcement of results. All protests are examined and resolved by the Chief Commissaire, whose 'field of play' decisions are final and without appeal.

Field of Play Decisions

'Field of play' decisions are related to the conduct and outcome of a race. They are decisions a commissaire makes in the live setting of the competition and are seldom subject to review by cycling associations, sport arbitrators, or courts. Indeed, a commissaire's exercise of discretion and judgment is beyond challenge, except to the extent that the rules of the race so provide.

For the decisions of commissaires to be reviewed, there must be some evidence of fraud, corruption, bad faith, malicious intent, prejudice, or arbitrariness on the part of the commissaires. A participant cannot complain about field of play decisions simply because they disagree with the commissaires. To be sure, commissaires will inevitably make mistakes or give rulings based upon their line of sight or position on the road, trail, or track. Nonetheless, the Court of Arbitration in Sport has stated that competitors "should have the benefit of honest 'field of play' decisions, not necessarily correct ones."[37]

Cycling governing bodies stress the importance of respecting the authority of the officials for various reasons. First, commissaires are selected for their expertise in officiating cycling, and as such, they have more expertise than arbitrators or judges. Second, interfering with field of play decisions would be disruptive to the races themselves; cycling events should not be constantly interrupted by appeals to courts. Third, the presence of an adequate number of commissaires, in addition to the introduction of technology such as electronic timing chips and photo finishes, help mitigate any potential mistakes. Finally, the reputation of commissaires would be adversely affected if their decisions were retrospectively judged as incorrect. For all of those reasons, participants in a cycling race are contractually bound, by the terms of their racing licence, to accept the field of play decisions of commissaires.

sports-related disputes

While field of play decisions are generally not reviewable, many other decisions made by sport-governing bodies and cycling associations may be challenged by athletes and other sport participants. Sports-related disputes may be of an administrative or commercial nature, touch upon terms of employment, or involve national team selection, government grants for training, harassment, doping, or disciplinary matters. In the cycling world, for instance, athletes have questioned their exclusion from provincial and national teams,[38] challenged decisions relating to funding programs,[39] argued over the interpretation of contractual agreements,[40] and even sued anti-doping agencies for invasion of privacy.[41]

The trend in the sports world is towards establishing a more accessible system for the resolution of disputes than can be offered by domestic courts. The aim is to produce a dispute resolution system where hearings are by and large expeditious, the costs are a fraction of that of litigation, there is a consistency of outcomes, and the adjudicators are selected for both their legal expertise as well as their sport-specific knowledge. Moreover, the use of alternative dispute mechanisms is supported by the federal government and is a prerequisite for government funding. Indeed, government backing for national sporting organizations like Cycling Canada is contingent on the existence of appeals policies and dispute resolution systems that provide for independent arbitration of disputes.[42]

As a result, international and domestic sports organizations have developed a range of mechanisms dedicated to the resolution of disputes outside of domestic courts. They include internal appeal procedures, a national program for sport arbitration and mediation, and an international specialist tribunal. In addition, there are specific tribunals for doping offences, and limited remedies available before domestic courts.

Arbitration and mediation are now the main ways to resolve sports-related disagreements. Arbitration is a procedure in which a dispute is submitted to one or more independent adjudicators designated by the parties to the disagreement. The arbitrator hears the evidence and makes a binding decision on the dispute, the parties having agreed in advance to comply with the decision. Once rendered, arbitral awards have the same enforceability as judgments of ordinary courts.

Mediation is a different type of voluntary process where a neutral mediator helps parties discuss a dispute and work toward a solution that is acceptable to all parties. The mediator does not render a decision; if parties cannot come to an agreement, mediation may be abandoned without a resolution.

Internal Appeals

Disagreements between cycling associations and their members are to be resolved through the internal appeals mechanisms set up by each body to review its own decisions. This means that the first point of resolution for disputes is Cycling Canada and its subsidiary organizations, namely provincial and territorial cycling bodies and local clubs. In fact, cycling participants may be bound to submit certain disputes to the internal administrative mechanisms set up by Cycling Canada or provincial and territorial cycling bodies as a condition of participation in sanctioned cycling activities.

Cycling Canada's Appeals Policy applies to decisions "relating to eligibility, selection, allocation of competitive opportunities, harassment, [and] discipline."[43] It does not apply to policy and procedures established by organizations external to Cycling Canada, nor does it apply to infractions for doping offences, which are dealt with pursuant to the Canadian Anti-Doping Program. Moreover, for any decision related to the federal Athlete Assistance Program, individuals must follow the appeal procedures set out in the Policies and Procedures of Sport Canada's Athlete Assistance Program.[44]

Decisions made by officials of Cycling Canada can be appealed on a limited number of procedural grounds. For instance, individuals can challenge decisions on the grounds that the decision maker did not have jurisdiction, failed to follow bylaws or approved policies, or made a decision that was influenced by bias or was grossly unreasonable.

Appeal requests are first assessed by the Case Manager appointed by Cycling Canada to oversee the management and administration of the appeals policy. If the Case Manager is satisfied there are sufficient grounds for an appeal, the Case Manager appoints a tribunal consisting of a single adjudicator who has the power to review and decide the appeal. The decision of the adjudicator is final and binding on the parties, but it can be reviewed pursuant to the rules of the Sport Dispute Resolution Centre of Canada (SDRCC).

National Program for Sport Arbitration and Mediation

Several countries have established national programs for the prevention, arbitration and mediation of sporting disputes. In Canada, the national program for the arbitration and mediation of sporting disputes is administered by the Sport Dispute Resolution Centre of Canada. The jurisdiction of the SDRCC extends to any dispute with 'national impact' handed down by a national sport organization or a multisport organization that affects one of its members. For instance, a decision made by an adjudicator appointed by Cycling Canada, or a panel selected under Sport Canada's Athlete Assistance Program to review the exclusion of a cyclist from federal funding, can be referred for review and arbitration to the SDRCC. Before a party can apply for SDRCC arbitration, the internal appeal process available through a sporting body must first be exhausted. The arbitration is then conducted under the auspices of the SDRCC and pursuant to its Code of Procedure.[45]

Court of Arbitration for Sport

At the international level, the Court of Arbitration for Sport (CAS) provides arbitration and mediation services to facilitate the settlement of sports-related disputes. Its jurisdiction extends to cyclists who compete at the international level, or national-level cyclists who have fully exhausted all national remedies. The CAS has two divisions: the Ordinary Arbitration Division which hears disputes over employment or commercial issues, and the Appeals Arbitration Division, which acts as a final court of appeal for disputes concerning the decisions of sport federations, including doping decisions.

Disputes Relating to Doping Infractions

Infractions for doping offences are dealt with pursuant to the Canadian Anti-Doping Program. Under the CADP, two appeals mechanisms have been established. A national-level athlete facing a finding that he or she has committed an anti-doping rule violation under the CADP can appeal the decision to a Doping Appeal Tribunal established by the SDRCC. Appeals involving international-level athletes must be appealed exclusively to the Court of Arbitration for Sport, the CAS having been designated as the mandatory appeal tribunal under the WADA Code.

Domestic Courts

While sport-governing bodies have set up an elaborate private system for resolving disagreements, it is also true that sport participants can take their disputes to domestic courts. However, what the courts can or will do is very limited. Indeed, domestic courts have a restricted 'supervisory' jurisdiction over the decisions of private organizations.

There are essentially two main grounds upon which a court will agree to examine a decision by a not-for-profit sport organization.[46] First, a court can review whether a sport organization acted properly according to its rules, policies, and procedures. This arises from the fact that the jurisdiction of a private decision-making body is founded on a contract that it has with its members, and a court is entitled to oversee the observance of contractual rights. A court can thus review an internal decision to see if proper procedures were followed in a specific case.

Second, a court can examine whether a private decision-making body has complied with the requirements of procedural fairness (also known as 'natural justice' or 'due process'). What is considered an appropriate degree of procedural fairness will depend on the administrative and factual context of each case. As a result, procedural safeguards may vary depending on the decision maker and the nature of the decision. But the duty of fairness generally requires that some measures be taken to ensure the following: prior notice of a decision; a reasonable opportunity to participate in the decision-making process; access to counsel; the provision of reasons for the decision; and the right to an unbiased adjudicator.

A court does not act as an appeal body; instead, it undertakes a limited review of the capacity of the sport body to make the decision and the legality of the decision-making process. In general, courts will not review the merits of a decision. Essentially, they will not intervene where a private organization has acted properly according to its policies and rules, no matter how unfair the outcome may seem.

anti-doping regulations

Doping involves athletes using prohibited substances or methods to enhance their sporting performances. Cycling as a sport has unfortunately been seriously affected by years of doping scandals, and Canada has not been spared of its share of cyclists who have resorted to the use of banned substances: several elite Canadian cyclists have either confessed to using performance-enhancing drugs, or been sanctioned for doping offences. The problem has even touched the amateur ranks of the sport: in 2012, a Canadian master-level cyclist tested positive for a banned substance during an in-competition test at an Ontario Cup road race.[47]

The doping problem in the sport of cycling has not been limited to the athletes themselves. In some cases, the use of performance-enhancing drugs has been part of organized doping programs run by many of the men's and women's pro teams. The US Anti-Doping Agency described United States Postal Service squad as running "the most sophisticated, professionalized and successful doping program that sport has ever seen."[48] A UK elite cyclist who retired in 2014, described how she resisted the pressure from her team to take "medicines" to help her improve her performances.[49] A Canadian cyclist admitted that she took EPO with the assistance of her coach, her physician, and with the knowledge of her father.[50]

Cycling governing bodies have also been criticized for how they handled doping scandals: former presidents of the UCI have been accused, at best, of mismanagement of anti-doping cases, and at worst, of covering up positive tests and protecting US cyclist Lance Armstrong.[51] Indeed, the Cycling Independent Reform Commission was established in 2014 to investigate the history of doping in cycling, including whether or not the UCI played a role in covering up such practices.[52]

The magnitude of the problem in cycling, and the accompanying concerns about the health and well-being of athletes, has led to numerous initiatives to reform the sport's approach to anti-doping. It has also meant that cycling is often the most intensely drug-tested sport. For instance, the Canadian Centre for Ethics in Sport (CCES) reported that it performed more anti-doping tests on cyclists than any other athletes during the period from July through September 2013.[53] The Cycling Anti-Doping Foundation, for its part, reported that the number of tests carried out across all the cycling disciplines in 2012 was 14,168.[54]

Anti-Doping Programs

Doping is regulated by sport-governing bodies and by international and national anti-doping organizations that have adopted harmonized anti-doping programs. First and foremost is the *World Anti-Doping Code*[55] (the WADA Code), a set of anti-doping policies, rules, and regulations formulated by

WADA and adopted by international sport federations and national anti-doping authorities. WADA also maintains the "Prohibited List" which identifies the substances and methods prohibited in sport.[56] It is important to note that a revised WADA Code will come into effect on 1 January 2015.

As the WADA Code is only binding on non-governmental sports organizations, another initiative was necessary to enlist the support of national governments in the fight against doping. This was achieved by the adoption of the first global anti-doping treaty, the *International Convention against Doping in Sport* (Convention).[57] The Convention was put forward by UNESCO, an agency of the United Nations that promotes education, science, culture, and communication. The treaty requires state parties to recognize the mandate of the World Anti-Doping Agency and the principles of the *World Anti-Doping Code*. Canada ratified the Convention in November 2005 and the treaty came into force in 2007.

Canadian cyclists are subject to the standards and rules of the WADA Code because the UCI, the Canadian Centre for Ethics in Sport — recognized by WADA as Canada's national anti-doping organization — and Cycling Canada have all implemented the Code's mandatory provisions.

The UCI has incorporated the WADA Code directly into the *UCI Cycling Regulations*.[58] In addition, the international federation adopted distinctive anti-doping measures in 2008. First, it created the Cycling Anti-Doping Foundation to manage its anti-doping program. The CADF is responsible for implementing cyclist testing, creating testing pools, managing bodily sample collections, and creating anti-doping educational programs. Second, the UCI has established the Athlete's Biological Passport Program. This innovative anti-doping program allows cycling authorities to monitor a number of biological variables over time to detect deviations considered abnormal in individual cyclists.

For its part, the CCES drafted and adopted the Canadian Anti-Doping Program[59] (CADP), a set of regulations that is compliant with the WADA Code. The CADP also represents the Canadian government's implementation of its international treaty obligations under the *International Convention against Doping in Sport*. The CADP outlines the rules governing in-and out-of-competition testing, the process to apply for Therapeutic Use Exemptions, and the consequences of doping violations.

Lastly, Cycling Canada has adopted the CADP. In fact, meeting the requirements of the CADP is a condition for the receipt of government funding by any sport organization in Canada, and for participation in the Olympic movement.

As a result of the interplay between all of these regulatory programs, Canadian cyclists are directly subject to the provisions of the CADP and the rules of the UCI, which in turn are both compliant with the WADA Code and its Prohibited List of Substances and Methods.

Doping Offences

According to the CADP and the WADA Code, doping offences can be categorized in two broad groups: first, 'doping violations' occur through the use of a prohibited substance or method; and second, 'doping-related violations' occur through a refusal to provide bodily samples for testing or other conduct that condones the use of banned substances or undermines doping controls.

Specific infractions include the following:

» the presence of a prohibited substance in an athlete's bodily sample;
» using a prohibited substance or method;
» refusing or evading a bodily sample collection;
» failing to file whereabouts information;
» tampering with the doping control process;[60]
» the possession of a prohibited substance or method;
» trafficking in any prohibited substance or method;
» the administration to any athlete of a prohibited substance or method;
» any type of complicity involving an anti-doping rule violation.[61]

The revised WADA Code to come into force in 2015 will add the offence of 'associating with a banned person' such as a coach or doctor.

If a cyclist fails to submit updated whereabouts information on a regular basis, they may receive what is called a 'filing failure.' If a doping control officer can't find the cyclist at the designated location, the violation is known as a 'missed test.' Any combination of three filing failures and/or missed tests in an eighteen-month period may result in an anti-doping rule violation.

Anti-doping infractions are known in law as 'strict liability' offences. This means that intention to commit the offence is not relevant: if a prohibited substance is found in the system of a cyclist, then a doping infraction has occurred regardless of whether the athlete had an intention to violate the anti-doping rules. Intention, however, can become a mitigating factor in setting the length and severity of the sanction.[62] But to avoid the strict liability rule, an athlete would have to show either a complete lack of fault, or no significant fault, in relation to the use of the prohibited substance or method.[63]

The WADA Code currently has a limitation period of eight years.[64] A limitation period is the time frame within which a person can be charged with committing a doping violation.

The eight-year limitation period posed a singular problem for Cycling Canada in 2013 when three of the nation's elite cyclists admitted to (or were accused of) having used banned substances ten years prior to their admissions. Given the number of years that had elapsed, their confessions could not result in any doping charges and Cycling Canada voiced concerns to the ICU about the challenges of responding to historic doping cases.[65] The issue seems to have been addressed in the revised WADA Code to be implemented in 2015: the limitation period was increased from eight to ten years.

Sample Collection Procedures

All athletes, coaches, team staff, and doctors associated with the sport of cycling are expected to know and comply with the anti-doping rules and procedures applicable to them.[66] The racing licence, a mandatory document for sanctioned bicycles races, is the contractual agreement by which a cyclist and other persons undertake to comply with the doping control tests of the UCI and the CADP.[67] Athletes must therefore be available for bodily sample collections, and they must cooperate with the doping control authorities during anti-doping controls. Bodily sample collections are carried out in all cycling disciplines, in-and-out-of-competition. The general rule is that cyclists who compete at the international and national levels may be tested anytime, anywhere. Cyclists are expected to take responsibility for what they ingest and use and to make sure that any medical treatment they receive does not violate any anti-doping rules. Ignorance of the rules does not constitute an excuse to an anti-doping offence.

International sporting federations, national sporting associations, and national anti-doping organizations are responsible for anti-doping controls. In cycling, the UCI has contracted the management of its anti-doping program to the Cycling Anti-Doping Foundation. In Canada, anti-doping controls are carried out by the CCES. In both cases, specially trained and accredited doping control personnel carry out all tests.

During sample collection sessions, cyclists have certain rights and responsibilities. Their rights include:

» the right to a representative;
» the right to an interpreter, if available;
» the right to ask for additional information regarding the sample collection process; and
» the right to request a delay in reporting to the doping control station for valid reasons providing they are chaperoned during the delay.[68]

Cyclists also have responsibilities. They must:

» remain within the sight of sample collection personnel throughout the doping control process;
» produce identification;
» comply with sample collection procedures;
» report immediately to the doping control station for testing unless delayed for valid reasons; and
» maintain control of their sample until it is sealed.[69]

The sample collected from the athlete is divided and sealed into two bottles, the 'A' and 'B' samples. The cyclist, a witness, and the doping control officer all sign a form attesting that proper collection procedures were followed.

Athletes may be required to take medications that happen to fall under the World Anti-Doping Agency's Prohibited List to treat an illness or medical condition. In that case, they can request a Therapeutic Use Exemption (TUE) authorizing them to take the needed medicine.

Cyclists Subject to Doping Controls

Under the WADA Code, international sporting federations and national anti-doping organizations are required to create pools of athletes who are subject to doping tests. For the sport of cycling, the Cycling Anti-Doping Foundation is responsible for creating the registered testing pool of cyclists who compete at a high level internationally. Other competitive cyclists in Canada fall into registered testing pools maintained by the CCES. The table below outlines the five different testing pools and categories of cyclists subject to doping controls, and their obligations under anti-doping rules:

Testing Pool	Category of cyclists	Obligations of Cyclists
UCI Registered Testing Pool	Cyclists who compete at a very high level internationally and who meet certain criteria, including (but not limited to) UCI rankings, classifications, race results, disciplinary hearing results, and other factors determined by the CADF.	» Must complete a number of mandatory medical tests throughout the year » Subject to in-and-out-of-competition tests » Must supply whereabouts information to UCI and CCES, including one sixty-minute time between 06:00 and 23:00 each day during which the cyclist will be available for testing at a specified location » Must submit a request to obtain a Therapeutic Use Exemption (TUE) to the CCES » Must complete the "True Champion or Cheat" Anti-Doping Education Program » Should maintain a comprehensive medical file
CCES Registered Testing Pools, split into two tiers: 1. National RTP Cyclists 2. General RTP Cyclists	Cyclists who compete at a national and/or international level, athletes who compete in a sport with a higher doping risk, and cyclists who receive funding from Sport Canada.	1. National RTP athlete » Subject to in-and-out-of-competition tests » Must supply whereabouts information to UCI and CCES, including one sixty-minute time between 06:00 and 23:00 each day during which the cyclist will be available for testing at a specified location » Must submit a request to obtain a TUE to CCES » Should maintain a comprehensive medical file 2. General RTP athlete » Subject to in-and- out-of-competition tests » Must supply whereabouts information to UCI and CCES (do not need to include a sixty-minute time slot for each day) » Must submit a request to obtain a TUE to CCES » Should maintain a comprehensive medical file

Testing Pool	Category of cyclists	Obligations of Cyclists
International Cyclists	Cyclists who compete outside of Canada, but are not included in the UCI Registered Testing Pool	» Subject to in-and-out-of-competition tests » Do not need to submit whereabouts information » Must submit a request to obtain a TUE to CCES » Should maintain a comprehensive medical file
Domestic Cyclists	Cyclists who compete at home, for example developing cyclists and Canada Games participants	» Subject to in-and-out-of-competition tests » Do not need to submit whereabouts information » TUE applications for all medications are only submitted when requested by the CCES following the receipt of results from a doping control session » Should maintain a comprehensive medical file

To be sure, internationally and nationally ranked cyclists are subject to the bulk of the sample collections and doping tests. But it is also true that more testing is now being done in the amateur ranks of cycling. It has been reported that CCES has conducted in-and-out-of-competition testing at the Masters level of competitive cycling (cyclists over thirty-five years of age).[70] In Quebec, the CCES and the provincial cycling federation are collaborating to increase doping controls at the amateur level. By raising membership and race entry fees, the Quebec provincial cycling federation is able to pay for spot tests of cycling's 'weekend warriors.'[71]

Other sporting bodies with a cycling component also have their own anti-doping programs. Craig, for instance, participates in Ironman events, run by the World Triathlon Corporation, a US for-profit company. The event agreements and waivers he signs acknowledge his willingness to be tested for drugs. Such testing is uncommon, but does happen. That testing reveals that doping among older, amateur athletes is not an imagined issue: age group athletes are occasionally caught and banned from events.

There has now been considerable discussion in sporting circles about relatively common testosterone replacement treatment, and how it may feature among middle-aged triathletes and cyclists.[72] And as he watches occasional pacelines of (illegally drafting) triathletes blow by him, the cynic in Craig can't help but wonder whether people willing to cheat so visibly in an event everyone does for fun may also cheat chemically. Craig may not be that big of a cynic: a recent German study of competitors at Ironman Frankfurt found that 13 percent of respondents had engaged in "physical doping" in the preceding twelve months (that is, taken banned substances to improve physical performance such as steroids, human growth hormone, EPO etc.).[73] These were not young, professional athletes, but rather age group amateur competitors. Moreover, they chose voluntarily to reveal their use in the survey, suggesting that the actual doping rate may be even higher.

Hearings

Under Cycling Canada's anti-doping policy, and according to CCES rules, the Sport Dispute Resolution Centre of Canada conducts the hearing for the athletes and other individuals alleged to have committed a doping violation. However, several steps must be followed before an athlete or other person is summoned to a hearing for a doping or doping-related violation.

In relation to an adverse doping control result, the UCI or CCES must first determine if the athlete has a Therapeutic Use Exemption, or is entitled to one. If not, the anti-doping authority then notifies the athlete (or other affected person) of the adverse doping result and of the athlete's right to request an analysis of the B Sample. The positive test of Sample 'A' does however lead to a provisional suspension from competition. If the B Sample is tested, and a prohibited substance or method is detected, the findings are reported to the cyclist or other affected person, and to Cycling Canada, the UCI and WADA. The procedures are slightly different if the UCI or CCES is in receipt of information that an athlete or another person may have committed a doping-related offence, for example, a failure to submit to a sample collection. In that case, the first step is for the UCI or CCES to conduct an investigation to determine whether there is a possible anti-doping rule violation.

In all cases, however, the matter is eventually referred to the Sport Dispute Resolution Centre of Canada (SDRCC) to determine whether an anti-doping rule violation had been committed and, if so, to identify the appropriate sanction against the athlete or other affected person. An individual may forego a hearing by acknowledging the violation of the anti-doping rules and by accepting the consequences. If a hearing is held, the athlete or other person has a right to a procedure which respects the following principles:[74]

- » a timely hearing;
- » a fair and impartial hearing body;

- » the right to be represented by counsel at the person's own expense;
- » the right to be fairly and timely informed of the asserted anti-doping rule violation;
- » the right to respond to the asserted anti-doping rule violation and resulting consequences;
- » the right of each party to present evidence, including the right to call and question witnesses;
- » the right to an interpreter at the hearing;
- » a timely, written, reasoned decision (specifically including an explanation of the reason(s) for any period of ineligibility).[75]

Under the CADP, the onus of proof first falls on the doping control authorities to show that there is a valid and accurate positive test result. In terms of the standard of proof, doping authorities must prove to "a comfortable satisfaction" that a violation occurred.[76] The onus then shifts to the athlete if they intend to argue either a complete lack of fault or no significant fault. The athlete's standard of proof is the more familiar civil standard of a "balance of probabilities."[77]

Hearings are held by a single arbitrator sitting as the Doping Tribunal, constituted and administered by the Sport Dispute Resolution Centre of Canada. The Tribunal's proceedings are confidential, but its decisions and written reasons are generally a matter of public record. The proceedings are normally conducted as an oral hearing, unless the athlete agrees to a documentary hearing. Appeals can be made to the Doping Appeal Panel of the SDRCC, except for international-level cyclists who can only appeal to the CAS.[78]

Sanctions

The consequences of doping violations are set out in the CADP[79] and the *UCI Cycling Regulations*.[80] All sanctions imposed are in compliance with the WADA Code.

The CADP rules apply in situations where (1) the CCES has initiated and directed the sample collection or discovered the violation, and (2) when the cyclist is a national or resident of Canada, or a licence-holder or member of a Canadian cycling association. Canadian international or national level cyclists who are tested at an international event may be subject to the rules of the UCI. If so, the results management and the determination of an anti-doping rule violation and consequences will be governed by the UCI anti-doping rules.

Under the CADP, a sanction is imposed once an anti-doping rule violation has been determined. This can be as a result of a cyclist admitting to a violation and waiving their right to a hearing, or a decision of an independent arbitrator after a doping tribunal hearing.

The sanctions for anti-doping offences range from among the following:

» a reprimand, if the cyclist can establish how a specified substance entered his or her body (or came into his or her possession) and that the substance was not to enhance the athlete's sports performance or mask the use of a performance-enhancing substance (applies to first offences only);[81]

» disqualification of individual results, including forfeiture of medals, points and prizes;[82]

» suspension from the sport for a period of ineligibility that can vary from a two-year ban (for first-time offenders and for most offences) to a lifetime ban (for violations involving trafficking and the administration of a prohibited method or substance, the minimum period of ineligibility is four years);[83]

» financial sanctions;[84]

» public disclosure;[85]

» loss of federal or provincial funding for life;[86] and

» ineligibility to compete in the next Olympic or Paralympic Games, or to represent Canada on an international team.[87]

The most common penalty for an anti-doping rule violation is a sanction imposing a period of ineligibility to participate in sport. It is important to note that the new WADA Code, to come into force in 2015, provides for tougher sanctions, including doubling the current sanction from two to four years for first-time offenders.

A sanction can be decreased or increased depending on the type of violation and the unique mitigating or aggravating circumstances surrounding each case. For example, decision-making bodies can take into account whether the offence is a first or a subsequent violation; whether the substance was a specified substance on the Prohibited List; whether the cyclist was able to prove "no fault" or "no significant fault" on their part; the extent to which a person cooperated with the investigation; and whether the offence involves a minor.[88]

In Canada, cyclists have faced a variety of sanctions for doping violations. Michael Barry received a six-month ban from competition and was stripped of all his race results between 13 May 2003 and 31 July 2006. Geneviève Jeanson, who waived her right to a hearing, was given a reduced sanction in light of her ready assistance with the investigation of André Aubut, her coach, and Maurice Duquette, her physician. She received a sport ineligibility period of ten years instead of a lifetime ban, along with permanent ineligibility for federal funding.[89] Both Aubut and Duquette were given lifetime ineligibility sanctions, the tribunal noting that the anti-doping rule violations of both men involved the administration of a prohibited substance to a minor.[90] This means neither can compete, coach, nor play any official role in any sport for the rest of their lives.

state-created laws and regulations

In addition to the private regulations established by sport and cycling associations, the sport of cycling and its participants may be subject to state-created laws and regulations.

the use of roadways

Race organizers may be prohibited by law from using specific highways and roadways.[91] For example, Ontario prohibits riding a bicycle on controlled-access highways.[92]

Furthermore, some Canadian jurisdictions have adopted roadway laws specific to bicycle racing. In Newfoundland and Labrador, the *Highway Traffic Act* prohibits a person from driving "a vehicle or bicycle in a race with another vehicle or bicycle on a highway."[93]

In Nova Scotia, the *Motor Vehicle Act* grants the Minister of Transportation the authority to close a highway for the purpose of a sporting event. The Act also allows the Minister to authorize "a bicycle race upon a highway that has not been closed for that purpose," and for the adoption of terms and conditions with which the participants in the bicycle race and the organizers must comply.[94]

Municipalities may also have regulations about the use of roadways and facilities under their jurisdiction[95] and may require permits to hold a cycling event on city roads, parks and trails.[96] Such permits typically outline the rights and responsibilities of race organizers. For instance, in 2013, the City of Ottawa cancelled permits issued to the Eastern Canadian Cyclocross Series after park staff alleged that damage was done to the trails used for the race.[97]

incorporation

National sport and cycling bodies are usually legally constituted under federal legislation. For instance, many such national organizations have until recently been incorporated under Section II of the *Canada Corporations Act*.[98] As discussed in Chapter 6, this law has now been replaced by the *Canada Not-for-Profit Corporations Act*[99] (*Can NPCA*) which came into force in the fall of 2011. To meet the new governance and incorporation requirements of the *Can NPCA*, federal not-for-profit organizations were required to draft new articles of incorporation before 17 October 2014 to avoid the dissolution of their association.[100]

To comply with the new law, some sport and cycling organizations were required to restructure their board of directors and revise their membership structure.[101] At its 2013 annual general meeting, Cycling Canada indicated that it was working on making significant changes to its bylaws to bring the association into line with the CNCA.

Each province and territory also has laws that govern the legal structure, fundraising activities, and operations of local not-for-profit organizations.[102] Such laws aim to ensure transparency and accountability in how provincial and territorial not-for-profit corporations are run. Incorporation may also provide rights for members of a not-for-profit association as well as to the organization itself. For instance, some provincial and territorial laws prohibit the use of a name that is the same as the name of an existing association if its use would be likely to deceive. In *Re Ontario Bicycle Moto Cross Association*,[103] the Ontario Cycling Association successfully challenged a group that had adopted a name that the OCA argued would confuse the public as to which of the two associations was the governing body for BMX bicycle racing.

human rights

In Canada, prohibitions against discrimination stem from the *Charter of Rights and Freedoms* and from federal, provincial, and territorial human rights legislation. These laws ensure that individuals, including athletes, can participate fully in their communities, their work places, and in society as a whole, free from discrimination and harassment.

Charter of Rights and Freedoms

The *Charter of Rights and Freedoms*[104] forms part of the Canadian Constitution[105] and guarantees fundamental civil and political rights to everyone in Canada. Some of the protections of the *Charter* include the freedom of religion, thought, expression and peaceful assembly. In addition, section 15 of the *Charter* prohibits certain forms of discrimination by providing the following right to equality: "Every individual is equal before and under the law and has the right to the equal protection and equal benefit of the law without discrimination and, in particular, without discrimination based on race, national or ethnic origin, colour, religion, sex, age or mental or physical disability." The right to equality is guaranteed not only on the nine enumerated grounds, but also on 'analogous grounds' of discrimination, including sexual orientation, marital status, and citizenship.

The *Charter* applies to the policies and actions of all levels of government. For example, provincial sport funding programs or municipal recreation facilities would come under the jurisdiction of the *Charter*, as such activities constitute government actions. Private individuals or corporations, such as national and provincial cycling associations, despite receiving government grants, are typically not part of the legal definition of "government action" and thus are not subject to *Charter* provisions.

To be sure, some sporting activities may constitute government actions. This principle was expounded in a 2009 decision in which several athletes argued that the exclusion of women's ski jumping at the Vancouver Olympic Games constituted sex discrimination prohibited by the *Charter*. The British Columbia Supreme Court held that the staging of the 2010 Olympic Games by the Vancouver Olympic Committee was a government activity given the significant involvement of the federal and provincial governments, and that exclusion of the women's event was discriminatory. However, since the refusal to offer a women's event was a decision of the IOC, an international sporting organization, it was beyond the reach of the Canadian *Charter*.[106]

In essence, sport and cycling bodies will be considered to be private organizations unless it can be said that they are controlled by government or carrying out a government program or policy. For this reason, the *Charter* has very little direct impact on Canadian sport, since most governing bodies are private entities.

Federal, provincial, and territorial human rights legislation

Human rights legislation exists in every province, territory and at the federal level. Such laws protect people against discrimination based on race, age, sex, sexual orientation, and several other grounds. Unlike the *Charter*, human rights legislation does prohibit discriminatory practices in both the private and public sectors by individuals or organizations, businesses, or government bodies.

Although there is some diversity among jurisdictions, human rights laws generally prohibit discrimination in employment, accommodation, and publicly available services. The jurisdiction of human rights laws is determined by the constitutional division of powers. The federal Act applies to areas under federal jurisdiction such as banking, national airlines, railways, or federal government employees. Provincial and territorial human rights laws apply to matters of provincial and territorial concern, such as school boards, city government, or restaurants.

Human rights systems across the country are generally complaint-based. This means that a cyclist who believes that he or she has been discriminated against must lodge a complaint with the relevant human rights commission. If a complaint is determined to be well-founded, human rights commissions generally attempt to mediate the dispute between the parties. Where mediation fails, a formal tribunal may be formed to hear the case and make a binding decision.

As discussed also in Chapter 6, since bicycle clubs and cycling associations offer services to the public at the national, regional, and local levels, their activities and programs are subject to the jurisdiction of federal, provincial, and territorial human rights legislation. For instance, when cyclist Robert Martens, a citizen of the Netherlands and permanent resident of Canada, was advised by Cycling Canada that he would not be able to participate in the 2005 National Cycling Championship, he filed a complaint with the British Columbia Human Rights Tribunal alleging that Cycling Canada discriminated against him on the basis of his place of origin. Cycling Canada policy stated that only Canadian Citizens were eligible for participation at national championships.[107] In response to Martens' complaint, Cycling Canada revised its eligibility policies[108] and participation in national championships is now open not only to Canadian citizens, but to permanent residents, landed immigrants, and as individuals with refugee status.[109]

'Reasonable and Justifiable' Distinctions

Not all types of distinctions or acts of discrimination are illegal. Human rights legislation does recognize that the general rule prohibiting discrimination does not apply if the discrimination is reasonable and justifiable. The leading case is *Bhinder v Canadian National Railway Company*,[110] where the

Supreme Court of Canada decided the requirement of wearing a hard hat is a *bona fide* occupational requirement and does not amount to discrimination on the basis of religion.[111]

It may therefore be legal to discriminate and segregate in organized sport, if the decision to discriminate can be reasonably justified, for instance, to ensure fair competition, the safety of participants, or to account for the physical differences in strength, stamina, and physique of the athletes. In cycling for instance, the following distinctions and restrictions are entrenched in the sport: single-sex competitions; restrictions based on disability; restrictions based on age; and team selection criteria based on nationality.

For a distinction to be considered reasonable, it must be shown that the discriminatory practice is justified on the basis of compelling empirical evidence, not just anecdotal observations or casual expressions of concern. It is also true that the Supreme Court has made it clear that a standard is not reasonably necessary if the service provider or employer has not fully considered alternatives that might allow the affected individual to participate in a non-discriminatory, or the least discriminatory, way. This is called the duty to accommodate. The duty to accommodate obligates the service provider or employer to adjust the service or the conditions of employment in order to accommodate the needs of individuals to the point of undue hardship.

Among the factors that may be considered in weighing undue hardship are financial cost, safety, disruption of the workplace or the service, and impact on other staff and clients. In *Youth Bowling Council of Ontario v Mc-Leod*,[112] the Ontario Divisional court held that undue hardship, in the sports context, was reached "when the proposed accommodation would impact significantly upon the way by which other participants would be required to play or would give the accommodated person an actual advantage over others."

So even if a cycling association believes it is reasonably justified to adopt a discriminatory practice or policy, it has a legal duty to accommodate individuals or groups discriminated against on the basis of a prohibited ground up to the point of undue hardship. The duty to accommodate could, as a result, involve making changes to a cycling organization's policies, bylaws, practices, and constitution to create equal opportunities for individuals protected under human rights laws.

Affirmative Action Programs

Human rights laws and statutes at the federal and provincial/territorial levels, as well as the Canadian *Charter of Rights and Freedoms*, make provision for 'special programs,' also known as employment equity or affirmative action programs. These programs are intended to correct the negative effects of historic or systemic patterns of discrimination that have worked to disadvantage certain groups of people. Such programs are not considered to contravene human rights legislation. For instance, Nicole has participated for years in a program that aims to encourage women to participate in competitive cycling, namely the Ottawa Bicycle Club's successful and long-standing Women's Time Trials Series. This program might meet the requirements of an affirmative action program.

Policies and Rules of Cycling Associations

Some sport and cycling organizations have adopted policies to prohibit discrimination and harassment.

At the international level, the UCI Constitution states that the federation will operate in compliance with the principles of "equality between all the members and all the athletes, licence-holders and officials, without racial, political, religious, or other discrimination."[113] The UCI rules also state that participants in cycling races are to "refrain from any acts of violence, threats or insults or any other improper behavior or from putting other persons in danger."[114] The *Olympic Charter* prohibits discrimination; in fact, part of the COC's role in Canada is to take action against discrimination in sport, currently defined by the *Olympic Charter* as "[a]ny form of discrimination . . . on grounds of race, religion, politics, gender or otherwise."[115]

The importance of inclusiveness is also underlined in the 2002–2012 *Canadian Sport Policy*, a statement that sets out the shared vision and goals of the 14 governmental jurisdictions for sport in Canada. The policy upholds the principle that "[s]port is welcoming and inclusive, offering an opportunity to participate without regard to age, gender, race, language, sexual orientation, disability, geography, or economic circumstances."[116] Moreover, national sport associations funded by Sport Canada are required to have an abuse and harassment policy,[117] and some provincial/territorial sport organizations are similarly required by their funders to implement policies to protect athletes from harassment.

The Constitution and ByLaws of Cycling Canada state that the organization "ensures equality of opportunity for cycling participation." Cycling Canada has implemented this principle in its 2010 *Policy to Address Discrimination and Harassment*.[118] The policy provides that individuals have "the right to participate and work in an environment which promotes equal opportunities and prohibits discriminatory practices." The policy specifically prohibits harassment, a form of discrimination that includes unwanted and uninvited behaviour that demeans, threatens, or offends. The policy applies to all employees as well as to all directors, coaches, athletes, team personnel, officials and members of the Canadian Cycling Association, and to discrimination and harassment that may occur at Cycling Canada activities and events. Furthermore, the policy sets up a complaint and investigation process.

Some provincial and territorial cycling associations have adopted similar policies. For instance, the Manitoba Cycling Association has a policy outlining its commitment to "providing an environment that is free from harassment/abuse (abuse) on the basis of race, nationality, ethnic origin, religion, age, sex, sexual orientation, marital status, family status or disability."[119] Cycling Nova Scotia has also adopted a policy on harassment.[120]

Gender Equality

The world-wide bicycle craze of the 1890s had a striking impact on the lives of women in the United States and Canada. For the first time, 'proper' ladies ventured outside of the parlour, away from chaperones, and into more practical clothes, to partake in the popularity of bicycling.[121] Women's rights and bicycling were so inextricably intertwined that in 1896 Susan B Anthony, a well-known American suffragist, declared bicycling had "done more to emancipate women than anything else in the world."[122] Yet sex segregation remains the primary organizing principle in all levels of the sport of cycling. From a legal perspective, the issue is to what extent are the distinctions made in sport between men and women discriminatory?

In Canada, sex discrimination in sport has been challenged before the courts. The watershed decision is that of *Blainey v Ontario Hockey Association*[123] which held it is illegal to prohibit a girl from trying out for boys' teams, regardless of the nature of the opportunities available for girls. Girls and women may choose to play on male teams, so long as they are at the same skill level, and there are no issues of physical safety.

Discrimination against women in sport goes beyond opportunities to participate; historically, a vast disparity has existed between men's and women's sports in the provision of training and playing facilities, proper competitive events, adequate equipment, professional coaching staff, and sufficient funding. In the cycling world, some disciplines fare relatively well in terms of gender equality. In mountain biking and cyclocross, the top-level races for women, such as World Cup events, are usually held with the men's events, and some have equal prize money.[124] In track cycling, race formats for men and woman are identical, or almost identical, for the individual sprint and keirin events. This is also true for BMX races. The Tour of Flanders and Flèche Wallonne hold similar elite men's and women's races on the same day. Finally, a campaign to have a women's event at the Tour de France was recently successful; organizers of the most prestigious bicycle race in the world introduced a women's race on the Champs-Élyseés to accompany the final stage of the 2014 Tour.

Nonetheless, gender equality remains an issue in competitive cycling. For instance, road cycling has been consistently criticized for offering women fewer race opportunities, poor or non-existent media exposure, shorter race distances, and salary and prize money inequity. Continued disparities between men and women at the highest level in cycling have led some to argue that women in cycling be given equal footing in the sport, similar to other endurance events such as triathlons and marathons. For instance, in triathlons, the distances and prize money have been the same since the beginning of the sport, and women generally compete in conjunction with men's events.

In Canada, the issue of equal prize money for men and women at bike races was raised in Toronto in the late 1980s. Some cycling advocates argued that the inequality in race rewards was discriminatory. In response, the Toronto municipal government adopted a bylaw mandating equality in prizes for all bicycles races that required civic approval for road closures.[125] The issue has however remained contentious; as recently as 2012, individuals in the cycling community in British Columbia called on the organizers of the Canadian Cyclo-cross Championships to provide equal prizing for elite men and women.[126] In 2013, the UCI finally took a stand on the issue: it directed that equal prize money for men's and women's races be awarded in most of the world championship events. In announcing the policy, the UCI stated that "no distinction should be made between the achievements of men and women."[127]

At least one provincial cycling association has formulated a dedicated gender equality policy. Cycling Nova Scotia has adopted guidelines on gender equality that state that the organization seeks to "attain and maintain equality for both genders in all aspects of participation and access within Bicycle Nova Scotia."[128]

Transgender and Intersex Athletes

Most sports organizations have traditionally been organized on the premise that human beings come in one of two sexes: male or female. Undoubtedly, transgender[129] and intersex[130] athletes do not easily fit into this entrenched binary sex classification and, as a result, their participation in sport has challenged the extent to which competitive athletic events can be truly inclusive, fair, and respectful of human rights. In Canada, cycling was one of the first sports to confront some of these issues.

Michelle Dumaresq, a transgendered woman, began competing in downhill mountain bike events in 2001, six years after completing sex reassignment surgery.[131] Her right to compete against female athletes was challenged by other competitive cyclists, and her racing licence was even suspended for a period by Cycling BC. To resolve the matter, Cycling Canada and the UCI required Michelle Dumaresq to provide a birth certificate that indicated she was female before they reinstated her licence in 2002 and allowed her to compete in the women's category.[132]

In Dumaresq's case, cycling authorities required proof that she was legally and medically considered a woman.[133] Today, the inclusion of transgender cyclists would likely be governed by an IOC policy known as the *Stockholm Consensus* that has been adopted by other sport-governing bodies. Formulated in 2003, the policy allows transgendered athletes to compete in their acquired gender if they meet the following criteria:

» they must have had gender reassignment surgery;
» they must have legal recognition of their assigned gender by the appropriate official authorities; and
» they must have at least two years of hormone therapy.[134]

These requirements are now binding on any transgendered athlete who wishes to take part in a sporting activity governed by the IOC. Canadian Cyclist Kristen Worley, a nationally ranked women's cyclist, was one of the first persons to try to compete in the Olympics as an openly transgendered, post-operative athlete under the rules of the *Stockholm Consensus*. She did not however make any of the qualifying times that Canada said were required for her to be able to compete in the Olympics.[135]

Intersex athletes have confronted a somewhat different challenge to participation in sport: sex verification testing. Sports organizations have long relied on scientific and medical professionals to determine an athlete's eligibility to compete in women's elite sporting events (men are rarely, if ever, subject to such testing). To be sure, sporting organizations have moved away from compulsory testing; the 1996 Atlanta Games were the last Olympics with mandatory sex-verification tests.[136] Yet women athletes can still be subject to medical evaluations of their gender, as evidenced by the 2009 testing of South African runner Caster Semenya.[137] In 2010, a panel of medical experts recommended that the IOC adopt the following approach to intersex athletes: "Athletes who identify themselves as female but have medical disorders that give them masculine characteristics should have their disorders diagnosed and treated."[138] After treatment, eligibility to compete would be decided on a case-by-case basis.[139]

The current policies of sport-governing bodies on the eligibility rules for transgendered and intersex athletes continue to be debated. Some critics have argued that the focus of policies should be on promoting broad inclusiveness in sports and respecting athletes' rights to bodily integrity, privacy, and self-identification.[140] This position is bolstered by the growing consensus that there is no clear or objective way to scientifically draw a bright line between male and female.[141]

At the very least, Canadian human rights laws require that cycling bodies ensure that transgender and intersex athletes are not subject to prejudice and discrimination. It is certainly consistent with Cycling Canada's policy to ensure "equality of opportunity for cycling participation" that transgender and intersex athletes should be welcome to participate in cycling and be treated with dignity and respect by teammates, competitors, coaches, commissaires, sport personnel, and spectators.

Cycling Canada seems to have taken a first step in that direction in the Michelle Dumaresq case. When Cycling Canada and the UCI reinstated Dumaresq's racing licence in 2002, her right to participate in female sports continued to be challenged by other cyclists, especially when Dumaresq earned a spot on the National Team and represented Canada at the World Championships.[142] At the 2006 Canadian Nationals, where Dumaresq placed first, the boyfriend of second-place finisher Danika Schroeter, jumped up onto the podium and helped Schroeter put on a t-shirt that read "100% Pure Woman Champ." In response, the Canadian Cycling Association suspended Schroeter for three months for her actions, stating that the "Canadian Cycling Association takes offences of this nature committed by its members very seriously. While athletes have the right to hold and express their opinions, they also have a duty to express them in a manner appropriate to sport and to Canadian society."[143]

tort law

As discussed in Chapters 3 and 6, everyone has a duty not to injure others. If a person harms another, they are liable to pay compensation for the damage suffered by the injured party. This branch of private law is called tort law in common law provinces, and civil responsibility in Quebec. It determines in what circumstances, and with what consequences, one person may be liable for injuring or harming another person.

In common law jurisdictions, tort law is developed for the most part by the courts, rather than by law-makers. In Quebec, the civil responsibilities of individuals are found in the *Quebec Civil Code*. The general principle, however, is the same for all Canadians: the law imposes a general duty on everyone to take reasonable care to avoid causing injury or harm to others.

As discussed in Chapter 6, in the sports world, tort law delineates the responsibilities of players, coaches, officials, spectators, and clubs to each other before, during, and after a sporting event. We repeat some of that discussion here, with a specific eye to racing events and competitive cyclists.

Tort law covers intentional acts, like physical assault, and negligent acts caused by carelessness. This means that tort actions may be in respect to sport-related injuries where a participant or spectator claims to have been injured by the intentional or negligent behaviour of another participant, organizer, or official.[144]

For a tort action in negligence to succeed, a person must have failed to carry out his or her duties to the standard of care required by the common law or by statute. This test is often explained as follows: what would a reasonable competitor, organizer, or official, in his or her place, do or not do? A commissaire could be held responsible for an injury suffered at a cycling event, if the commissaire was negligent in ensuring the safety of the race. Race organizers, for their part, may be similarly liable for injuries caused to spectators at a cycling event if they failed to act reasonably. Coaches may also have a duty to select training venues and equipment that are reasonably safe for cyclists.

The usual remedy for tortious harms is an award of damages: a form of monetary compensation paid to the injured party to compensate for actual and anticipated losses. For instance, damages can be awarded for pain and suffering, medical expenses, and lost earnings.

In assessing damages, courts have found that injuries sustained by competitive cyclists in collisions with motor vehicles may warrant the awarding of general damages, which include the loss of opportunities. The effects of an injury from a collision may be inconsequential to the ordinary person but could be significant to a competitive cyclist. Indeed, courts have held that because competitive cycling is not only an international athletic activity, but also an event at the Summer Olympics, athletic prowess has an economic value.[145] Therefore, the loss of a competitive cycling career has been considered as a non-pecuniary loss for which an injured athlete can be awarded general damages.[146]

criminal code

Criminal law sets a standard of conduct for people to follow, including individuals involved in sporting activities. In Canada, the *Criminal Code* is a federal law and it applies across the country. A breach of the *Criminal Code* can result in criminal prosecution and criminal sanctions, including imprisonment. Criminal law is thus another set of legal rules which delineate the responsibilities of clubs, players, coaches, referees, and spectators to each other during the sporting event itself and before and after the competition.

Violence, abuse, or corruption in the context of a sporting event or an athletic relationship could amount to a criminal offence. For instance, injurious behaviour in sport, while considered part of some sports, may lead to assault and battery charges if the conduct changes from competing against another athlete to intentionally inflicting harm on another. Criminal law further prohibits assault, harassment, sexual assault, uttering threats, and the sexual abuse and exploitation of children. As discussed in Chapter 6, section 153(1) of the *Criminal Code* prohibits a person who is in a position of trust or authority towards a young person from engaging in any sexual activity with that young person, even where the activity is consensual.[147] Criminal offences prohibiting physical and sexual abuse are of particular relevance to the world of sport, where the maltreatment of a number of athletes by powerful and publicly respected coaches has been widely reported in Canada.[148] Finally, the *Criminal Code* also outlaws sports gambling.[149]

family law

Parents have a legal obligation to provide financial support to their children. Under child support legislation, courts may consider a child's involvement in competitive and elite sports as an additional cost to be shared between parents. For instance, section 7 of the *Federal Child Support Guidelines*[150] authorizes a court to augment a child support payment in relation to several categories of special or extraordinary expenses, including "extraordinary expenses for extracurricular activities." In deciding whether to increase the amount of child support to account for the cost of a child's participation in sports, a court must consider whether the expenses are reasonable and necessary, and for extracurricular activities, if they are, in addition, "extra-ordinary."

The cost of high performance athletic training has been considered by the courts to be an extraordinary expense in relation to child support.[151] Courts have held that it can be in a child's best interest to participate in sports at an advanced level. Generally, this has been the case when a child has significant talent and his or her participation in elite sports could create educational and professional opportunities in the future. The equipment, travel, and coaching costs of competitive cycling can be significant, and if a parent has the means to support the child, a court could grant a request to increase child support payments to help defray the expenses of a child's participation in competitive cycling.

In *Willock v Willock*,[152] the British Columbia Supreme Court was asked to decide if an adult child involved at the elite level of competitive cycling could continue to receive child support from her father, pursuant to the provincial *Family Relations Act*.[153] Under the provincial legislation, much like the federal *Divorce Act*, a "child" is defined as including a person "who is 19 years of age or older and, in relation to the parents of the person, is unable, because of illness, disability or other cause, to withdraw from their charge or to obtain the necessaries of life."[154] The issue in *Willock* was whether training as an athlete constituted an "other cause," which made the adult daughter economically unable to withdraw from her parents' charge. At the time, she trained full-time and received support from Cycling Canada, and became a member of the national team with ambitions to compete at the Olympics. The court held that although the child was over nineteen, she was unable to contribute to her support while training as an elite cyclist. As a result, the father was required to pay child support.[155]

income tax act

Professional and amateur cyclists may be subject to special taxation rules in Canada. Because athletes receive compensation for their athletic endeavours in many forms, such as endorsements or prize money — and because they may train and live abroad — it is beyond the scope of this book to give a detailed account of the tax liabilities of Canadian amateur and professional cyclists. We shall nevertheless outline the most common tax rules that affect cycling associations and athletes.

Registered Canadian Amateur Athletic Associations (RCAAA)

A number of sport and cycling organizations, such as Cycling Canada, the COC, and the Canada Games Council, are registered as Canadian Amateur Athletic Associations under the federal *Income Tax Act*. As RCAAAs, they must comply with a number of requirements under the federal legislation. For instance, RCAAAs are required to have, as their exclusive purpose and function, the promotion of amateur athletics in Canada on a nation-wide basis. RCAAAs can conduct business featuring professional athletes, but these activities must be "ancillary and incidental" to the exclusive purpose and function of promoting amateurs athletes.[156]

Similar to registered charities, RCAAAs can issue official donation receipts for income tax purposes for gifts they receive from corporations or individuals. If an RCAAA fails to comply with the law, they can be subject to an array of sanctions, ranging from monetary penalties, the suspension of the authority to issue official receipts, and the revocation of the association's status.

Amateur Athlete Trust Accounts

Under the *Income Tax Act*, athletes can defer paying tax on funds related to athletic participation in international sporting events. The rules apply to athletes who are, in a taxation year, a member of a registered Canadian Amateur Athletic Association, such as Cycling Canada, and eligible to compete in international sporting events as a Canadian national team member. Eligible cyclists can place the income they receive from endorsements, prizes, rewards, and other remuneration related to their athletic endeavours in a trust account. The funds, and the income generated, will be taxed only upon the date of distribution to the athlete, or eight years after the last year in which the athlete was eligible to compete as a Canadian national team member.[157]

It should be noted that high-performance cyclists who receive allowances from the Sport Canada Athlete Assistance Program are not required to pay income tax on such funds, and do not need to place this revenue in an amateur athlete trust account.

Children's Fitness Tax Credit

Under the *Income Tax Act*, parents can claim to a maximum of $500 per child for fees paid relating to the cost of enrolling a child in a program of physical activity. This is known as the 'Children's Fitness Tax Credit.'[158] The tax credit applies to a child under sixteen, or for children with disabilities, for a child under the age of eighteen. To qualify, a recreational or competitive cycling program must be ongoing, supervised, suitable for children, and include a significant amount of physical activity contributing to cardiorespiratory endurance and to at least one of the following: muscular strength, muscular endurance, flexibility, or balance.

immigration

Under Canadian immigration laws, cyclists and coaches who are nationals of certain countries need a Temporary Resident Visa (TRV) to enter Canada if they wish to participate in cycling events being held in this country. Canada has imposed such visa requirements on a large number of countries, and athletes have been denied entry into Canada for sporting events.[159] To be issued a TRV, foreign athletes and coaches are required to show that they have enough funds to support themselves while in Canada. In addition, they have to prove that they have sufficient ties to their home country and will leave Canada at the end of their stay.

Canadian immigration law normally requires that foreign nationals obtain a valid authorization to engage in employment in Canada. Exemptions are provided, however, for foreign-based athletes and coaches. Pursuant to the *Immigration and Refugee Protection Regulations*, foreign professional or amateur athletes who enter Canada to participate in sports activities — either as individual participants, or as members of a foreign-based or a Canadian amateur team — do not require a work permit to take part in competitions.[160] The immigration regulations extend similar exemptions to foreign coaches, trainers, and other essential members of the team, as well as judges, referees, and sport officials involved in an international amateur sports competition.[161] In addition, a family member of a foreign athlete may apply for a study permit if the athlete is participating in sporting events in Canada.[162]

Finally, if a foreign national is hired as a professional cycling coach or athlete in Canada, they will require a Canadian work permit.

citizenship

Citizenship entitles individuals to certain government benefits and to voting rights, but also obligates them to perform specific duties, such as paying taxes. The Canadian *Citizenship Act*[163] sets the rules for how and under what circumstances a person may become a citizen of Canada. In this country, a citizen is a person who is Canadian by birth, or who has applied and obtained Canadian citizenship (called 'naturalization').

Certain competitive sporting activities require that participants be Canadian citizens. For instance, members of national sporting teams competing in international events must be Canadian citizens. While such restrictions may amount to discrimination based on nationality, ethnicity, place of origin, or citizenship, some courts have upheld sport eligibility rules that favour Canadian citizenship.[164] In Ontario, the *Human Rights Code* explicitly permits restrictions based on Canadian citizenship for sporting activities.[165]

Cycling bodies also allow rules to restrict participation based on citizenship. For instance, in 2005, the UCI amended the eligibility rules to stipulate that only a citizen of a country could be a National Title holder.[166] As a result, Cycling Canada adopted a policy that only Canadian citizens are eligible to participate in national championship events and in the selection processes for national pools or teams; permanent residency was no longer a valid status.[167]

This policy change adversely affected cyclist Robert Martens, a citizen of the Netherlands and permanent resident of Canada, who was advised by Cycling Canada that he would not be able to participate in the 2005 National Cycling Championship in Kamloops, British Columbia. Martens filed a complaint with the British Columbia Human Rights Tribunal alleging that Cycling Canada discriminated against him on the basis of his place of origin.[168] In response to Martens' concerns, Cycling Canada reviewed its eligibility policies.[169] As a result, it is now the case that participation in national championships is open to Canadian citizens, permanent residents and individuals with refugee status. Prize money is based on order of finish, regardless of citizenship.[170] However, only Canadian citizens have access to Canadian titles, Canadian championship podium positions, UCI points, and Canadian championships medals.

The UCI regulations further prohibit individuals with more than one citizenship status to change the nation they represent. Individuals with dual citizenship status must, when applying for their racing licence for the first time or within two years of gaining a different citizenship, choose the country they wish to represent at the time of application. The choice is final for all athletes over the age of eighteen.[171]

Obtaining Canadian citizenship can thus be a crucial step for a cyclist wishing to compete for Canada at the international stage. Unfortunately, the delays in obtaining Canadian citizenship can be substantial. For instance, it took a year and a half for cyclist Jasmin Glaesser, born in Germany but living in Coquitlam, British Columbia, to obtain her Canadian citizenship. Her application was processed just in time for Glaesser to compete in the 2011 Pan-American Games and later win a bronze medal in the women's team pursuit at the 2012 London Olympics.[172] Citizenship applications for some high-performance athletes have been expedited to allow them to compete for Canada at the international level.[173] The federal minister of Citizenship and Immigration can do this pursuant to a section of the *Citizenship Act*, which states that the minister may grant Canadian citizenship "to alleviate cases of special and unusual hardship or to reward services of an exceptional value to Canada."[174]

official languages

English and French are the official languages of Canada. A key principle of the federal *Officials Languages Act*[175] is that Canadians have the right to communicate with, and receive services from, federal institutions in either official language.

While Sport Canada is subject to the provisions of the *Official Languages Act*, sport-governing bodies are non-governmental organizations and are not directly regulated by the federal legislation. However, national sporting and cycling associations have official language obligations arising out of their contractual agreements with Sport Canada. Sport Canada has stated that linguistic duality is an essential feature of the sports system and that all persons, regardless of language or culture, should be able to participate in sport.[176] To achieve this goal, Sport Canada requires sport organizations to meet certain official language requirements as a condition of funding, and contribution agreements contain an official languages clause.[177] Sport Canada may withhold funds if sport bodies do not meet their contractual obligations in regard to official languages.

Cycling Canada has stated in its constitution that the organization recognizes Canada's two official languages equally.[178]

trade-marks

A trade-mark is a word, name, symbol, or design, used to identify and distinguish a company's goods or services from the products of another manufacturer in the marketplace. Trade-mark registration in Canada is a matter of federal jurisdiction, governed by the *Trade-marks Act*.[179] If registered, a trade-mark improves the rights of the owner and provides some protection against claims of infringement or misuse by others.

Canadian bicycle companies involved in sponsoring cycling teams have taken action over the possible infringement of their trade-marks. In *TBG The Bicycle Group Inc v Rona Inc*,[180] the hardware and home renovation company Rona filed an application to register the trade-mark "ÉQUIPE CYCLISTE RONA CYCLING TEAM." At the time, Rona was sponsoring a women's cycling team that included Canadian cyclist Geneviève Jeanson. Rona wanted to launch a range of official products bearing the team name and design, and was seeking the protection afforded by registration of the trade-mark. Rona's application was opposed by the Canadian bicycle manufacturer Kona. In addition to the sales of bicycles, clothing, and equipment, Kona was involved in organizing mountain bike races and was the sponsor of mountain bike and cyclocross teams. The Canada Trade-marks Opposition Board rejected Rona's application because it agreed that there was a reasonable risk of confusion with Kona's existing trade-mark.

In another case, the bicycle manufacturer Trek, also involved in the sponsorship of cycling teams, lost its bid to prohibit the registration by the Canadian Lung Association of the trade-mark "BICYCLE TREK FOR LIFE & BREATH" in relation to an annual charity bicycle ride. In that case, the Trade-marks Opposition Board concluded there was no reasonable chance of confusion between the two trade-marks.[181]

conclusion

Bicycle racing is a complex undertaking. Riders are licensed, selected, and regulated. Their regulations govern their behaviour in terms of doping, and their conduct during races. An international infrastructure with Canadian equivalents exists to organize athletes and events. As in any complex social system, disputes are inevitable, and bicycle racing includes a customized dispute settlement regime. Surrounding this entire apparatus at greater or closer distances are federal, provincial, and municipal laws that affect how athletes behave, and bicycle racing associations are created, how they operate, and how they interact with athletes, coaches, officials, spectators, and others involved in the sport.

endnotes

1   *Ross v Orr* (1894), 25 OR 595 (HCJ).

2   Union cycliste internationale, *UCI Constitution*, art 2, online: www.uci.ch/mm/
    Document/News/Rulesandregulation/16/26/19/STA-20140926-E_English.pdf [*UCI Constitution*].

3   *Ibid.*

4   For a list of the regulations, see Union cycliste internationale, "Rules," online:
    www.uci.ch/inside-uci/rules-and-regulations/regulations/.

5   The CADF has now outsourced the supervision of this program to the Athlete Passport Management Unit (APMU) of the Lausanne Anti-doping Laboratory (LAD).

6   *UCI Constitution*, above note 2, ss 74–78.

7   Cycling Canada, "Cycling Canada to Fund 72 Cyclists in 2014" (23 January 2014),
    online: www.cyclingcanada.ca/sport/cycling/news/sport-canada-to-fund-72-cyclists-in-2014/.

8   International Olympic Committee, *Olympic Charter* (9 September 2013), online:
    www.olympic.org/Documents/olympic_charter_en.pdf.

9   Canadian Olympic Committee, *General By-Law*, Recitals, s 8(k) [COC, *By-Law*].

10 SC 2003, c 2, s 10 [*Can PASA*].

11 *Ibid*, s 5.

12 Sections 7 and 8 of the Canadian Anti-Doping Program in sport [CADP] set out the procedures to be followed in cases of violation of anti-doping rules and refer more precisely to the Sport Dispute Resolution Centre of Canada [SDRCC] as the authorized doping tribunal. See Canadian Centre for Ethics in Sport, *Canadian Anti-Doping Program*, online: www.cces.ca/files/pdfs/CCES-POLICY-CADP-E.pdf.

13 Canadian Cycling Association, "History," online: www.canadacup.ca/cca/about/history.shtml.

14 Canadian Cycling Association, "CCA Changes Name to Cycling Canada" (23 May 2012), online: www.canadiancyclist.com/dailynews.php?id=24159.

15 The Canadian Cycling Association is incorporated in accordance with Part II of the *Canada Corporations Act*, RSC 1970, c C-32 (the organization is currently working to modify its bylaws to meet Industry Canada's new guidelines in accordance with the updated *Canada Not-for-Profit Corporations Act*, SC 2009, c 23 [*Can NPCA*]).

16 Cycling Canada, "Provincial and Territorial Cycling Associations," online: Cycling Canada www.cyclingcanada.ca/provincial-territorial-cycling-associations/. The list consists of: Cycling British Columbia, online: www.cyclingbc.net; Alberta Bicycle Association, online: www.albertabicycle.ab.ca; Saskatchewan Cycling Association, online: www.saskcycling.ca; Manitoba Cycling Association, online: www.cycling.mb.ca; Ontario Cycling Association, online: www.ontariocycling.org; Fédération Québécoise des sports cyclistes, online: www.fqsc.net; Vélo New Brunswick, online: www.velo.nb.ca; Bicycle Nova Scotia, online: www.bicycle.ns.ca; Bicycle Newfoundland and Labrador, online: www.bnl.nf.ca; Cycling Association of Yukon, online: yukoncycling.com; Cycling PEI, online: www.sportpei.pe.ca.

17 *Ontario Cycling Association, Affiliated Racing Team, "2014 Team Affiliation Package," electronic document, online: Ontario Cycling Association* www.ontariocycling.org/

ocamedia/web_doc%2Fclub_forms%2F20140409-122838-2014+Team+Affiliation+
Package+%26+Application+-+2014+April+Version+5.pdf.

18   Union cycliste internationale, *UCI Cycling Regulations, Part 1 General Organi-*
sation of Cycling as a Sport, s 1.1.001, online: www.uci.ch/mm/Document/
News/Rulesandregulation/16/26/49/PartI-Generalorganisationofcyclin-
gasasport-01.05.2014-ENG_English.pdf [*UCI Cycling Regulations, Part I*].

19   *Ibid*, s 1.1.004:

> Anyone requesting a licence thereby undertakes to respect the constitution and
> regulations of the UCI, the UCI continental confederations and the UCI member
> Federations, as well as to participate in cycling events in a sporting and fair
> manner. He shall undertake, in particular, to respect the obligations referred to
> in article 1.1.023.
>
> As from the time of application for a licence and provided that the licence is
> issued, the applicant is responsible for any breach of the regulations that he
> commits and is subject to the jurisdiction of the disciplinary bodies.
>
> Licence holders remain subject to the jurisdiction of the relevant disciplinary
> bodies for acts committed while applying for or while holding a licence, even if
> proceedings are started or continue after they cease to hold a licence.

20   *Ibid*, s 1.1.002.

21   *Ibid*, s 1.1.010.

22   See Cycling Canada, "National Insurance Program," online: Cycling Insurance
www.cyclinginsurance.ca/.

23   *UCI Cycling Regulations, Part I*, above note 18, s 1.006.1:

> Federations shall issue licences according to such criteria as they may deter-
> mine. They shall be responsible for monitoring compliance with these criteria.
>
> Before the licence is issued, the licence holder and the national federation must
> ensure inter alia that the licence holder is adequately insured against accidents
> and civil responsibility in every country where he practises competitive cycle
> sport or training throughout the year for which the licence is issued.

24   See *Cowie v Canadian Cycling Association* (2007), online: Sport Dispute Resolution
Centre of Canada www.crdsc-sdrcc.ca/resource_centre/pdf/English/0_SDRCC%20
07-0062.pdf; See also *Dionne v Canadian Cycling Associations* (2004), online: Sport
Dispute Resolution Centre of Canada www.crdsc-sdrcc.ca/resource_centre/pdf/
Summary/0_SDRCC%2004-0019-summary.pdf, where a cyclist argued that Cycling
Canada departed from its selection criteria and as a result treated him unfairly [*Dionne*].

25   *UCI Cycling Regulations, Part 1*, above note 18, s 1.2.080.

26   *Ibid*, s 1.2.079.

27   *Ibid*; provincial and national cycling bodies may also have their own codes of conduct: see, for example, Ontario Cycling Association, *Code of Conduct*, online:
www.ontariocycling.org/high-performance/code-of-conduct/.

28   *UCI Cycling Regulations, Part 1*, above note 18, s 1.2.081.

29   *Ibid*, s 1.2.082.

30   *Ibid*.

31   *Ibid*, s 1.3.031.

32 *Ibid*, s 1.2.083.

33 Union cycliste internationale, *UCI Cycling Regulations, Part 2 Road Races*, s 2.2.024, online: Union Cycliste Internationale www.uci.ch/mm/Document/News/Rule-sandregulation/16/11/53/2-ROA-20140815-E_English.pdf [*UCI Cycling Regulations, Part 2*], except for UCI World Tour events, Women's World Cup events, and time trial events.

34 *UCI Cycling Regulations, Part 1*, above note 18, s 2.

35 *Ibid*; see also Union cycliste internationale, *Technical Regulations For Bicycles: A Practical Guide To Implementation*, online: Union cycliste internationale http://62.50.72.83/Modules/BUILTIN/getObject.asp?MenuId=MTkzNg&ObjTypeCode =FILE&type=FILE&id=NTIoMDY&LangId=1.

36 *UCI Cycling Regulations, Part 2*, above note 33, s 2.2.023; the main reasons for restricted gearing are purportedly to prevent injury and to encourage development of good pedalling technique.

37 *Yang v Hamm* (2004), CAS 2004/A/704 (Court of Arbitration for Sport).

38 *Dionne*, above note 24; see also *Shaw v Canadian Cycling Association (Cycling Canada)* (2012), online: Sport Dispute Resolution Centre of Canada www.crdsc-sdrcc.ca/resource_centre/pdf/English/0_SDRCC%2012-0181.pdf.

39 *Perras v Canadian Cycling Association* (2008), online: Sport Dispute Resolution Centre of Canada www.crdsc-sdrcc.ca/resource_centre/pdf/English/435_SDRCC%20 08-0069.pdf.

40 See Martin Delgado, "Bradley Wiggins in court battle over his £5m Tour win: Cyclist Disputes £740,000 Bill from His Management Team" *Daily Mail* (18 January 2014), online: Daily Mail www.dailymail.co.uk/news/article-2541847/Bradley-Wiggins-court-battle-5m-Tour-win-Cyclist-disputes-740-000-bill-management-team.html.

41 "Jeannie Longo attaque l'agence de lutte contre le dopage" *Midi libre* (3 December 2013), online: Midi libre www.midilibre.fr/2013/12/03/cyclisme-jeannie-longo-attaque-l-agence-de-lutte-contre-le-dopage,791711.php.

42 Government of Canada, Canadian Heritage, *Sport Canada Contribution Guidelines Sport Support Program National Sport Organization Component*, s 3.1.5, online: Canadian Heritage www.pch.gc.ca/eng/1360946745826/1360951317553.

43 Canadian Cycling Association, *Appeals Policy*, s 3, online: Canadian Cycling Association www.cyclingcanada.ca/wp-content/uploads/2012/05/appeals_policy.pdf.

44 *Ibid*, s 4(b).

45 Sport Dispute Resolution Centre of Canada, *Canadian Sport Dispute Resolution Code*, online: www.crdsc-sdrcc.ca/eng/documents/CODE2011FINALEN.pdf.

46 See the landmark UK case: *Lee v Showmen's Guild of Great Britain*, [1952] 2 QB 329; see also *Senez v Montreal Real Estate Board*, [1980] 2 SCR 555 (the Supreme Court of Canada reviewed the relationship between a member and a voluntary association in a Canadian context); see also *Lakeside Colony of Hutterian Brethren v Hofer*, [1992] 3 SCR 165 at 175 (the Supreme Court of Canada affirmed the statement of Stirling J in the case of *Baird v Wells* (1890), 44 Ch D 661 decided in 1890: "[the] only questions which this court can entertain are: first, whether the rules of the club have been observed; secondly, whether anything has been done contrary to natural justice; and, thirdly, whether the decision complained of has been come to *bona fide*.")

47   "Cyclist Suspended for Testosterone Violation" *Canadian Centre for Ethics in Sport* (8 August 2012), online: www.cces.ca/en/news-208; see also Richard Poplak, "Why Do Some Amateur Cyclists Resort to Doping?" *The Globe and Mail* (20 July 2013), online: www.theglobeandmail.com/sports/why-do-some-amateur-cyclists-resort-to-doping/article13329812/?page=all (he received a two year suspension from the sport).

48   Statement from USDA CEO Travis T Tygart Regarding the US Postal Service Pro Cycling Team Doping Conspiracy (10 October 2012), online: Cycling Investigation cyclinginvestigation.usada.org/.

49   "Nicole Cook's Retirement Statement" *The Guardian* (14 January 2013), online: www.theguardian.com/sport/2013/jan/14/nicole-cooke-retirement-statement.

50   The coach and doctor were banned for life from participating or competing within the Canadian sport system. The cyclist received a ten-year ban, a sanction mitigated because of her cooperation with the investigation; see Sport Information Resource Centre, Press Release, "CCES Announces Results for 2008-09 Anti-Doping Program" (28 May 2009), online: www.sirc.ca/news_view.cfm?id=28548.

51   "Lance Armstrong Claims Verbruggen Aided in Doping Cover Up" *Cycling News* (18 November 2013), online: www.cyclingnews.com/news/lance-armstrong-claims-verbruggen-aided-in-doping-cover-up.

52   Union cycliste internationale, Press Release, "Cycling Independent Reform Commission Appeals for Testimony to Assist its Investigation into Cycling's Past" (11 January 2014), online: www.uci.ch/inside-uci/about/.

53   Canadian Centre for Ethics in Sport, *CCES Quarterly Statistics* (6 January 2014), online: www.cces.ca/files/pdfs/CCES-MR-2013JulSepDetails-E.pdf.

54   Union cycliste internationale, Press Release, "CADF: Review of 2012 Anti-Doping Activities," online: www.uci.ch/pressreleases/press-release-cadf-review-2012-anti-doping-activities/.

55   World Anti-Doping Agency, *World Anti-Doping Code*, online: WADA https://wada-main-prod.s3.amazonaws.com/resources/files/wada-2015-world-anti-doping-code.pdf [WADA Code].

56   World Anti-Doping Agency, "2014 List of Prohibited Substances and Methods," online: WADA list.wada-ama.org/prohibited-in-particular-sports/prohibited-substances/.

57   UNESCO, *International Convention against Doping in Sport* (19 October 2005), online: unesdoc.unesco.org/images/0014/001425/142594m.pdf.

58   Union Cycliste internationale, *UCI Cycling Regulations, Part 14 Anti-Doping*, online: www.uci.ch/mm/Document/News/Rulesandregulation/16/26/70/14ant-E_English. PDF [*UCI Cycling Regulations, Part 14*].

59   *Canadian Anti-Doping Program*, above note 12.

60   "CCES Responds to Salas Comments on Sanction" *Canadian Cyclist* (23 January 2014), online: www.canadiancyclist.com/dailynews.php?id=27050&title=cces-responds-to-salas-comments-on-sanction.

61   *Canadian Anti-Doping Program*, above note 12, rr 7.23–7.37.

62   For cases where mitigating factors were considered, see *Lindman-Porter v Canadian Cycling Association* (2005), online: Sport Dispute Resolution Centre of Canada www.crdsc-sdrcc.ca/resource_centre/pdf/English/398_SDRCC%2005-0027.pdf;

Canadian Cycling Association v Rolland Green (2005), online: Sport Dispute Resolution Centre of Canada www.crdsc-sdrcc.ca/resource_centre/pdf/English/0_SDRCC%2005-0025.pdf.

63 *Canadian Anti-Doping Program*, above note 12, rr 7.44–7.45; Rachel Corbett, Hilary Findlay, & David Lech, *Legal Issues in Sport: Tools and Techniques for the Sport Manager* (Toronto: Emond Montgomery Publications, 2008) at 82.

64 WADA Code, above note 55, art 17.

65 "Hesjedal Admits to Doping: 'I Chose the Wrong Path'" *Velonews* (30 October 2013), online: velonews.competitor.com/2013/10/news/cycling-canada-concerned-about-hesjedal-doping-allegations_306627.

66 WADA Code, above note 55, art 2.

67 *UCI Cycling Regulation, Part I*, above note 18, s 1.1.004:

> Anyone requesting a licence thereby undertakes to respect the constitution and regulations of the UCI, the UCI continental confederations and the UCI member Federations, as well as to participate in cycling events in a sporting and fair manner. He shall undertake, in particular, to respect the obligations referred to in article 1.1.023.

> As from the time of application for a licence and provided that the licence is issued, the applicant is responsible for any breach of the regulations that he commits and is subject to the jurisdiction of the disciplinary bodies.

> Licence holders remain subject to the jurisdiction of the relevant disciplinary bodies for acts committed while applying for or while holding a licence, even if proceedings are started or continue after they cease to hold a licence.

68 Canadian Centre for Ethics in Sport, *Athletes' Rights and Responsibilities*, online: www.cces.ca/en/samplecollection/rightsandresponsibilities.

69 *Ibid.*

70 "Globe & Mail Issues Correction to Wheels of Bloor" *Pedal Mag* (23 July 2013), online: Pedal Mag http://pedalmag.com/globe-mail-issues-correction-to-wheels-of-bloor/; "Wheels of Bloor Tested by CCES" *Pedal Mag* (6 June 2013), online: www.pedalmag.com/wheels-of-bloor-team-tested-by-cces/; Poplak, above note 47.

71 *Ibid.*

72 See, most famously, Andrew Tilin, *The Doper Next Door: My Strange and Scandalous Year on Performance Enhancing Drugs* (Berkeley, CA: Counterpoint, 2011).

73 Pavel Dietz et al, "Associations between Physical and Cognitive Doping — A Cross-sectional Study in 2997 Triathletes" (2013) 8(11) PLoS ONE e78702, online: www.irishtriathlon.com/wp-content/uploads/2014/01/ironman-triathlon-doping-study.pdf.

74 *UCI Cycling Regulations, Part 14*, above note 58, Chapter IX.

75 *Canadian Anti-Doping Program*, above note 12, r 6.21d)(i).

76 *Ibid*, r 7.81; this standard of proof is greater than the Canadian civil threshold of proof on a "balance of probabilities," but less than the criminal standard of "proof beyond a reasonable doubt."

77 *Ibid.*

78 *Ibid*, r 8.20: Appeals involving International-Level Athletes "In cases arising from Competition in an International Event or in cases involving International-Level Athletes, the decisions of the Doping Tribunal may be appealed exclusively to the CAS in accordance with its rules and procedures." According to UCI rules, a decision may not be appealed. Indeed, according to *UCI Cycling Regulations, Part 14*, above note 58, r 278:

> The decision by the hearing panel of a *License-Holder's* National Federation shall not be subject to an appeal before another body (appeals board, tribunal, etc.) at National Federation level. If such an appeal is entered, it must be declared inadmissible. Any other decision is void as of right. However, the UCI may ask the Court of Arbitration for Sport (CAS) to pronounce nullity where appropriate upon supplementary application in an appeal procedure against the decision of the competent body. This application may be made at any time during the procedure before the CAS.

79 *Canadian Anti-Doping Program*, above note 12, rr 7.38–7.62.

80 Union cycliste internationale, *UCI Cycling Regulations, Part 10 Continental Championships*, online: www.uci.ch/mm/Document/News/Rulesandregulation/16/26/66/vt_10cont-E_English.PDF.

81 *Canadian Anti-Doping Program*, above note 12, r 7.42.

82 *Ibid*, rr 7.5–7.10.

83 *Ibid*, rr 7.38–7.41.

84 *Ibid*, r 7.58.

85 Canadian Centre for Ethics in Sport, "Anti-Doping Sanctions," online: www.cces.ca/en/sanctions [CCES Sanctions].

86 *Canadian Anti-Doping Program*, above note 12, r 7.57.

87 CCES Sanctions, above note 85.

88 *Canadian Anti-Doping Program*, above note 12, rr 7.40 and 7.44–7.47.

89 Canadian Centre for Ethics in Sport, "Cyclist's On-air Admission to Using EPO Results in Investigation, Sanction," online: www.cces.ca/en/news-99-cyclist-s-on-air-admission-to-using-epo-results.

90 *Ibid*; Canadian Centre for Ethics in Sport, "Doctor Receives Lifetime Ban from Sport Following Investigation into Administration of EPO to a Cyclist," online: www.cces.ca/en/news-10.

91 *Motor Vehicle Act*, RSBC 1996, c 318, s 183(2)(h) [*BC MVA*]; *The Highway Traffic Act*, CCSM c H60, s 150(5); *Vehicles on Controlled-access Highways*, RRO 1990, Reg 630, s 1(1); *Highway Safety Code*, CQLR c C-24.2, art 295(4.2); *Highway Traffic Act*, RSPEI 1988, c H-5, s 194(2)(h); *Highway Traffic Act*, RSNL 1990, c H-3, s 129(2)(h) [*NL HTA*].

92 Ont *Vehicles on Controlled-Access Highways*, s 1(1).

93 *NL HTA*, s 168.

94 *Motor Vehicle Act*, RSNS 1989, c 293, art 163(2), 163(3).

95 See, e.g., *BC MVA*, s 124.2(1); *Motor Vehicles Act*, RSY 2002, c 153, s 126(2)(b) [*YT MVA*].

96 See, e.g., *BC MVA*, s 124.2(1); *YT MVA*, s 126(2)(b).

97 "City Pulls Bike Racing Permits after Park Damaged" *CBC News* (4 November 2010), online: www.cbc.ca/news/canada/ottawa/city-pulls-bike-racing-permits-after-park-damaged-1.869052.

98 Above note 15.

99 Above note 15.

100 All not-for-profit corporations that were incorporated under the *Canada Corporations Act* were required to apply for a certificate of continuance to transition to the *Canada Not-for-Profit Corporations Act* before 17 October 2014.

101 Moreover, organizations who are Registered Canadian Amateur Athletic Associations under the *Income Tax Act*, RSC 1985, c 1 (5th Supp), must have their articles of incorporation approved by the Canada Revenue Agency.

102 The Ontario Cycling Association is incorporated under the Ontario *Corporations Act*, RSO 1990, c C.38.

103 (1986), 11 CPR (3d) 335 (Companies Branch, Ministry of Consumer and Commercial Relations, Ontario).

104 *Canadian Charter of Rights and Freedoms*, Part I of the *Constitution Act, 1982*, being Schedule B to the *Canada Act 1982* (UK), 1982, c 11.

105 *Constitution Act, 1982*, Schedule B to the *Canada Act 1982* (UK), 1982, c 11.

106 The court found that the skiers had suffered discrimination, and the source of the discrimination was the IOC, but the organization was beyond the reach of Canadian courts: *Sagen v Vancouver Organizing Committee for the 2010 Olympic and Paralympic Winter Games (VANOC)*, 2009 BCSC 942.

107 *Martens v Canadian Cycling Assn*, 2006 BCHRT 434 [*Martens*].

108 Canadian Cycling Association, *Final Report of the Canadian Cycling Association (CCA) Task Force on Eligibility of Landed Immigrants to participate in National Championship sporting* events, online: www.canadian-cycling.com/cca/documents/information/finalreport_eligibility.pdf.

109 However, only Canadian citizens have access to Canadian titles, Canadian championship podium positions, UCI points, and Canadian championships medals. Prize money, however, is based on order of finish, regardless of citizenship or nationality; see Canadian Cycling Association, *Race Guide: Canadian Championships*, online: www.canadian-cycling.com/disciplines/sites/default/files/12_V24-05_Guide%20technique.pdf [*Race Guide*].

110 [1985] 2 SCR 561; see also *British Columbia (Public Service Employee Relations Commission) v British Columbia Government Service Employees' Union*, [1999] 3 SCR 3.

111 This meant that the employment of a Sikh worker who wished to wear a turban could be terminated if he refused to wear a hard hat.

112 (1994), 20 OR (3d) 658, aff'g (1990), 75 OR (2d) 451 (Div Ct).

113 *UCI Constitution*, above note 2, art 3.

114 *UCI Cycling Regulations, Part I*, above note 18, s 1.2.079.

115 COC, *By-Law*, above note 9, s 8(j).

116 Canadian Heritage, "Sport in Canada in 2012," online: www.pch.gc.ca/sportcanada/pol/pcs-csp/2003/103-eng.cfm.

117 Amanda Heron, "A Study of National and Provincial Sports Organizations' Athlete Protection and Harassment Policies and Procedures" (2012) at 7, online: University

of Ottawa www.sante.uottawa.ca/pdf/AstudyofNationalandProvincialSport Organizations.pdf.

118 Canadian Cycling Association, *Policy to Address Discrimination and Harrassment* (January 2010), online: www.canadian-cycling.com/cca/about/documents/ discrimination_harrassment.pdf.

119 Manitoba Cycling Association, *Harassment Policy*, online: www.mbcycling.ca/ wp-content/uploads/2010/03/HARASSMENT-POLICY.pdf.

120 Bicycle Nova Scotia, "Policy Statement on Gender Equity and Harassment," online: www.bicycle.ns.ca/BNS_Forms/Equity_Harassment_Policy.pdf.

121 Sue Macy, *Wheels of Change: How Women Rode the Bicycle to Freedom (With a Few Flat Tires along the Way)* (Washington, DC: National Geographic Children's Books, 2011).

122 Annie Londonderry, *Women on Wheels: The Bicycle and the Women's Movement of the 1890s*, online: www.annielondonderry.com/womenWheels.html.

123 (1986), 54 OR (2d) 513 (CA).

124 "The Long, Hard Road to Equal Pay for Women's Cycling and Sport as a Whole" *The Guardian* (6 March 2014), online: www.theguardian.com/sport/100-tours-100-tales/2014/mar/06/equal-pay-womens-sport-cycling-koppenbergcross.

125 Laura Robinson, "Bio," online: www.femlaw.queensu.ca/conferencesFLSQ/ lauraRobinson.html; Laura Robinson, "Jack Layton: Our Friend on a Bicycle" *Pedal* (22 August 2011), online: www.pedalmag.com/jack-layton-our-friend-on-a-bicycle/.

126 "Debate over Equal Prize Money Flares Up in BC Prior to CX Nationals This Weekend" *Pedal* (16 November 2012), online: www.pedalmag.com/debate-over-equal-prize-money-flares-up-in-bc-prior-to-cx-nationals-this-weekend/.

127 Sarah Barth, "UCI Approves Equal Prize Money in Men's and Women's Races in Most World Championship Events" *Road.cc* (22 December 2012), online: www.road.cc/content/news/72424-uci-approves-equal-prize-money-mens-and-womens-races-most-world-championship. The 2014 women's Tour of Britain will also offer absolute parity with men in terms of prize money and backup.

128 Bicycle Nova Scotia, *Policy Statement on Gender Equity and Harassment*, 2013, online: www.bicycle.ns.ca/BNS_Forms/Equity_Harassment_Policy.pdf.

129 The term "transgender" generally describes "people whose gender identity (sense of themselves as male or female) or gender expression differs from that usually associated with their birth sex": American Psychological Association, "Answers to Your Questions about Transgender People, *Gender Identity and Gender Expression*," online: APA www.apa.org/topics/sexuality/transgender.aspx. This may lead some to seek "gender reassignment," which usually involves hormones or surgery, to bring their physical characteristics into conformity with their gender identity.

130 Intersex conditions include atypical developments of physical sex characteristics, including abnormalities of the external genitals, internal reproductive organs, sex chromosomes, or sex-related hormones. Some examples include external genitals that cannot be easily classified as male or female, or inconsistency between the external genitals and the internal reproductive organs: American Psychological Association, "Answers to Your Questions About Individuals With Intersex Conditions," online: APA www.apa.org/topics/sexuality/intersex.aspx.

131   John Billman, "Michelle Raises Hell" *Outside* (1 April 2004), online: www.outside
      online.com/outdoor-adventure/biking/mountain-biking/Michelle-Raises-Hell.html.

132   "UCI Finalizes Decision regarding Canadian Transgendered Athlete" *Pedal* (29 Au-
      gust 2002), online: www.pedalmag.com/uci-finalizes-decision-regarding-canadian-
      transgendered-athlete/.

133   *Ibid.*

134   International Olympic Committee, "Statement of the Stockholm Consensus on Sex
      Reassignment in Sports" (12 December 2003), online: www.olympic.org/documents/
      reports/en/en_report_905.pdf.

135   Worley has stated that she considers it unfair that the IOC required her to come out
      in such a public way, when all she wanted to do was be recognized for the woman
      that she is: Lena Hoober, "Guest Post: Trans Athletes In the Olympics" (3 July 2012)
      Medal Heads (blog), online: www.medalheads.wordpress.com/2012/07/03/guest-
      post-trans-athletes-in-the-olympics/.

136   For a history of sex testing, see: Vanessa Heggie, "Testing Sex and Gender in
      Sports; Reinventing, Reimagining and Reconstructing Histories" (2010) 34:4 En-
      deavour 157, online: National Center for Biotechnology Information www.ncbi.nlm.
      nih.gov/pmc/articles/PMC3007680/. The IOC used to carry out mandatory gender
      exams at the Olympics, but those checks were dropped in 1999 because the screen-
      ing process — chromosome testing — was deemed unscientific and unethical.

137   Jeré Longman, "South African Runner's Sex-Verification Result Won't Be Public"
      New York Times (19 November 2009), online: www.nytimes.com/2009/11/20/
      sports/20runner.html?_r=0.

138   Gina Kolata, "I.O.C. Panel Calls for Treatment in Sex Ambiguity Cases" *New York
      Times* (20 January 2010), online: www.nytimes.com/2010/01/21/sports/olympics/
      21ioc.html.

139   *Ibid.* Some have expressed concerns however that the "treatment" required by
      international sporting agencies will mean subjecting individuals to invasive and
      irreversible medical procedures that are not required for health reasons: Rebecca
      Jordan-Young, Peter Sönksen, & Katrina Karkazis, "Sex, Health, and Athletes"
      (2014) BMJ 2926, online: www.bmj.com/content/348/bmj.g2926.

140   Rebecca Jordan-Young & Katrina Karkazis, "You Say You're a Woman? That Should
      Be Enough" *New York Times* (17 June 2012), online: www.nytimes.com/2012/06/18/
      sports/olympics/olympic-sex-verification-you-say-youre-a-woman-that-should-be-
      enough.html?_r=0. In 2012, in *XY v Ontario (Minister of Government and Consumer
      Services)*, 2012 HRTO 726, the Ontario Human Rights Tribunal held that the *Vital
      Statistics Act* requirement that an individual seeking to change the sex designation
      on his or her birth registration supply medical certificates confirming that he or
      she has undergone transsexual surgery was discriminatory. See Jena McGill & Kyle
      Kirkup, "Locating the Trans Legal Subject in Canadian Law: *XY v Ontario*" (2013) 33
      Windsor Rev Legal Soc Issues 96.

141   Canadian Centre for Ethics in Sport, *Sport in Transition: Making Sport in Canada
      More Responsible for Gender Inclusivity* (July 2012) at 13–14, online: www.cces.ca/
      files/pdfs/CCES-PAPER-SportInTransition-E.pdf.

142 "Worlds MTB National Team Controversy" *Pedal*, online: www.pedalmag.com/worlds-mtb-national-team-controversy/.

143 The CCA found that Schroeter's conduct was in breach of its rules governing the conduct of racers, which read, in part, "All license holders shall at all times be properly dressed and behave correctly in all circumstances . . . They shall refrain from any [. . .] insults or any other improper behavior [. . .] They may not in word, gesture, writing or otherwise harm the reputation or question the honour of other license holders [. . .] The right of criticism shall be exercised in a motivated and reasonable manner and with moderation." See Canadian Cycling Association, News Release, "CCA Rules to Suspend Danika Shroeter (Maple Ridge, B.C.) for Three Months" (31 July 2006), online: www.canadian-cycling.com/cca/media/news/news_0731_206.shtml.

144 See, for example, *Buchan v United States Cycling Federation, Inc*, 277 Cal App (3d) 887 (1991) (a cyclist, who suffered a traumatic brain injury, blamed race organizers for a spill in which sixty-five competitors fell because they authorized an inexperienced twenty-year-old novice racer to compete). See also Ashley Pescoe, "Cole Porter's Estate Files Lawsuit after Fatal Tour De Fair Haven Crash" *NJ.com* (8 January 2014), online: www.nj.com/monmouth/index.ssf/2014/01/cole_porters_estate_files_lawsuit_after_fatal_tour_de_fair_haven_crash.html.

145 *Gillmour v Laird*, [1989] BCJ No 15 at para 2 (SC) [*Gillmour*].

146 See *Goncalves v Maguire*, [1987] OJ No 1520 (Dist Ct); *Apostolopoulos v Fraser*, [1993] BCJ No 199 (SC); *Finnigan v Morrison*, [1993] BCJ No 907 (SC); *Gillmour*, above note 145.

147 *R v Audet*, [1996] 2 SCR 171; *R v Weston*, [1997] AJ No 263 (QB).

148 For instance, one cyclist was reportedly the target of verbal abuse by her coach, and it has been reported that the coach threw a race radio at her because he was upset with her performance: see Randy Starkman, "Jeanson's Story a Sorry One" *The Star* (22 September 2007), online: www.thestar.com/sports/olympics/2007/09/22/jeansons_story_a_sorry_one.html; see also Laura Robinson, *Crossing the Line: Violence and Sexual Assault in Canada's National Sport* (Toronto: McClelland & Stewart, 1998); Canadian Academy of Sport and Exercise Medicine, *Canadian Academy of Sports and Exercise Medicine Discussion Paper: Abuse Harassment and Bullying in Sport* (December 2010), online: Sport Law www.sportlaw.ca/wp-content/uploads/2011/03/CASEM-Discussion-Paper-December-2010.pdf; Peter Donnelly & Robert Sparks, "Child Sexual Abuse In Sport" in Peter Donnelly, ed, *Taking Sport Seriously: Social Issues In Canadian Sport*, 2d ed (Toronto: Thomson Educational Publishing, 2000) at 108–11; Sheldon Kennedy & James Grainger, *Why I Didn't Say Anything: The Sheldon Kennedy Story* (Toronto: Insomniac Press, 2006).

149 *Criminal Code*, RSC 1985, c C-46, s 202.

150 SOR/97–175.

151 See *Bland v Bland*, 1999 ABQB 236.

152 2005 BCSC 1697.

153 RSBC 1996, c 128.

154 *Ibid*.

155 See also *Olson v Olson*, 2003 ABCA 56; *Maxwell v Maxwell*, 2007 BCSC 45.

156 *Income Tax Act*, s 149.1(6.01): A Canadian amateur athletic association is considered to devote its resources to its exclusive purpose and exclusive function to the extent that it carries on

    (a) a related business; or

    (b) activities involving the participation of professional athletes, if those activities are ancillary and incidental to its exclusive purpose and exclusive function.

157 *Ibid*, s 143.1.

158 *Ibid*, s 118.03.

159 Alison Korn, "Runners Denied Entry into Canada" *Toronto Sun* (9 April 2010), online: www.torontosun.com/sports/columnists/alison_korn/2010/04/09/13526661.html; Peter Kamasa, "Four Africa Volleyball Teams Denied Canadian Entry Visas" *The New Times* (29 August 2012), online: www.newtimes.co.rw/news/index.php?i=15099&a=57646.

160 *Immigration and Refugee Protection Regulations*, SOR/2002-227, s 186(h).

161 *Ibid*, s 186(m).

162 *Ibid*, s 215(2)(g).

163 RSC 1985, c C-29.

164 *Beattie v Acadia University* (1976), 18 NSR (2d) 466 (CA). For a discussion of eligibility rules, see John Barnes, *Sports and the Law in Canada*, 3d ed (Toronto: Butterworths, 1996) at 64.67.

165 *Human Rights Code*, RSO 1990, c H.19, s 16(2).

166 *UCI Cycling Regulation, Part 1*, above note 18, s 1.2.028.

167 Cycling Canada, *National Team Selection Policy: General Conditions and Criteria for Selection to All National Team Programs* (29 November 2013), online: www.cycling-canada.ca/wp-content/uploads/2014/01/2014-01-21-Cycling-Canada-General-Selection-Policy.pdf.

168 *Martens*, above note 107.

169 Canadian Cycling Association, *Final Report of the Canadian Cycling Association (CCA) Task Force on Eligibility of Landed Immigrants to Participate in National Championship Sporting Events* (27 November 2008), online: www.canadian-cycling.com/cca/documents/information/finalreport_eligibility.pdf.

170 *Race Guide*, above note 109.

171 *UCI Cycling Regulation, Part I*, above note 18, s 1.1.033.

172 Kathryn Bertine, "Jasmin Glaesser Races to London" *ESPN* (20 July 2012), online: www.espn.go.com/espnw/athletes-life/article/8180815/riding-pros-jasmin-glaesser-races-london.

173 "Feds Urged to Fast-track Ping-pong Athlete's Citizenship" *CBC News* (14 October 2012), online: www.cbc.ca/news/politics/feds-urged-to-fast-track-ping-pong-athlete-s-citizenship-1.1225412.

174 *Citizenship Act*, s 5(4).

175 RSC 1985, c 31 (4th Supp).

176 Canadian Heritage, "Linguistic Barriers to Access to High Performance Sport," online: www.pch.gc.ca/pgm/sc/pubs/obstacles_linguistiques-linguistic_barriers/101-eng.cfm.

177 Canadian Heritage, *Sport Canada Contribution Guidelines Sport Support Program National Sport Organization Component 2012–2013*, s 3.1.2, online: www.pch.gc.ca/eng/1360946745826/1360951317553.

178 Canadian Cycling Association Constitution and By-Laws (January 2010), art 7, online: www.canadian-cycling.com/cca/documents/information/cca_bylaws08.pdf.

179 RSC 1985, c T-13.

180 (2006), 56 CPR (4th) 159 (TMOB).

181 *Trek Bicycle Corp v Canadian Lung Assn*, [2000] TMOB No 81. Other trade-mark disputes: Nigel Wynn, "Specialized Withdraws Action against Cafe Roubaix in Trademark Dispute" *Cycling Weekly* (11 December 2013), online: www.cyclingweekly.co.uk/news/latest-news/specialized-withdraws-action-against-cafe-roubaix-in-trademark-dispute-22586; "Alberta Bike Shop in Trade Mark Dispute with Specialized" *Cycling 4 women* (7 December 2013), online: Canadian Cyclist www.canadiancyclist.com/cycling4women_news.php?id=26885&title=alberta-bike-shop-in-trade-mark-dispute-with-specialized.

Index